The Last Days of
Richard III
and the fate of
his DNA

The Last Days of
Richard III
and the fate of
his DNA

John Ashdown-Hill

In memory of Joy Ibsen,
Richard III's niece in the sixteenth generation,
without whose help the final chapters could not have been written.

Duérmete, rosal,	Sleep, my rose,
que el caballo se pone a llorar.	for the horse is starting to weep.
Las patas heridas,	Hooves wounded,
las crines heladas,	mane frozen,
dentro de los ojos	a silver dagger
un puñal de plata.	in his eyes.
Bajaban al río.	Down they went to the river.
¡Ay, cómo bajaban!	Oh, how they went down!
La sangre corría	The blood was flowing
más fuerte que el agua.	faster than the water.

Federico García Lorca, *Bodas de Sangre* [*Blood Wedding*] act 1, scene 2
(translation J. Ashdown-Hill)

'… the truth is that those of us who were alive then
never knew what really happened'

J.K. Rowling, *Harry Potter and the Deathly Hallows*, p. 129

Front: Richard III Paston Portrait © Society of Antiquaries of London

First published 2010
This fully revised and updated edition published 2013

The History Press
The Mill, Brimscombe Port
Stroud, Gloucestershire, GL5 2QG
www.thehistorypress.co.uk

British Library Cataloguing in Publication Data.
A catalogue record for this book is available from the British Library.

ISBN 978 0 7524 9205 6

Typesetting and origination by The History Press
Printed in Great Britain

Contents

List of Illustrations

Illustrations not otherwise attributed are the property of the author.

1. The royal family in 1484: Queen Anne Neville, King Richard III, and Edward of Middleham, Prince of Wales. Engraving of 1844, after the Rous Roll.

2. Queen Anne Neville's grave was originally marked by a brass memorial in the Abbey Church at Westminster. This lost monument – the only brass memorial to a queen in England – may once have carried a figure similar to that shown in one version of the contemporary Rous Roll.

3. Nowadays Anne's place of burial is marked only by a plaque with this modern brass shield displaying her coat of arms.

4. The Gatehouse of the Priory of the Knights of St John of Jerusalem (Knights Hospitaller), Clerkenwell. Richard III came here on Wednesday 30 March 1485, possibly to perform the royal ritual of touching for the 'King's Evil', and issued a public denial of rumours that he planned to marry his illegitimate niece, Elizabeth of York.

5. The seal of Richard III's nephew, John de la Pole, Earl of Lincoln. (© Colchester and Ipswich Museum Service)

6. Richard III's nephew, Edward of Clarence, Earl of Warwick. Engraving of 1859, after the Rous Roll.

7. Richard III's nieces (the four eldest surviving daughters of Edward IV and Elizabeth Woodville): Elizabeth, Cecily, Anne and Catherine. Fifteenth-century stained glass from Little Malvern Priory, Worcs. (© Geoffrey Wheeler). Unlike the figures from the Royal Window at Canterbury (which have been heavily restored), these are authentic contemporary representations of Richard III's nieces.

8. Copy of Richard III's earliest surviving portrait. © The Dean and Chapter of Leicester.

9. Richard III's preferred prospective bride, Infanta Joana of Portugal (© Geoffrey Wheeler). Redrawn from the portrait attributed to Nuño Gonçalves in the Museu de Aveiro.

10. Richard III's alternative prospective bride, Infanta Isabel of Spain (© Geoffrey Wheeler). Redrawn from 'Our Lady of Grace with the family of the Catholic Monarchs', painting of *c.* 1485, the Cistercian Monastery, Burgos.

11. Henry VI as a saint, from the fifteenth-century rood screen, Eye church, Suffolk.

12. A medieval Corpus Christi procession: a bishop, walking beneath a canopy, carries the Host in a monstrance.

13. & 14. Courtyard of St Mary's Guildhall, Coventry, showing the north-west view and south-east view. Richard III probably stayed at the Guildhall while attending the Coventry Corpus Christi celebrations in June 1485. (© Robert Orland)

15. Kenilworth Castle, where Richard III stayed in May–June 1485. Engraving of 1829.

16. The approach to the hunting lodge, Bestwood Park (Sherwood Forest), where Richard III stayed for about a week in mid-August 1485. (© John Beres)

17. Deer were probably Richard III's quarry at Bestwood Park. Fifteenth-century wood carving from the Guildhall, Eye, Suffolk.

18. The outer wall and gateway of Nottingham Castle where Richard III stayed from late June to August 1485. (© Anne Ayres. Image courtesy of the Richard III Society Nottinghamshire and Derbyshire Group)

31. Portrait in oils of Barbara Spooner (Mrs William Wilberforce) after the pastel portrait by John Russell. Barbara was Richard III's niece in the twelfth generation. (Private collection, reproduced by courtesy of the owner)

32. Alice Strettell (Comyns Carr), at the age of twenty-three. Alice was Richard III's niece in the fourteenth generation, the wife of an Edwardian theatre producer, a friend of Dame Ellen Terry and goddaughter of the author, Charles Kingsley. Photograph taken in 1873, at the time of her marriage.

33. Alice Strettell's only daughter, Dorothy ('Dolly') Comyns Carr, at the age of three. Dolly was Richard III's niece in the fifteenth generation. Photograph of a sketch by E.A. Abbey, published in *Mrs J. Comyns Carr's Reminiscences*, 1925.

34. Alma Strettell (Harrison), Richard III's niece in the fourteenth generation. Photograph of the portrait by John Singer Sargent published in *Mrs J. Comyns Carr's Reminiscences*, 1925. Alma was a writer, a friend of the artists Sargent and Burne Jones, and a close friend of Queen Elisabeth of Romania.

35. Alma Strettell's younger daughter, Sylvia Harrison, Richard III's niece in the fifteenth generation. Photograph of the portrait by John Singer Sargent published in *Mrs J. Comyns Carr's Reminiscences*, 1925.

36. Alma Strettell's elder daughter, Margaret Harrison (Nowell; Armstrong), Richard III's niece in the fifteenth generation. Photograph courtesy of Margaret's granddaughter, Anna Lee Frohlich.

37. Charlotte Vansittart Neale (Mrs Frere), Richard III's niece in the thirteenth generation, and niece of Barbara Spooner (Wilberforce). (Photograph courtesy of Mrs J. Ibsen)

38. Charlotte Vansittart Frere (Mrs Stokes), Richard III's niece in the fourteenth generation. (Photograph courtesy of Mrs J. Ibsen)

39. Muriel Stokes (Mrs Brown), Richard III's niece in the fifteenth generation. (Photograph courtesy of Jeff Ibsen)

40. Joy Brown (Mrs Ibsen), direct descendant in the sixteenth generation (and in an all-female line) of Richard III's sister, Anne of York, Duchess of Exeter. (Photograph courtesy of Mrs J. Ibsen)

41. A tentative plan of the Franciscan Priory in Leicester, based on the excavations of August 2012, and on plans of similar priories. 'X' marks the site of Richard III's grave.

42. Richard III's grave, showing the position in which his body was found. The feet were missing, due to nineteenth-century trenching. The skeleton in this photograph is not the original.

43. Facial reconstruction, based upon Richard III's skull.

Illustrations in the Text

Introduction

There have been innumerable books about Richard III, but this one is unique because it combines the true story of the last five months of Richard's life with the true story of the fate of the king's body and DNA after his death.

First and foremost, my study focuses upon a detailed exploration of the last 150 days of the life and reign of England's most controversial king, examining in detail what Richard did from Friday 25 March 1485 (the first day of the medieval English New Year) up to Monday 22 August that same year. It also considers what thoughts may have preoccupied Richard during those last five months of his life.

It is surely a great mistake – almost bound to lead to errors – to view historical events in the light of hindsight. Yet most accounts of Richard III have been greatly overshadowed by the Battle of Bosworth – an event of which Richard himself never heard. The *fact* of that final battle cannot, of course, be ignored – but neither should Richard's unawareness of it. Therefore, this book deliberately seeks to see things as they might have appeared to contemporaries, most of whom must simply have assumed, at the beginning of 1485, that Richard III still had many years of life and reign ahead of him.

It then becomes clear that Richard himself also assumed that he would continue to reign victoriously. Despite the gloomy view presented by previous writers, during what we now know to have been the last months of his life the king was not simply winding down and waiting for his cousin, known as Henry 'Tudor', to come and defeat him.[1] On the contrary, he was preoccupied with ordinary events and activities, with his own day-to-day life, and with the proper government of his country. At the same time he was also busy with important plans for the future – real plans at the time – even though ultimately destined to come to nothing.

This study also consciously seeks to avoid overshadowing *Richard's* actions with reports of the doings of his rival, the so-called Henry 'Tudor'. Since the latter was ultimately victorious (with the result that he and his supporters were around subsequently to talk to early historians), it is unfortunately the case that most previous books about Richard III actually tell us more about what the future Henry VII was doing between March and August 1485. By contrast, *this* book concentrates on Richard's activities.

In order to establish the context for some of the important happenings and concerns of those last 150 days, the account actually opens about ten days earlier, thus encompassing the sickness and death of Richard's consort, Queen Anne Neville. It also glances back even further, to the death of Richard's only legitimate son and heir, Edward of Middleham, thereby setting in context the problem of the succession, which was unquestionably one of the principal concerns occupying Richard's mind during those last few months of his life.

But this book also differs from every other book on Richard III in another respect. Its story does not simply end on Monday 22 August with Richard's death. The second part of this study goes on to cut through five centuries of persistent mythology and recount the *true* fate of Richard's body.

First, we examine the immediate aftermath of the Battle of Bosworth: how Richard's dead body was transported back to Leicester, placed on public view, and subsequently buried in the choir of the Franciscan Priory Church. New insights into the handling of the corpse are offered, based upon a careful consideration of the most contemporary accounts available, and informed by the recorded treatment of the remains of other vanquished leaders, both in England and elsewhere in Europe, at about this period. Detailed evidence of Richard's burial is drawn from the recent excavations on the Greyfriars site in Leicester – an archaeological project which was principally inspired by the first edition of this very book.

We also examine the subsequent commemoration of Richard's burial in Leicester. We trace the erection, about ten years after Richard's death, of his alabaster tomb – exploring when, why and by whom this monument was constructed, and what subsequently became of it. As a result, a new and more subtle interpretation of Henry VII's attitude to his predecessor emerges. Then we look at the post-Dissolution monument, which was erected in Richard's honour, and on his grave site, by a former mayor of Leicester after the Greyfriars church had been destroyed.

Finally, the reader is taken on into totally new territory, exploring the ultimate fate of Richard III's mortal remains, and revealing the fascinating story of how his DNA was found by the author, alive and well, and living in Canada. The penultimate chapter recounts the fascinating history of that key all-female line of descent, which permitted DNA evidence to be used to confirm the identity of the body excavated from the now-famous Greyfriars car park in Leicester.

No previous writer has explored the story of Richard III in these ways. Thus, even those readers who are very familiar with the events of Richard's short life are sure to find here fascinating new information and fresh insights. For those readers who are new to the field of Ricardian controversy, this book offers a stimulating and thought-provoking introduction to an enigmatic king whose life and death continue to excite widespread interest.

⚜⚜✠✠⚜

The general background to Richard III's reign is the dynastic dispute popularly known as 'The Wars of the Roses', and the background to *that* is the deposition of Richard II in 1399, followed by the Lancastrian usurpation of Henry IV. Modern attitudes to the rival claims to the throne of the houses of Lancaster and York are often as partisan as those of the fifteenth century. Thus the attitudes adopted by historians tend to reflect the personal preferences of the writer. Since this probably cannot be avoided, the next best thing is to be honest about it; to admit that, when the facts are open to dispute, the picture presented will reflect the writer's personal opinion; and to acknowledge that this is not quite the same thing as objective certainty.

Let me begin, therefore, by saying that I believe that the members of the house of York had a good claim to the throne – superior to that of their Lancastrian cousins. I also believe that Richard III personally had a sound claim to the throne in 1483: a claim superior to that of his nephew, Edward V. I set out in detail the reasoning behind this opinion in my earlier book, *Eleanor, the secret Queen*, and in a number of papers, and it will be reiterated in the appropriate chapter of my forthcoming book on *Royal Marriage Secrets* (The History Press, 2013).

Briefly, however, the background to Richard III's reign, as I see it, is that in 1461 – in the person of Richard's elder brother, Edward IV – the house of York assumed the Crown. Edward's accession could certainly be called usurpation. The fact that (unlike Richard III's accession) it is *not* usually so called is just one of many examples of the curious double standards, which seem to be unthinkingly applied to the events of this period by many writers.

Rather like his grandson, Henry VIII, King Edward IV made a complete muddle of his royal marriage policy. He entered into clandestine and overlapping contracts with at least two English noblewomen, while at the same time also permitting negotiations for a foreign royal bride to be conducted on his behalf. As a result he engendered, by his second and bigamous clandestine marriage to Elizabeth Woodville, a family of children who were technically illegitimate. When this fact was brought into the open by the expert canon lawyer Bishop Robert Stillington of Bath and Wells, in the summer of 1483, there was little option but to set those spurious heirs aside. Even though the eldest boy had by then been named Edward V, and his younger brother Richard, Duke of York, it became obvious that by reason of bastardy neither was now eligible to hold those titles, and the Crown must pass to the nearest available legitimate heir – Richard III.

Inevitably, this caused a split in the Yorkist ranks. The Woodville family had tried hard to forestall any enquiry by keeping the future Richard III in the background and hastening to get Edward V crowned with all possible speed. When this move failed, some members of the Woodville family fled, ending up in the 'Tudor' (*soi-disant* Lancastrian) camp. Other key Yorkist supporters, like Lord Hastings, while far from sympathetic to the Woodville cause, nevertheless balked at the drastic step of setting aside Edward IV's Woodville children. In the rather black and white politics of 1483 – and given that the final decision of the royal council went against his opinion – Lord Hastings ultimately had to pay for the uncompromising stance he took on this question with his life.

Nevertheless, through the dramatic events of that key summer of 1483, Richard III was supported by *all* the living members of the royal house of York, and also by his cousin, the Duke of Buckingham. Buckingham's subsequent defection and betrayal came as a great shock to Richard, who was in some ways politically naïve, and often over-kind and generous.

Despite an inevitable degree of public confusion regarding the complex legal points at issue, Richard's accession seems generally to have been accepted, and the new royal family was well received on its public appearances around the country. However, yet another break in the anticipated order of succession had now occurred. Such upsets were always liable to cause trouble. Richard's position was additionally undermined by the death of his only legitimate son, Edward of Middleham – a bereavement which was not only a personal tragedy for Richard, but also left him as a king without a direct heir, and with a consort whose own health was also failing. It is at roughly this point that we take up Richard III's story.

1

'Your Beloved Consort' [I]

The first symptom had probably been a little cough, a dry tickle in the queen's throat, so slight as to be barely noticeable. At first, only those who were very frequently in Anne Neville's presence might have noticed the cough's persistence, for at times it may have seemed to go away, allowing the slender woman respites of peace. Yet each time the cough will have returned, gradually growing more noticeable, while the queen herself grew weaker. Increasingly she doubtless found that she tired quickly and seemed to have little energy. [2]

We have no record of the medicines she took, but presumably the usual simple remedies of the period were tried. Thus the Duke of Norfolk may have suggested that sucking a small piece of sugar candy, or sipping a little honeysuckle water or wine, could be of help in such cases. He had purchased similar medicines for his own first wife, Catherine, in the early stages of *her* fatal illness. [3] But in the long run sugar candy and honeysuckle water had failed to cure Lady Howard. In Anne's case, too, although such palliatives may have helped a little at first, as time went on her cough must have become more persistent and more troublesome.

Anne had been well enough to participate in the festivities of the court at Christmas, accompanied by the Lady Elizabeth, eldest daughter of the late King Edward by his bigamous pretended marriage to Lady Grey. According to the Crowland chronicler, the feast was celebrated with great (even excessive) splendour. He comments in acidulated tones upon the quantity of singing and dancing, and upon the 'vain changes of dress – similar in colour and design – of Queen Anne and of the Lady Elizabeth, eldest daughter of the late king'. [4] Yet soon after Christmas Anne's condition probably worsened, as other and more distressing symptoms began to manifest themselves. Her voice will have grown hoarse. She must often have found herself short of breath, and no doubt her appetite, which may never have been large, progressively decreased.

With failing health came symptoms of which only the queen herself, her intimate body servants, and her husband will have been aware: probably her monthly cycle had now ceased, even though Anne was not yet thirty years of age. Had this fact been more widely known it would have caused grave disquiet in the court, since at this time Richard III was a king with no direct heir. To the great distress and anguish of both his parents, Edward of Middleham, the only child of the royal couple, had died earlier that same year.[5] For the stability of the nation and the dynasty it was, therefore, a matter of some urgency that a replacement heir be engendered as soon as possible.

The king and queen had their own separate bedchambers, as was the norm in upper-class households. Nevertheless, Richard and Anne, who had known one another since childhood, and who were cousins as well as marriage partners, had always been close. For the greater part of their married life they had been in the habit of sleeping together. However, as Anne's health worsened the king was advised by doctors to cease sharing her bed.[6] If consumption (tuberculosis) was the cause of Anne's distress, no doubt her continuous dry, hoarse cough made sleep difficult for both of them. Moreover, she had probably begun to suffer from night sweats, so that Richard would wake in the small hours to find their shared bed soaked and cold. The fact that the king and queen no longer slept together came to be whispered in corners. Royal sexual activity has always been a topic of prurient public interest, and throughout the court, behind hands, the reason for this change in sleeping arrangements became the subject of murmured speculation and gossip.[7]

As the days slowly began to lengthen, the queen will have become increasingly listless. Day by day she must have grown paler and thinner. The napkin with which she covered her lower face when she coughed may now have begun to be speckled with blood. By Collop Monday it must have been abundantly clear to all who saw her that Anne would not be able to take part in the Ash Wednesday fast, nor would her weakened body be capable of sustaining the abstinence of the Lenten diet, which would follow.[8] She would almost certainly need to avail herself of the dispensation which the Church had always accorded to the sick in such circumstances.

Having spent the Christmas season at the royal Palace of Westminster, the court had remained in residence there as the year of grace 1484 drew towards its close.[9] Apart from any other consideration, it may have been thought undesirable to attempt to move the ailing queen. By this time, all at court must have known that she was gravely ill. As is usual in such cases, the relatively sudden onset of her malady gave rise to rumour, and some of those whose meat and drink is to gossip about the affairs of others, began to hint that the only explanation they could think of for such a rapid deterioration in health was poison. Typically, their ill-informed gossip demonstrated little more than their lack of solid information. But, also as usual, that fact did nothing to stop the spread of the malicious tittle-tattle.

The end for Queen Anne came just over a week before the year's end. On Wednesday 16 March a grave portent appeared in the heavens. Just after nine o'clock in the morning, as the Benedictine monks in nearby Westminster Abbey were singing the office of Terce, the spring sunlight filtering through the stained-glass windows on the south side of the choir faltered, and the Latin words in their breviaries and antiphoner became hard to see.[10] Outside the abbey church, the brightness of the morning was fading. In the south-eastern sky, the shadow of the moon's disc crept slowly across the face of the sun until the light of the latter was almost completely obscured. The resulting near-total darkness lasted for almost five minutes, no doubt engendering a delicious *frisson* of fear amongst the superstitious.[11] A solar eclipse was thought to be among the most dreadful of omens, so it probably came as a surprise to no one when the great bell of Westminster began to toll, announcing the passing out of this sinful world of the poor sick queen.[12]

In the Palace of Westminster, the royal chaplains intoned the Litany and murmured the prayers for a passing soul over Anne Neville's frail, wasted body. 'Go forth, Christian Soul, out of this world, in the name of God the Father, who made you; in the name of God the Son, who redeemed you, in the name of God the Holy Spirit, who was poured out upon you.' The rapid muttered Latin of their voices went on to invoke the Holy Mother, and all the angels and saints, to receive the dead queen at the gate of Heaven and conduct her soul into paradise. One can only try to imagine what might, at this time, have been going through the mind of the bereaved king, who in less than a year had lost both his only legitimate child, and his wife. There is no reason to doubt Richard's affection for Anne Neville, and 'one of his last acts prior to the queen's decease, and at a time when her dissolution was hourly expected, was reportedly a grant of £300 to that university which in the preceding year had decreed an annual mass for "the happy state" of the king and "his dearest consort, Anne"'.[13]

Human sexuality encompasses a varied spectrum. The basic black and white terminology popularly employed to pigeonhole it does scant justice to its complex shadings. Nevertheless, the pigeonholes do have their uses. Thus we may observe that in modern terms there had been straight Plantagenets and gay Plantagenets; promiscuous Plantagenets and faithful Plantagenets. Richard's eldest brother, Edward IV, was certainly one of the promiscuous Plantagenets, so much at the mercy of his own libido that he committed grave errors as a result, with very serious consequences for his dynasty. But Edward IV's father, Richard, Duke of York, and the king's younger brothers, George, Duke of Clarence, and Richard III, all seem to have been amongst the continent Plantagenets. Although his had been a marriage arranged for political and economic reasons, the Duke of York seems to have genuinely come to love Cecily Neville, and to have been faithful to her. Their children were numerous; the couple spent a great deal of time together, and we know of no mistresses.[14] Similarly George, Duke of Clarence, seems to have been faithful to Isabel Neville, even though his reasons for marrying her in the first place may have included more than a hint of politics. No mistress or bastard of the Duke of Clarence is named in any surviving source.

Richard III seems to have been cast in very much the same mould as his father and his brother, Clarence. Although he is known to have had two illegitimate children, John and Catherine, these would seem to have been engendered during Richard's teens, at an age when young people are prone to experiment with sex. After Richard married Anne Neville there is no evidence of infidelity on his part, and no more bastards are known to have been born.[15] But unlike his parents' marriage, that of Richard III was not conspicuously fruitful. He and Anne produced only a single child, Edward of Middleham. Whether there had also been other pregnancies which did not run to term, we cannot now know, but even if there were none, there is no reason to suppose that Richard was not an attentive husband. Indeed, the fact that, during Anne's last illness, his avoidance of her bed gave rise to comment and gossip speaks volumes, for it can only mean that for Richard to sleep apart from his wife was considered highly unusual, and that all the court knew this. Presumably then, for most of their married life, Richard and Anne must regularly have shared a bed. Their lack of a large family was, therefore, probably due merely to biological chance.[16]

From the little evidence we have, it is legitimate to deduce that the relationship between Richard III and Queen Anne Neville was a close one throughout, and that their shared grief at the loss of their only child may have deepened that relationship. There is, therefore, every reason to presume that Anne's death at a comparatively young age (even though it was neither sudden nor unexpected) will have caused the king much pain, particularly since this loss followed so closely upon the heels of his earlier grief at the death of his son. In March 1485 Richard III, bereft of his immediate family, probably felt very much alone. He was a religious man.[17] What had happened to him since he accepted the Crown may have raised difficult questions in his mind, resurrecting the ghost of those problems that he had perforce confronted eighteen months earlier. Had his answer been the right one? At the heart of all his concerns lay the perennial problem of the succession to the English throne.[18]

The queen had died at the Palace of Westminster on Wednesday 16 March. No detailed records survive of the arrangements for her exequies, but based on what is known of the funeral arrangements for Edward IV (who also died at Westminster), we may assume that later that same day her dead body was taken into the hands of the embalmers, who then proceeded to prepare Queen Anne for her burial.[19] On 17 March Anne's corpse, royally robed, was doubtless borne into the palace chapel of St Stephen (whose site is now occupied by the chamber of the House of Commons) to lie in state there for a week. On the afternoon of Thursday 24 March it would then have been carried in solemn procession to nearby Westminster Abbey, where *Placebo* and *Dirige* (the offices of Vespers and Matins for the Dead) would have been celebrated into the night while the body, now enclosed in its coffin, lay before the high altar on a great hearse surrounded by candles. It was on the morning of Friday 25 March – Feast of the Annunciation of the Blessed Virgin Mary, and according to the English calendar, the first day of the new year of 1485 – that solemn Requiem Mass for Queen Anne Neville was celebrated in the abbey church, ending with the queen's interment in a grave, which had been newly opened for her beneath the pavement on the right-hand side of the high altar.[20] Although little evidence now survives, there is no doubt that Queen Anne Neville's interment was accompanied by the full panoply of a medieval royal funeral. Indeed, while it gives no details, the late fifteenth-century Crowland Chronicle assures us that, as one would expect, she 'was buried … with honours no less than befitted the burial of a queen'.[21] However, in accordance with established royal protocol the king himself was doubtless absent – at least officially – from all these ceremonies.[22]

⚜⚜⚜

The liturgical season did not lend itself to any prolonged period of royal seclusion for the private indulgence of grief. Lent was rapidly drawing to its close, and inevitably Richard must have appeared in public on Sunday 27 March, to take part in the Palm Sunday procession at Westminster. Palm Sunday marks the start of Holy Week, during which further important religious observances will have required the king's presence. Subsequent English sovereigns were wont to touch for the 'King's Evil' (scrofula) during Holy Week – as well as at other times of the year.[23] This miraculous royal healing ceremony was exclusive to the kings of England and France. The period around Easter was considered particularly appropriate for 'touching', since in France – and probably also in England prior to the Reformation – it was thought important for the monarch to be in a 'state of grace' (having confessed, received absolution and taken Holy Communion) before beginning the rite.[24]

This healing ritual was enacted in England from at least the time of Henry II, founder of the Plantagenet dynasty.[25] Indeed, from the fourteenth century, if not before, it seems to have been regarded as offering an acid test of the validity of the monarch's claim to the throne.[26] By the reign of Henry VII a special order of service had been established for 'touching', which, however, 'incorporates much older material'.[27] Specific records of numbers and dates of 'touchings' during the Yorkist period are lacking, but this in itself is not particularly surprising. The rite was by this time so routine as to excite little comment. Moreover, the system of accounting had been changed, so that disbursements under the general heading of 'royal alms' were no longer itemised in detail.[28] We can nevertheless be quite certain that Edward IV performed the ritual, since Sir John Fortescue (then a Lancastrian supporter) denied that Edward's 'touching' could be efficacious, on the grounds that Henry VI was the true anointed king.[29] Richard III must also have 'touched'. Failure to do so would inevitably have cast doubt on the legitimacy of his royal claim.

The duty involved was not a particularly pleasant one. After having confessed and taken communion, the king was required to rinse his hands, then press them upon the suppurating sores of each of the afflicted, while one of his chaplains intoned the Latin words: *Super egros manus imponent et bene habebunt* ('They will lay their hands upon the sick and they will recover': Mark, xvi, 18). The ceremony could be held in either a secular or a religious building. In England it took place with the king seated, the sick being brought before him.[30] After their sores had received the royal touch, each was given a coin. By 1485 this was almost certainly one of the recently introduced gold 'angels', depicting the Archangel Michael overcoming evil, and bearing the legend: *Per crucem tuam salva nos Christe Redemptor* ('Christ, Redeemer, save us by your cross').[31] On Wednesday 30 March, five days after his queen's burial, we know that Richard III was at the Priory of the Knights of St John of Jerusalem (Knights Hospitaller) in Clerkenwell[32] – where he made an important public statement, which we shall examine in detail in the next chapter. Since the Hospitallers were specifically dedicated to the care and healing of the sick, it is possible that this Holy Week visit by the king was in order to conduct the royal 'touching' ceremony at the knights' priory on this occasion.

The following day was Maundy Thursday, and the king must have attended the mass of the Last Supper, most probably at St Paul's Cathedral. After the gospel reading from the thirteenth chapter of St John had been intoned, in accordance with ancient custom Richard III donned an apron and went down on his knees. He then proceeded to wash the feet of thirty-two poor men while the choir chanted a series of antiphons, from the opening words of the first of which this whole day derives its English name.[33] Having washed the feet of the poor in imitation of Christ, Richard then gave to each of the thirty-two men the apron he had worn to wash that man's feet, together with the towel with which he had dried them. Additional gifts followed, including for each man a gown, a hood, a pair of shoes, bread, fish, wine and a purse containing thirty-two silver pennies. Both the total number of poor men and the number of pennies distributed to each of them reflected the years of the king's age.[34]

Friday 1 April found the king on his knees again, for the penitential rite of 'creeping to the cross', which was the main focus of the Good Friday liturgy. For preference, the cross adored by medieval English kings on this occasion was the reliquary Cross Gneth captured by Edward I from the Welsh and containing a fragment of the True Cross. From the reign of Edward III this was normally kept at St George's Chapel, Windsor. Since Richard III was in London on Good Friday 1485, either this royal reliquary cross was brought to him from Windsor, or a different cross must have been used on this occasion. At the appropriate point of the Good Friday liturgy 'the king would … prostrate himself, and then – without getting up – slowly approach the symbol of the crucifixion' in a semi-prostrate condition.[35]

Early in the fourteenth century this Good Friday veneration of the cross – practised universally throughout the Church – had acquired in the chapel royal an additional element, which all subsequent English monarchs then observed until the Reformation. After his adoration of the cross, the king would make a special and unique offering, originally comprising newly minted gold and silver coins. These he would then redeem by replacing them with an equivalent offertory in the form of old coins. Meanwhile, the new coins of the first offering would be taken away to be made into 'cramp rings', which were believed to be capable of relieving muscular cramp, spasms and even epilepsy.[36] These rings were given away, and were much sought-after. From the reign of Henry VI the offering ceremony was simplified slightly. Thereafter, gold and silver from the treasury to the value of twenty-five shillings was made into cramp rings prior to Good Friday. It was then these ready-prepared rings that the king first offered to the holy cross, and subsequently redeemed with coins to the same value.[37] All English monarchs from Edward II to Mary I seem to have observed this custom. 'For two reigns only the evidence is lacking – those of Edward V and Richard III … [The relevant accounts] from Richard III's reign seem to have been lost or destroyed.'[38] However, there is no reason to suppose that Richard would have neglected this Good Friday ritual, or failed to produce and distribute cramp rings on the two Good Fridays that fell within his reign.

In accordance with tradition, no mass was celebrated on Good Friday, being replaced by the special liturgy for this day, which, as we have seen, included the veneration of the cross. The king may also have attended the gloomy office of *Tenebrae*, when the church was lit by only a single candle.[39] If he did so, the reiterated words of the third responsory of the third nocturn for Good Friday may well have resounded in his ears like an echo of his own private sorrows:

Caligaverunt oculi mei a fletu meo, quia elongatus est a me, qui consolabatur me. Videte, omnes populi, si est dolor similis sicut dolor meus.

My eyes are dim with weeping, for the one who comforted me is far away from me. O all you people, see whether there be any sorrow like mine.

2

'It Suits the King of England to Marry Straight Away' [1]

By 1485, having successfully overcome challenges to his tenure of the throne, Richard III appeared firmly established as King of England. However, he had unfortunately become a king without an heir. While not a disaster, this was certainly a problem – albeit one which could hopefully be remedied relatively easily, now that the queen too was dead. The background to Richard's problem was the fact that for a hundred years England had been experiencing disputes over the royal succession. This sorry story had begun with another king called Richard, who had likewise found himself with no direct heir. That fact and its sequel were well remembered. It is therefore quite certain that Richard III must have realised he had a problem and that something needed to be done about it. Indeed, it is clear that Richard's diplomatic activity during the five months from March to August 1485 was precisely focused upon rapidly resolving this dilemma by providing a new queen consort for the kingdom – hopefully leading in due course to a new heir to the throne.

As a matter of fact, the king was not childless. As we have seen he had a son and a daughter, both probably born long before his marriage to Anne Neville. Richard's son, John of Gloucester (or John de Pountfreit), might possibly have been conceived during Richard's first solo expedition: a visit to the eastern counties in the summer of 1467, at the invitation of Sir John Howard.[2] If so, John of Gloucester will probably have been born in about March 1468, and he might even have derived his first name from Sir John Howard, who could have been his godfather. These can only be speculations, because nothing has so far been discovered relating to John of Gloucester's birth.[3] However, if he *was* born in about March 1468, that same month in 1485 would have marked his seventeenth birthday. It is therefore interesting to note that it was on 11 March 1485 that King Richard announced John's appointment as Captain of Calais. The royal patent refers to 'our dear bastard son, John of Gloucester, whose disposition and natural vigour, agility of body and inclination to all good customs, promises us by the grace of God great and certain hope of future service'. Richard goes on to note that John is still a minor, and makes provision to take charge himself of subordinate Calais appointments until John 'reaches the age of 21 years'.[4] It is clear from this patent and appointment that Richard III hoped his illegitimate son would become a future support to the dynasty. At the same time, his uncompromising revelation of John of Gloucester's bastard status precludes any notion that the king would ever have sought to make this lad his heir. Both the house of York as a whole and Richard III personally based their claims to the throne on the principle of absolute legitimacy. We can therefore be confident that Richard would never have countenanced the notion of such an advancement for his own illegitimate son.[5]

Richard was still a young man, and the death of Queen Anne Neville (however sad this may have been in itself) did offer him the possible hope of future royal heirs. He had only to remarry. There can be no doubt whatever that his immediate advisers, well aware of the fact that his consort was dying, had already urged him to begin seeking a new queen even before Anne had breathed her last.[6] In the secrecy of the royal council it seems clear that well before 16 March the *desiderata* for a future consort had already been thoroughly thrashed out. A foreign princess was preferable. This would conform with the traditional pattern established for medieval English kings, while at the same time avoiding the dangers inherent in advancing the daughter of any particular English noble family.[7] Naturally the chosen princess should be of an age to bear children. However, it seems also to have been decided to take advantage of the situation to try to end once and for all the dynastic feud between the heirs of York and Lancaster. That this was the case emerges quite clearly from the points put forward subsequently by the royal councillors of Portugal, to their sovereign and his sister, as one argument in favour of the royal marriage pact proposed to them by Richard III. The Portuguese Council of State recommended the projected English royal marriage to their king's sister for various reasons, but most specifically 'for the concord in the same kingdom of England that will follow from her marriage and union with the king's party, greatly serving God and bringing honour to herself[8] by uniting as one the party of Lancaster, and York – which are the two parties of that kingdom out of which the divisions and evils over the succession are born'.[9]

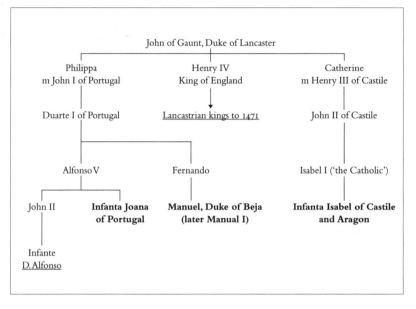

FAMILY TREE I: The heirs of the house of Lancaster (simplified). The three individuals directly involved in the 1485 marriage plans of Richard III are shown in bold type.

In the legitimate male line the house of Lancaster had been extinct since the death of Henry VI in 1471, and there were also no living descendants of any of the Lancastrian kings in legitimate female lines. However, there *were* living descendants both of Henry IV's sister, and of his half-sister. The most direct heirs of these two Lancastrian princesses in 1485 were respectively King John II of Portugal and Queen Isabel of Castile.[10] Both Portuguese and Spanish infantas were therefore strongly favoured as possible brides, although preference seems to have been accorded to Portugal, probably because the Portuguese royal house of Avis had a stronger dynastic claim than the Castilian royal house of Trastámara to be the senior surviving Lancastrian heirs.[11]

Proof that a second wife for the king had already been discussed before the first had died lies in the fact that, on Tuesday 22 March, less than a week after Anne Neville's death, and before her body had even been buried, Sir Edward Brampton, a converted Portuguese Jew who had long served King Edward IV, was sent back to his former homeland to offer, on Richard's behalf, for the hand of King John II's elder sister, the Infanta Joana.[12] It is also as a result of Brampton's negotiations in Portugal that we have knowledge of the alternative English plan for a marriage with the Spanish infanta, in case the Portuguese match should come to nothing. In fact, the contemporary commentator Álvaro Lopes de Chaves, writing retrospectively in about 1488, reported that the Portuguese Council of State had been very anxious to ensure that the Portuguese marriage proposal was accepted. Behind their forceful support of the proposed Anglo-Portuguese marriage pact lay the councillors' openly expressed fear that if the Portuguese marriage did not take place, Richard III 'could marry the Infanta Doña Isabel of Castile [*sic*] and make alliance with *those* kings, and become your enemy and opponent'.[13] Indeed, knowing that such an alliance with England was only too likely to prove agreeable to 'the Catholic Kings' of Spain, the Portuguese royal advisers reiterated their anxiety, strongly underlining the risk that if the projected marriage with their own Infanta Joana were not quickly brought to a successful conclusion, 'the sovereigns of Castile may give him [Richard] their eldest daughter as his wife'.[14] The Portuguese councillors were also well aware that Richard III was in a hurry to remarry, since they commented specifically on the fact that 'it suits the king of England to marry straight away'.[15]

In fact, the marriage proposal brought to Portugal by Sir Edward Brampton was for a double alliance. Richard III himself would marry Joana, while his niece, Elizabeth of York, would marry John II's cousin Manuel, Duke of Beja (who later became King Manuel I). This point too is established beyond question by Álvaro Lopes de Chaves who referred to a 'marriage between the daughter of King Edward of England ... and the Duke of Beja Dom Manuel ... which said marriage had previously been appointed by Edward Brampton on his coming as ambassador of King Richard (brother to the said King Edward) to swear the betrothals and commit the Princess Joana in marriage'.[16] On the Portuguese side it was hoped that, in return for the proposed matches, Richard would provide King John II with English help against dissident members of the aristocracy, who were being supported from Castile.

Brampton's overtures were later followed up by someone described as the Count or Earl of Scales [Scalus].[17] In earlier publications relating to this subsequent visit, both Barrie Williams and his modern Portuguese source, Gomes dos Santos, mistakenly assumed that the activities of this 'Count Scales' represented a follow-up embassy from Richard III. In addition, Williams embroils himself in vain speculations as to the identity of 'Count Scales'.[18] Unfortunately, he is at sea in suggesting that *Richard* Woodville might have inherited the Scales title from his elder brother, Anthony. In fact this title had merely been acquired by Anthony Woodville as a result of his marriage to the Scales heiress. Nevertheless, it is known that Anthony attempted to bequeath it to his other brother *Edward*.[19] This attempt had no legal validity, but it explains why Edward Woodville might have called himself 'Lord Scales' – and indeed, the Portuguese records establish beyond question that in fact he did so.

They also prove that Edward Woodville's visit to King John took place *after* Richard III's death, in 1486, at a time when Edward was returning home to England after taking part in the ongoing Spanish *reconquista* of the southern kingdom of Granada.[20] Thus his visit would be too late in its timing to have any interest for us in the present context, were it not for the fact that the *soi-disant* 'count' sought to revive half of Richard III's proposed Portuguese marriage pact – namely the part involving the marriage of one of his nieces to Dom Manuel, Duke of Beja (King John's cousin). By seeking to revive this proposal, Sir Edward explicitly drew attention to the fact that Richard III's initial overtures in 1485 had included such plans for the marriage of one of Edward IV's daughters with Dom Manuel. We shall return to this interesting second aspect of Richard III's Portuguese marriage project shortly.

As for the Infanta Joana, she was a few months older than her prospective husband, having been born in February 1452. She was deeply religious, and had already rejected previous offers of marriage from several other European rulers. However, either because she herself was genuinely interested in the proposed English royal marriage, or because she was placed under considerable pressure by her brother, King John, Joana seems to have given very serious consideration to the idea of marriage to Richard. In fact, had the latter not lost the Battle of Bosworth, the Portuguese royal marriages would very probably have taken place.[21]

As has already been noted, of the two princesses who were apparently regarded as the leading potential contenders for the English consort's crown, it must have been the fact that the Infanta Joana was the most senior living heir of the house of Lancaster (after her brother, King John) which chiefly influenced Richard III and his council in her favour, for in other respects she might well have been considered less than ideal. As a childless and hitherto unmarried princess, thirty-three years of age, her chances of bearing for Richard the all-important son and heir he so badly needed must, in retrospect, be regarded as somewhat questionable. There is no doubt that, in terms of age, the fourteen-year-old Spanish infanta, Doña Isabel de Aragón y Castilla, who shared Richard III's birthday (2 October) but who was eighteen years his junior, would have been a far more promising prospective mother of a future prince of Wales.[22]

As we have seen, the proposed Portuguese marriage was part of a package deal. Not only was Richard III to marry Joana, but also his niece, Elizabeth of York – the eldest illegitimate daughter of Edward IV by Elizabeth Woodville – was to marry the Portuguese prince Manuel, Duke of Beja, cousin (and eventual successor) of King John II. The subsequent attempts on the part of 'Count Scales' to revive this second marriage proposal were aided by the fact that Richard III's negotiations had apparently never referred to

Elizabeth of York by name, but had simply spoken of '[a] filha del Rej Duarte' ([the] daughter of King Edward).[23] For Richard III this circumlocution may have been advantageous in that it skirted round the potentially tricky problem of Elizabeth of York's status. In 1485 she was, of course, a mere royal bastard and not an English princess – but unfortunately for Richard there were no legitimate English royal daughters then available for the marriage market. Without actually being openly deceitful, the terminology employed by Richard's envoys tended to imply that the proposed bride was an English princess – and indeed, probably the most senior royal daughter available.[24]

There may also have been one other advantage. If anything should happen to Elizabeth, one of her sisters could easily be substituted for her without the need for renegotiations. This was a period when death readily claimed young victims, and even promising royal sprigs did not always manage to successfully complete their journey into adulthood. Some children of Edward IV by Elizabeth Woodville had already died young.[25] The names of Elizabeth, Cecily and Anne of York may have meant little even to King John II, while his cousin, Dom Manuel (who was to marry this English girl), was at that time a relatively minor member of the Portuguese royal house, whose marriage negotiations probably did not demand the detailed precision which would, for example, have surrounded the betrothal of King John's son and heir. But undoubtedly both the Portuguese king and his cousin had heard of King Edward IV himself. Thus 'King Edward's daughter' was in every way a convenient phrase.

Later, this rather vague terminology proved fortunate for 'Count Scales', because at the time of his negotiations in 1486 Elizabeth of York was actually no longer available (having recently married Henry VII). However, Cecily of York was then on the marriage market. The annulment of Cecily's previous marriage at about this juncture – and at the behest of Henry VII – may have been no accident, for she was more or less of an age with Dom Manuel. Failing her, her younger sister Anne could also have been considered. Indeed, evidence survives that Anne of York *was* put forward as a candidate for the hand of Dom Manuel. This evidence comprises a papal dispensation permitting such a marriage in spite of the fact that the proposed partners were related within the prohibited degrees.[26]

Given all these points, it is not surprising that, in 1486, 'Count Scales' continued to refer vaguely to 'the daughter of King Edward' in his Portuguese marriage negotiations. Moreover, the existence of the dispensation of 1491 strongly suggests that Edward Woodville may have been acting on direct instructions from Henry VII who, in one way or another, was intent on picking up and carrying into effect at least some of the matrimonial projects of Richard III.[27]

There were two reasons why Richard III should have included Elizabeth of York in his marriage plans in 1485. The first was the fact that, as we have already noted, no legitimate English princesses were available as marriage pawns. The second point is the fact that one of Richard III's promises to the girl's mother, Elizabeth Woodville – solemnly made towards the end of the eleven months (April 1483–March 1484), during which the latter had remained in sanctuary with her daughters at Westminster Abbey – had been that, if she would emerge from her self-imposed seclusion, she and her daughters would be well treated and that suitable marriages would be arranged for the girls:

Memorandum that I Richard by the grace of God king of England and of Fraunce and lord of Irland in the presens of you my lords spirituelle & temporelle and you Maire and Aldermen of my Cite of London promitte & swere *verbo Regio* & upon these holy evangelies of god by me personally touched that if the doghters of dam Elizabeth Gray late calling her self Quene of England that is to wit Elizabeth Cecille Anne Kateryn and Briggitte wolle come unto me out of Saintwarie of Westminstre and be guyded Ruled & demeaned after me than I shalle see that they shalbe in suertie of their lyffes and also not suffer any maner hurt by any maner persone or persones to theim or any of theim in their bodies and persones to be done by wey of Ravisshement or defouling contrarie to their willes not theim or any of theim emprisone within the Toure of London or other prisone but that I shalle put theim in honest places of good name & fame and theim honestly & curtesly shalle see to be(e) foundene & entreated and to have alle thinges requisite & necessarye(te) for their exibicione and findings as my kynneswomen And that I shalle do marie sucche of theim as now bene mariable to gentilmen borne and everiche of theim geve in mariage lands & tenementes to the yerely valewe of CC marc for terme of their lyves and in like wise to the other doghters when they come to lawfulle Age of mariage if they lyff and suche gentilmen as shalle happe to marie with theim I shalle straitly charge from tyme to tyme loyngly to love & entreat theim as their wiffes & my kynneswomen As they wolle advoid and eschue my displeasure And over this that I shalle yerely fromhencefurthe content & pay or cause to be contented and paied for thexibicione & finding of the said dame Elizabeth Gray during her naturelle liff at iiij termes of the yere that is to wit at pasche Midsomer Michilmesse & Christenmesse to John Nesfelde one of the squires of my body (&) for his finding to attende upon her the summe of DCC marc of lawfulle money of England by even porcions And moreover I promitte to theim that if any surmyse or evylle report be made to me of theim or any of theim by any persone or persones that than I shalle not geve thereunto faithe ne credence not therefore put theim to any maner ponysshement before that

they or any of theim so accused may be at their lawfulle defence and answere
In witnesse wherof to this writing of my othe & promise aforsaid in your said
presences made I have set my signemanuelle the first day of Marche the first
yere of my Reigne.[28]

Richard had already taken positive steps to demonstrate that this had been
no empty promise on his part. In 1484 he had arranged the marriage of his
own illegitimate daughter, Catherine, to one of his supporters, the Earl of
Pembroke, and although the precise date is not on record it was probably at
about the same time that he also arranged the marriage of his niece, Cecily
(the second surviving daughter of Edward IV and Elizabeth Woodville), to
Ralph Scrope, a younger brother of Thomas, 6th Baron Scrope, who was
another of Richard's supporters.[29]

Cecily's Scrope marriage was a perfectly respectable one for the bastard
daughter of a deceased monarch. But the Portuguese royal marriage that was
now in prospect for her elder sister went far beyond Richard's promise to
marry the girls to gentlemen born, and must have delighted their mother,
Elizabeth Woodville. This marriage would heal the split in the Yorkist ranks
by offering the Woodvilles a dynastic alliance, which would pose no threat
to Richard. Had the marriage taken place, it would instantly have restored
Elizabeth of York to legitimate royal rank. Indeed, it would one day have
made her Queen of Portugal – though no one could possibly have foreseen
that in March 1485. The young girl herself was very excited by the proposal,
and apparently wrote to her uncle's right-hand man, John Howard, Duke
of Norfolk, imploring him to urge the king, on her behalf, to press on with
the project.[30] The fact that Elizabeth of York's letter to Norfolk was written as early as mid-February 1484/85 shows that key members of the royal
council were already aware of the possibility of a double royal marriage pact
with Portugal at least four weeks *before* Queen Anne Neville breathed her last.
But naturally no such plans could proceed until Richard's first consort died,
and the fact that Anne was lingering in mortal illness seems to have led the
young Elizabeth of York to remark, in a rather thoughtless and unkind way –
excusable perhaps on the grounds of her youth and her eagerness to be a
princess once again – that 'she feared the queen would never die'.[31]

It may also have been some ill-considered, indiscreet remark on the part
of Elizabeth of York or some member of her mother's family that led to the
leaking out of rumours of marriage plans for both the girl and the king.
These rumours were promptly misunderstood. Instead of a dual marriage
pact with the house of Avis, what began to be spoken of in England was
a single marriage, between Richard III and his niece. Such rumours gave
cause for concern, and their circulation was discussed by the royal council.

As a result, 'Sir Richard Ratcliffe and William Catesby ... told the king to his face that if he did not deny any such purpose' there could be serious consequences.[32] Convinced of the need for some official statement, the king then acted very quickly to scotch this unfortunate misunderstanding. On the Wednesday of Holy Week (30 March), at the Priory of St John in Clerkenwell, in the presence of the mayor and citizens of London, he publicly and very firmly denied any plans for a marriage between himself and Elizabeth of York, commanding the mayor to arrest and punish anyone found spreading this tale.[33] A couple of weeks after Easter, on 19 April, he wrote in similar terms to the city of York. Given that his own legitimacy as king depended absolutely upon the bastardy of his late brother's Woodville children, it must have seemed vital to Richard to set the record straight in respect of this unfortunate rumour.[34]

ᏸᏰᏓᏓ

In addition to his own illegitimate children, and the prospect of future children as a result of his projected second marriage, Richard III also had other potential Yorkist heirs to hand. It is often stated that when his own son died he named one of his nephews, either Edward, Earl of Warwick (son of the Duke of Clarence) or John de la Pole, Earl of Lincoln (son of the Duchess of Suffolk), as heir to the throne.[35] In fact there is no evidence that either nephew was ever formally designated as Richard's heir, and the fact that various authors have given conflicting accounts of their supposed elevation merely serves to underline the lack of proof. Indeed, as affairs stood in April 1485 there was no conceivable reason for precipitate action on the part of the king. As we have seen, in this first full month of the medieval English year of 1485, Richard III was undoubtedly planning to remarry. He thus had every prospect of a legitimate son of his own as heir to the throne. Hence there was no necessity to designate an alternative heir. So far as Richard was aware, many years of his reign still lay before him, offering him ample time and opportunity to train his as yet unborn son for future kingship.[36]

However, likely looking Yorkist princes such as his nephews were still an investment for the future. Hopefully both Lincoln and Warwick would become bulwarks supporting and maintaining the royal house of York well into the sixteenth century. Thus there was every reason to train and promote them – not as future monarchs, but as key supporters for the throne. The elder of the two, the Earl of Lincoln, was certainly given some preferment, and this must be seen as part of that same policy which led Richard to give John of Gloucester the Calais post. The king was firming the foundations of his dynasty by promoting its future senior members to important posts, in which they could learn the business of government, while at the same time themselves becoming known to the aristocracy and to the country as a whole.

Lincoln had been born in about 1460. He was the eldest son of Richard's sister, Elizabeth of York, and her husband, John de la Pole, Duke of Suffolk. Edward IV had created him Earl of Lincoln on 13 March 1467, and he had subsequently received knighthood, together with Edward's own sons, on 18 April 1475. He had attended Lady Anne Mowbray on the occasion of her marriage to Edward IV's second son, Richard of Shrewsbury, Duke of York, in January 1478; had borne the salt at the baptism of Edward's daughter Bridget in November 1480, and (in the absence of the future Richard III himself) had acted as the chief mourner at the funeral of King Edward IV in 1483. He then went on to carry the orb at Richard III's own coronation.[37] By 1485 he was already a young adult.

> Lincoln supported Richard against the rebels of October 1483 and was rewarded the following April with land worth £157, and the reversion of Beaufort estates worth a further £178 after the death of Thomas, Lord Stanley, who had been granted a life interest in the land which his wife, Margaret Beaufort, had forfeited for her part in the rising. In the following month Lincoln was granted an annuity of £177 13s. 4d. from the duchy of Cornwall until the reversion materialized.[38]

Prior to his early demise, Richard III's own son, Edward of Middleham, Prince of Wales, had briefly held the important post of Lieutenant of Ireland.[39] This post was normally exercised through a deputy, so that the boy's youth would not have been of much significance. It is noteworthy that, following Edward of Middleham's death, Richard appointed his nephew, the Earl of Lincoln, to this post. Given that the Plantagenet dynasty as a whole (and the house of York in particular) had always acknowledged that the right to the Crown could be transmitted through the female line, Lincoln must certainly have been regarded as a potential heir to the throne. Indeed, it is arguable that he automatically became the heir presumptive following Edward of Middleham's death – given that the sons of Edward IV were all illegitimate, and, therefore, excluded, while the Earl of Warwick, son of Richard III's brother, the Duke of Clarence, was ruled out by reason of Edward IV's act of attainder against his father. The king's eldest sister, Anne of York, Duchess of Exeter, had given birth to two children, one by each of her two successive husbands. However, both of these had been girls, and while the capacity of female heirs to *transmit* rights to the throne was recognised, the possibility of a female heir actually succeeding to the English throne in person had not yet been conceded. It is, therefore, entirely plausible that after the death of the Prince of Wales, Richard III regarded Lincoln as his interim heir. Nevertheless, no specific statement to that effect was issued – and indeed, none would have been strictly necessary.

In addition to being appointed to the lieutenantship of Ireland (21 August 1484), Lincoln was given further prominence by being granted also the presidency of the council in the north. This was a body established in the summer of 1484 'as the successor to the prince's council, which had itself replaced Gloucester's ducal council as a way of maintaining Richard's authority in the north'.[40]

The other Yorkist princeling in whom Richard III clearly took an interest is Edward, Earl of Warwick (1475–99), the only surviving son of the Duke and Duchess of Clarence, and thus the nephew both of Richard III and of Queen Anne Neville. But for Edward IV's act of attainder against his father, the young Earl of Warwick would actually have ranked higher in terms of the succession to the throne than Richard III himself. However, as things stood in 1485, Edward IV's act of attainder against Clarence ruled Warwick out of the succession entirely. Even so, acts of attainder were not irreversible – though given Warwick's seniority in the royal bloodline, Richard III would have needed to handle with some care any reversal of the attainder which excluded this particular nephew from the throne.

Warwick had been born in February 1475 at Warwick Castle, and was named for his godfather and uncle, Edward IV, who had given him the title 'Earl of Warwick' at his baptism. In a sometimes puzzling and misleading note on him for the *Oxford Dictionary of National Biography*, Christine Carpenter states that 'on his father's attainder in February 1478, Edward's lands, consisting essentially of the Warwick earldom as it stood at Clarence's death, were taken into royal custody. This was officially for his minority only, and he was indeed subsequently on occasion referred to as Earl of Warwick. In practice, however, the attainder was never reversed.'[41] Carpenter's last sentence is nonsensical. Edward's tenure of the earldom of Warwick was incontrovertible, since it was an inheritance derived from his *mother*, not his father. Moreover, he had explicitly and personally been granted this title by Edward IV in 1475. His tenure of it was, therefore, unaffected by his father's attainder. Following his father's execution, in 1481 Warwick was made the ward of Thomas Grey, Marquess of Dorset. He had attended his uncle Richard III's coronation in July 1483, and been knighted on the occasion of the investiture of his cousin Edward of Middleham, as Prince of Wales, in September the same year. Like his other cousin Lincoln, Warwick was a member of the council in the north.[42] In Warwick's case (given his youth) this membership was probably largely nominal in 1485, but it certainly indicates Richard III's intention that this nephew, too, should be trained to play some role in the politics of the future.

3

'Tapettes of Verdoures with Crownes and Rooses'[1]

In terms of rising, going to bed and eating meals, Richard III presumably lived out the last five months of his life on a day-to-day basis not dissimilar to that of most of his wealthier subjects. Certain aspects of this fifteenth-century routine would have differed from modern norms. It might, therefore, be helpful at this point to explore the kind of timetable which would have governed Richard's daily existence. At the same time we may also examine such evidence as we possess regarding the physical setting against which those last weeks and months of Richard's life were lived; the attire he wore, and the kind of activities which engaged him.

The obvious essentials of the daily human round of activities have not changed. However, in the fifteenth century Christian religious observance certainly played a greater part in day-to-day life than it appears to do for the majority of English households today. At dawn, when the bells of monastic, conventual, collegiate and cathedral churches rang for the early morning office, it was not necessary for lay people to be up and about, nor were they expected to take any formal part in the worship. Nevertheless, it was expected that if the sound of the bells happened to awaken them, they would utter some of the better-known set prayers, either in Latin or in the vernacular, before pulling up their blankets and going back to sleep.[2] By the 1480s the simple and easily memorised thrice-daily devotion of the *Angelus* had reached England, where its spread had been encouraged by Richard III's erstwhile supposed sister-in-law, Elizabeth Woodville.[3]

Attendance at mass certainly was expected, and a late fourteenth-century description of how mass was celebrated indicates that this differed very little from the modern rite. It comprised introit, *Kyrie*, *Gloria*, prayers, epistle, *Alleluia*, sequence, gospel-reading, offertory, *Sanctus*, prayers of consecration, *Pater noster*, *Agnus Dei*, post-communion chant, and final prayers.[4] However, the main objects of attendance at mass at this period were seen as being 'to *hear* His blessed mass and to *behold* His blessed sacrament'.[5] Actually receiving Holy Communion was much rarer than it is today, but we may suppose that Richard III probably attended mass on a daily basis. As we shall see shortly, there is evidence that his nephew, Edward V, did so as Prince of Wales.

The fact that Richard is known to have possessed a Book of Hours,[6] clearly designed for use rather than show, and containing some annotations in his own hand, strongly suggests that one regular feature of the king's waking life was the private recitation in his oratory of the cycle of prayer comprising the 'Little Office of the Blessed Virgin Mary'. This simplified version of the full Divine Office (as celebrated by all the regular and secular clergy) had originated in the ninth or tenth century for the use of those members of the educated laity who wished to participate on a regular basis in the *Opus Dei* – the formal prayer of the Church. The daily recitation of the entire Little Office was certainly not compulsory. Nevertheless, it seems probable that Richard III's day would have been punctuated by regular short sessions of prayer.

In addition to this religious timetable (*horarium*), Richard's life was conditioned by the secular timetable of a regular daily routine. It is possible that the passage of time was marked in his palaces by the bells and hour hands of weight-driven clocks. The king's distant cousin, John Howard, Duke of Norfolk, certainly possessed one.[7] Five hundred years or more ago there would probably have been some important differences in the hours of rising and going to bed, and also in the matter of mealtimes. In exploring this point, we must remember that, even today, there can be quite significant differences between individuals and households regarding times of rising and going to bed, and in respect of mealtimes – not to mention the names given to different meals, and the kinds of food that compose them. It would not be unreasonable to anticipate that similar variations also existed in the past. Any attempt to impose uniformity upon the fifteenth-century daily routine is, therefore, probably doomed to failure. Modern authorities on late medieval meals and mealtimes have certainly produced quite a variety of different models for the supposedly typical everyday timetable of fifteenth-century England. The apparent discrepancies may well reflect genuine variations in the fifteenth-century source material. There is no reason to suppose that the daily round of a particular individual or family was any more stereotypical in the late Middle

Ages than it is today. Yet despite probable individual variations, it is perhaps possible to suggest in broad terms some ways in which the fifteenth-century routine differed from that of the present day.

In accordance with the precepts of the Medical School of Salerno, the twelfth-century Italian poet, John of Milan, had advised: 'rise at 5, dine at 9, sup at 5, retire at 9, for a long life'.[8] His recommended times of rising and going to bed are both probably a good deal earlier than would be considered normal by the majority of the population nowadays. We may also observe that John made no mention of breakfast. This was not merely an Italian peculiarity, for in early medieval England too, breakfast seems to have been virtually non-existent. Even today, not everyone takes breakfast. However, by the fifteenth century it does seem to have become the accepted practice in at least some English households to break one's fast early in the day. Late medieval breakfast was a modest meal, so that 'to be able to have merely a "*sop in wine*" (bread or toast soaked in wine) every day for one's morning repast was considered luxurious'.[9] The 'full English breakfast' now apparently regarded as traditional in hotels and guest houses, was as yet unheard of in the fifteenth century.

Peter Hammond has concluded from his research that the better-off fifteenth-century peasants probably consumed three meals a day, comprising an early breakfast, dinner at 9.00 or 10.00 am, and supper eaten before nightfall (and thus perhaps as early as 3.00 pm in winter). Sixteenth-century writers certainly seem to have considered three meals a day to be reasonable – though some authorities have argued that breakfast was only eaten by children and workmen. The household accounts of Dame Alice de Bryene at the beginning of the fifteenth century, assume that breakfast will be provided for all, 'though the 1478 household ordinance of Edward IV specifies that only residents down to the rank of squire should have breakfast, except by special order. Edward, Prince of Wales, son of Edward IV, breakfasted after morning mass. The time was only specified as *a convenyent hower*, although to break one's fast after devotions was the generally recommended procedure.'[10] It would certainly have been considered inappropriate in the fifteenth century (or indeed at any time up until the second half of the last century) for any faithful Catholic to break his or her fast *before* going to mass, if he or she intended to participate fully in the liturgy and take Holy Communion, since the Church's regulations stipulated that the night fast should not be broken prior to receiving Communion.[11]

Other writers have suggested that by the fifteenth century, slightly later mealtimes than those proposed by Hammond were becoming the norm. 'Meal times in Britain have varied greatly over the years. In the fourteenth century breakfast was taken at five; dinner at nine and supper at four. In the fifteenth and sixteenth centuries breakfast had advanced to seven; dinner eleven and supper six. Towards the end of the sixteenth century dinner advanced to midday.'[12] Hammond has already suggested that the supper hour may have been determined by the onset of darkness. This being so, the availability of artificial lighting may well have played some part in the choice of times, particularly during the winter months. A wealthy establishment such as the royal household would have been in a position to sup as late as six o'clock if it wished, even during the winter months, since it would have enjoyed ready access to artificial means of lighting.

The onset and disappearance of daylight may not have been the only considerations:

> For the Medieval physician the justification for mealtimes involved in part a perception that one felt healthier if one ate only when one became hungry. To eat, therefore, before a previous meal had made its way completely out of the stomach was declared to be a most dangerous practice. Given that the average 'modern' digestive system seems comfortably able to handle only two substantial meals in a day, and given that the professional cook was required to lay on nothing less *than* substantial meals, the two-meal pattern remained the norm for most of Medieval Europe.[13]

Terrence Scully has argued that:

> breakfast, at first a concession, of an unseemly if not totally dissolute sort, became seen as less disgraceful to the extent that it was just an immaterial trifle. The license was justified – an excess, which strict Medieval morality might judge to be a variety of sin – by designing it on the one hand either to give the peasant and craftsman something to sustain their morning's labour, or, on the other, in the case of the aristocrat, merely to hold hunger awhile in abeyance until a meal that was really worthy of his or her status could be prepared. We find the morning collation justified in particular in the case of the aristocrat who was forced so often to be on the road visiting the various outlying parts of his estate, but who was unwilling to set out at daybreak on an empty stomach.[14]

Scully goes on to suggest that typical breakfast foods may have been quite wide-ranging, including: ale, beer or wine; preserved fish of various kinds; bread or toast (possibly soaked in wine); cheese and beef. If so, the choice between meat, fish and 'white meat' (cheese and eggs) will have been largely determined by the liturgical calendar. Meat could not be eaten on Fridays (nor, in more religious households, on certain other days), and during the season of Lent both meat and 'white meats' were completely forbidden.

As for the choice between the more homely ale (brewed without hops) or beer (brewed with hops), and imported wine, that presumably was largely conditioned by the affluence of the household, though personal preference may also have played some part. Thus (although this specific reference is not to breakfast) the household accounts of John Howard (later Duke of Norfolk) seem to indicate that Howard himself preferred wine, while his second wife, Margaret Chedworth, was fond of ale or beer.[15]

In the middle and upper echelons of society the daytime meal ('dinner') and the evening meal ('supper') both seem to have consisted of a number of courses, each course comprising many dishes. Surviving menus from late fourteenth-century France appear to indicate that there was little difference between 'dinner' and 'supper' in terms of the likely size of the meal.[16] These sample menus also show that medieval 'courses' bore little relationship to the modern conception of this word. Only rarely, for example, does the final course of either meal seem to have comprised exclusively sweet dishes.[17]

In the case of Richard III we may tentatively conclude that, being a young and active man with a heavy workload, both as Duke of Gloucester and as king, he probably rose early in the morning. As a religious man he is unlikely to have broken his fast before attending mass in the morning. He probably did so after mass with a light meal, perhaps of bread and watered wine. Generally, he may have dined as late as eleven o'clock in the morning – but possibly a little earlier, and he probably supped at around five or six o'clock in the evening. Evidence from his physical remains shows that he had a diet high in protein, and apparently enjoyed eating marine fish and seafood.

In wealthy households, cooking was an art, producing complex and elaborate dishes. The English *cuisine* of the fifteenth century seems to have enjoyed a higher reputation than in subsequent centuries. At all events, in 1500 a Venetian ambassador remarked that the English 'take great pleasure in having a quantity of excellent victuals, and also in remaining a long time at table, being very sparing of wine when they drink it at their own expense'.[18] Possibly one reason why English cooking was more highly regarded at this period was because it was reputedly quite closely modelled upon that of France. One modern assessment considers that effectively 'there were three basic rules: never do anything simply, keep adding spices and totally obscure the original flavour'.[19] Many fifteenth-century recipes survive, and those who wish to attempt to taste the flavours of the period are easily able to experiment with them.[20]

On formal occasions, Richard's courtiers would have been served great banquets. The coronation banquet served in 1420 to Catherine of France (consort of Henry V) gives some idea of such a meal.[21] A somewhat similar elaborate banquet is recorded as having been served in the summer of 1483, on the occasion of Richard III and Anne Neville's coronation. Like the banquet for Queen Catherine, this had comprised three courses, and at Richard's banquet these courses consisted of fifteen, sixteen and seventeen dishes respectively.[22] On such occasions each course often ended with a 'subtlety': a sculpture in sugar or marzipan, often based upon a Biblical or mythological theme. Vegetables did not figure prominently in high status fifteenth-century menus, though John, Lord Howard (the future Duke of Norfolk) certainly ate 'selad' on occasions.[23] At aristocratic and royal tables, 'trumpets signalled the arrival of a course, and music was played during the feasting, as well as performances being given by dancers, acrobats and others … The serving of food was attended by elaborate ceremony, and preceded by the washing of hands (very necessary since much eating was done with the fingers dipped into communal dishes). The water was sometimes perfumed with rose leaves, thyme, lavender, sage, camomile, marjoram or orange peel, or a combination of these.'[24] A grand banquet must surely have been served to Richard III and his court on Sunday 3 April 1485, for this was Easter Sunday, the greatest feast of the year, marking the formal ending of the Lenten diet of abstinence.

⚜✕⚜

Although by 1485 death had deprived Richard III of all his brothers, of his wife, and of his only legitimate son, he had not been left entirely without family. As we have seen, he took an interest in his nephews and nieces, and also in his illegitimate offspring. Two of his sisters were still alive,[25] and although one of them, Margaret, was living in the Low Countries as the dowager Duchess of Burgundy, there is no reason to suppose that Richard was not in touch with her.[26] The other sister, Elizabeth, Duchess of Suffolk, was the mother of the young Earl of Lincoln, whom Richard was actively promoting, so it is likely that she too was in regular contact with the king. Richard had lost his father at an early age, and it is perhaps doubtful how well he remembered him.[27] His mother was still alive, and seems to have remained always very close to her son. It was the dowager Duchess of York's London house (Baynard's Castle) which had been Richard's headquarters during the difficult summer of 1483 and during the events leading up to his proclamation as king – a move which Cecily Neville had clearly supported. After his accession Richard kept in close contact with his mother, and it is not surprising, therefore, to discover that, in the aftermath of Anne Neville's death, and at a time when he was actively planning to remarry in the hope of producing an heir to the throne, Richard III went to see the Duchess of York. At an earlier period of her widowhood, Cecily Neville had often resided at Clare Castle in Suffolk when she was not at her London house.[28] By 1485, however, she was living in semi-retirement and her principal residence seems to have been Berkhamsted Castle in Hertfordshire. As we shall see later, on Tuesday 17 May Richard paid a visit to his mother at Berkhamsted.[29] No doubt he wished to keep her up to date regarding the progress of negotiations for his second marriage.

On this and other occasions Richard III almost certainly travelled on horseback, as the much older (but hale and hearty) John Howard, Duke of Norfolk, seems normally to have done. Nevertheless, there was a royal carriage available, which had been used by his elder brother, the late king.[30] Whether Edward IV had used a carriage for ceremonial reasons, or simply because he had grown fat, unfit and somewhat lazy, it is difficult to say.[31] A vehicle which is probably of the same general type as that used by Edward IV is illustrated in the Luttrell Psalter. It has four wheels. The panelled wooden lower part of the body is carved with gothic tracery and was probably brightly painted and gilded. The upper part is covered by what appears to be painted canvas stretched over wooden half hoops. The shape is somewhat similar to that of the wagons used many centuries later in the American west by European settlers, but the canvas of the upper section of the medieval version was stretched taut and, like the base, was brightly painted. The vehicle illustrated in the Luttrell Psalter was drawn by five horses. Richard III may, on occasions, have made use of such a royal carriage.

Richard III's homes as king were the various royal palaces, castles and hunting lodges. In the London area these included the royal apartments at the Tower of London, the Royal Wardrobe and the Palace of Westminster, and Richard is known to have resided at different times at all three of these. Not one of them survives today in a form which he would recognise. The Royal (Great, or King's) Wardrobe is probably the least known of the three, and only the memory of its name is now preserved. It stood to the south-east of St Paul's Cathedral, at the northern end of St Andrew's Hill just to the north of St Andrew's church, having been moved to this site (formerly the mansion of Sir John Beauchamp) in 1360.[32] On its eastern side ran Apple Hill, and the Wardrobe was entered from Carter Lane. An enclosed bridge from the building ran across the upper end of St Andrew's Hill to a walled garden, just behind the Dominican (Blackfriars) Priory. Members of the Yorkist royal family regularly stayed there, including both Edward IV and Richard III. In the summer of 1468 it was from the Wardrobe that Margaret of York set out on her wedding journey to Flanders. The accommodation comprised a great hall with glazed windows, a 'King's Hall', chambers for both the king and the queen, and a chapel, together with kitchens and closets.[33] The Wardrobe survived until it was destroyed in the Great Fire of London in 1666, and it is depicted on Elizabethan plans of London.[34] During the reign of Edward IV the keeper of the Great Wardrobe, and also of the Privy Palace at Westminster, was Peter Curteys, but he seems to have fled into sanctuary at Westminster Abbey with Elizabeth Woodville and her children, and was accordingly dismissed from both his offices by Richard III at Michaelmas 1483. In his place, Richard appointed Robert Appulby.[35]

Elizabethan plans also depict the once extensive royal palace at the Tower of London, which in the late medieval period filled much of the area between the old Norman keep (the White Tower) and the outer walls flanking the River Thames on the southern side of the enclosure. Most of this late medieval royal residence at the Tower is also now destroyed. The old Palace of Westminster occupied more or less the same site as the present Victorian gothic confection, but was a much less grandiose and more higgledy piggledy collection of buildings. In Richard III's lifetime there was no bridge across the Thames at Westminster. But one could descend via Westminster Stairs to the water on the Westminster side and pick up a boat for the short river crossing, ascending at the other (Lambeth) side, where a second set of steps led up from the Thames just to the north of the Archbishop of Canterbury's London palace, giving access to the marshland, farmland and open countryside beyond.

Like the houses of the gentry and aristocracy, the royal palaces will have been adorned with tapestries. It is known, for example, that in 1480 Edward IV had acquired 'two peces of arras of the story of Paris and Elyn' as a gift from his sister, the Duchess of Burgundy.[36] He also acquired 'a curtyne of paled verdour rede and blue with riban of grene threde and rynges of latone'.[37] Verder(s) was tapestry decorated with foliage and flowers, but without human figures. This particular royal curtain was evidently composed of two strips of verders, one basically red, and the other basically blue, sewn together side by side to make up a hanging in the royal livery colours of the house of York. It was hemmed with green ribbon, and hung from brass curtain rings. It is perhaps worth observing at this point that notions of matching colour schemes seem to have had little or no place in the taste of the fifteenth century, either in matters of furnishing or in matters of dress. In both clothing and in interior decoration the whole gamut of varied and bright colours seems to have been combined.

At about the same time as acquiring the Paris and Helen tapestries, Edward IV had also obtained two new *spervers* (sets of bed hangings). These were apparently for members of the royal family, and either or both sets may well have still been in use in Richard III's household in 1485. One of Edward's canopies was made of red, green and white striped velvet, while the second was of white and blue velvet, *per pale*,[38] and lined with black buckram. Both sets of hangings comprised a tester, seler and valances. White and blue were the livery colours of the house of Burgundy, so it is possible that the set of blue and white bed hangings had been ordered for the king's sister, Margaret, Duchess of Burgundy, to use on the occasion of her visit to England in 1480. The seler was the bed canopy itself. The tester was the matching curtain, which hung down from the canopy at the head of the bed, and the valance was the matching fringe of cloth hanging down around the sides of the bed. There were also side and foot curtains, which could be drawn at night to enclose the royal bed. These curtains were made of sarcenet, which was a much lighter-weight fabric. The curtains, the seler and the valance were all decorated with multicoloured silk fringes.[39]

Edward IV's own bed at this period (1480) comprised a mattress stuffed with feathers, which would have been supported on a wooden framework with a woven webbing of taut ropes. The royal bed had bolsters stuffed with feathers, upon which rested pillows of fustian stuffed with down. The bed was made up with sheets of Holland cloth. Other contemporary beds prepared for the Burgundian ambassadors at the Erber[40] were supplied with counterpanes of red worsted, while the bed provided for the dowager Duchess of Burgundy herself rejoiced also in a pair of blankets.[41] However, the design of the covers (*tapettes*) for the king's own bed was far more regal and heraldic. These covers were made *per pale* of red and blue verders adorned with crowns and roses. Thus Edward IV in 1480 – and very probably also Richard III five years later – slept under a bedspread in the colours of the Yorkist royal livery, adorned with royal emblems.[42]

A great deal of information is available about clothing owned by Edward IV in or about 1480, and this helps us to form an impression of how his younger brother may have been dressed five years later. Edward IV had possessed a great variety of items of attire – and the surviving list is probably far from exhaustive. His garments had included long gowns, demi-gowns, doublets, hose and cloaks. Richard III's wardrobe must have been composed of a similar range of garments.[43]

Specifically, Edward IV had possessed at least twenty-four shirts of Holland cloth.[44] He also owned a long gown of blue cloth of gold upon satin, lined with green satin; another of black velvet lined with tawny damask; one of purple velvet lined with black satin; and two more of green velvet and of white velvet respectively, each upon velvet tissue cloth of gold and lined with black satin; another of velvet upon black cloth of gold, furred with ermine; one of crimson cloth of gold; and one of green damask. The king possessed a number of doublets, mostly of black satin, at least one of which was lined with Holland cloth, also another doublet of purple satin, and one of crimson velvet. He had a demi-gown of tawny velvet lined with black damask; another of green velvet lined with black damask; another of black velvet lined with purple satin; another of purple velvet lined with green sarcenet; and another of green velvet lined with black sarcenet. He had a number of tippets (hoods for cloaks) made of black velvet and an assortment of leather shoes and leather patens. Many of his shoes were of Spanish or Spanish-style leather ('cordwain'),[45] some being lined and others not. He also owned shoes and patens of black leather, black leather knee boots, and five pairs of boots of tan ('tawny') Spanish leather, together with a pair of long spurs, parcel-gilt. Edward IV also owned handkerchiefs and ostrich feathers, at least one cloak of black camlet, two pairs of green hose, and two pairs of black hose.[46]

Richard III seems to have been fond of hunting, and we shall have more to say on this point in a subsequent chapter. He also possessed a library, and was therefore presumably interested in reading.[47] Other distractions which may have been available to him included games of various kinds. Playing cards and dice were certainly in existence. John Howard, Duke of Norfolk, apparently possessed at least one chess set (possibly two). There is also evidence that tennis was being played in England at this period.[48]

One of the things which Richard III seems to have done in about April 1485 was to have his portrait painted. The earliest representation of Richard surviving today (with the exception of manuscript illustrations) is a small panel portrait in the possession of the Society of Antiquaries of London, and a copy of this is reproduced here (figure 8). The Society of Antiquaries portrait dates from the first decade of the sixteenth century, but was presumably copied from an earlier version, painted during Richard's lifetime. The portrait shows the king gazing to the viewer's left, and wearing a black velvet hat with a jewelled brooch, a crimson doublet, recalling the doublet of crimson velvet owned by Edward IV, and a gown or demi-gown of cloth of gold which again recalls items from the wardrobe of his elder brother. Richard has a thin face with a sad look about it.[49] His long hair is dark brown, like that of Edward IV.[50] There is no indication in the painting that the sitter suffered from any kind of physical deformity, but the curvature of Richard's spine was reported to produce only a slight variation in the height of his shoulders (see below). Such a small portrait could have been produced – and reproduced – quite quickly.[51]

Richard's sad expression in this portrait would certainly have been appropriate in April 1485, following his recent bereavements. However, there is another reason for assigning the painting of this portrait to about this period. The king's right hand holds a ring, which he is in the process of either placing upon, or removing from, the fourth finger of his left hand. Although the wedding ring finger was probably not fixed at this period, his gesture may imply thoughts of marriage.[52] Thus the original portrait may have been painted after the death of Queen Anne Neville, when new marriage plans were in prospect between 16 March and 22 August 1485. The painting was possibly intended to be sent to Portugal, with perhaps a second copy sent to Spain, to be shown to the infantas who were being wooed as prospective consorts. The comparatively small size of the portrait would appear to be consistent with this explanation, since it would have made the original easy to transport.

It was certainly not unusual for portraits of prospective royal *brides* to be dispatched to their prospective husbands in this way and at about this period. There is less evidence for the sending of such portraits on the part of the proposed husbands. However, the Infanta Joana of Portugal was known to be a hard matrimonial nut to crack. She had already turned down several potential spouses, including Charles the Bold of Burgundy and the King of France. Richard may therefore have felt that a special effort was called for. There is also a possible parallel example in the somewhat similar, oval-topped panel portrait of Henry VII that was painted by Michael Sittow in 1505, and which depicts Henry wearing the collar of the Order of the Golden Fleece. A copy of this representation may have been intended for the widowed Joanna the Mad, Queen of Castile and dowager Duchess of Burgundy, whom Henry was then hoping to marry as his second wife. It is thus feasible that several copies of Richard's portrait were produced: one for immediate dispatch to Portugal, another for use in Spain, with perhaps a third to be held in reserve in case both the Portuguese and Spanish negotiations foundered and it subsequently proved necessary to look further afield. It would then presumably have been from one of the reserve portraits retained in England that the extant example was reproduced, some twenty years later.[53]

<hr />

In addition to extraordinary activities such as sitting for a marriage portrait, during the period from March to August 1485 the king continued to occupy himself with the day-to-day business of government and running the royal household. A selection of the sort of business with which he occupied himself during these months includes:

Wednesday 9 March 1484/85, Westminster: warrant to Henry Davy to deliver to John Goddeslande 'foteman unto the lord Bastard two silk doublets, one silk jacket a gown, two shirts and a bonnet'.[54]

Friday 11 March 1484/85, Westminster: 'letter of passage' for Friar John Forde of the Dominican (Black) friars to go to Rome with one servant and his luggage.[55]

Tuesday 29 March 1485, London: 'warrant to the maister of thordenance to delyver unto [William Combresale] … fyfty bowes a hundred Shef of Arowes oon Barelle of gonnepowder fyfty Speres armed and thre cartes of rennyng ordenance for the defense of Harwiche'.[56]

Tuesday 12 April 1485, London: passport for Henry Delphaut (servant of Captain Salasar), together with his servants and horses, who are on their way to the (arch?)duke of Austria.[57]

Wednesday 13 April 1485, London: licence to John Rede to attend the General Chapter of the Premonstratensian Order in France.[58]

Friday 22 April 1485: Lord Maltravers commissioned to keep the Feast of St George at Windsor Castle in the king's absence.[59]

Sunday 24 April 1485, London: approval of the election of Dom William Senons, OSB as the new abbot of St Mary's Abbey, York.[60]

Friday 29 April 1485, Westminster: commission 'to take Carpenters & Sawyers … for the hasty spede of the kings werkes in the towre of London & Westminstre and also to take marke felle hewe and cary almoner tymber aswele okes Elmes as other tymbre needful for the said werkes'.[61]

Saturday 7 May 1485, Westminster: reprimand to the bailiff of Ware (Herts.) for allowing able-bodied male inhabitants of the town to waste time in playing cards, bowls and tennis instead of practising archery, and for allowing them to poach the royal pheasants, partridges, rabbits and hares.[62]

Friday 27 May 1485, Kenilworth: licence to Thomas Wright of Banbury to transport to Calais 200 sheep and 100 mares.[63]

Monday 6 June 1485, Kenilworth: payment of £15 19s. 10d. for repairs carried out at Sudeley Castle; also payment of £115 18s. for twenty tuns and one hogshead of wine delivered to the Castle of Kenilworth.[64]

There were also royal authorisations for the obtaining of hawks for hunting, which we shall consider in greater detail later (see below, chapter 6).

Incidentally, of the game mentioned as being hunted by the inhabitants of Ware in 1485 (all of which will have been familiar to Richard III), partridges and hares were native species. It has been suggested by some authorities that the bronze pheasant (*Phasianus colchicus*) was also a native species,[65] though others have argued that this large game bird was introduced to England by the Romans. It was unquestionably the Romans who brought the rabbit to these islands. Unfortunately, the English (or Grey) partridge (*Perdix perdix*) which Richard knew, and probably hunted and on occasions ate, is now by no means common. Those lucky enough to see a partridge in England nowadays will be much more likely to encounter the French (Red-legged) partridge (*Alectoris rufa*), first introduced to England only in the seventeenth century. Even the modern English pheasant is not quite the bird which Richard III will have known, as the possibly native bronze pheasant has been almost swamped by much more recent importations of the ring-necked pheasant (*Phasianus torquatus*) from China. While the latter species very closely resembles the traditional English bronze pheasant, it is easily distinguished from it by the white ring which encircles the neck of the cock bird, hence its name.

4

Tombs of Saints and Queens

According to the rather muddled and incomplete account of the events of 1485 given by the Crowland Chronicle, it was somewhere around the octave of Easter (Sunday 3 April–Sunday 10 April) that rumours of an impending rebellion reached the ears of the king.[1] The Crowland chronicler also reports that as early as the Feast of the Epiphany (6 January 1484/85) Richard had already received the news that an invasion on the part of his second cousin once removed, Henry 'Tudor', *soi-disant* 'Earl of Richmond', was likely to take place in 1485.[2]

On his mother's side, this Henry 'Tudor' (the future King Henry VII) was a descendant in a legitimised (but originally bastard) line from John of Gaunt, Duke of Lancaster. On his father's side he happened also to be a nephew of Henry VI – although his descent from Henry VI's mother had brought him no English royal blood whatsoever. It has also been suggested that Henry 'Tudor''s father, Edmund, was not really the son of Owen Tudor. Edmund 'Tudor''s real father may well have been Edmund Beaufort, first (second) Duke of Somerset, another of the legitimised Beaufort descendants of John of Gaunt, Duke of Lancaster.[3] If so, this descent might possibly have reinforced Henry Tudor's claim to the Crown of England, though it would undermine his right to the surname Tudor (a surname, which, in practice, he and his descendants rarely used).

In point of fact, in putting forward his royal claim Henry never mentioned details of any of his real lines of descent. In 1484–85 his claim as advanced in France was founded upon the transparent lie that he was a younger son of the late Henry VI.[4] Previously, Henry had tried another ploy. In 1483 he had sought unsuccessfully to advance a claim to the throne on the strength of a proposed future marriage with Elizabeth of York. Subsequently, he would claim the throne on the vaguely worded grounds of Lancastrian blood (with the details carefully left unspecified) coupled with the right of conquest. Interestingly, Henry VII was never to publicly proclaim his genuine but tenuous blood ties to the Plantagenet royal family. It was left to Richard III to attempt to explain those.

Far from being cowed and defeatist at the news of the forthcoming invasion, Richard was reportedly delighted. He believed that the coming of Henry 'Tudor' (as modern writers generally call him) against him would finally settle this matter, and that thereafter he would be able to reign in peace.[5]

It was doubtless in response to the latest intelligence regarding the threatened invasion (and the machinations of the King of France, which Richard certainly knew to lie behind it) that during the month of April a royal fleet was stationed in the Channel, under the command of Sir George Neville.[6] Richard III had himself served as Admiral of England during the reign of his elder brother, and had enjoyed a long and close association with Sir John Howard (later Lord Howard, and ultimately Duke of Norfolk) who had held office under Richard as Admiral of the Northern Seas, and who, in the summer of 1483, had succeeded him as Admiral of England. One may therefore assert with some confidence that Richard possessed a clear notion of the importance of the navy to the defence of the realm. Indeed, previous writers have acknowledged that he took care to maintain and augment the navy left to him by Edward IV.[7] Under its flagship, the carvel *Edward*, this fleet had been assiduously built up by the late king – a fact of which little account has hitherto been taken.[8]

However, Richard was embarrassed by a lack of ready money – a problem exacerbated by the fact that in the summer of 1483 Sir Edward Woodville had made off with a substantial portion of the royal treasury. King Richard himself had condemned in Parliament the so-called 'benevolences', or forced gifts, which his elder brother and preceding sovereigns had used as a form of taxation. Now, finding himself in a similar quandary to many of his predecessors, he was more or less compelled to adopt a not dissimilar solution. Instead of 'benevolences', however, he now introduced a system of forced loans. The difference between Richard's expediency and the system of 'benevolences' was that Richard III now issued receipts for the money he obtained from his subjects, accompanied by an undertaking to repay it. Given his subsequent defeat, it is impossible to know whether or not the money would ultimately have been repaid. It is nevertheless clear that Richard was trying, for no one had even pretended that the earlier 'benevolences' would ever be paid back!

Although he had been at Windsor from 18–20 April, Richard III was in London on St George's Day (23 April) 1485, and therefore did not attend the annual Garter Feast at St George's Chapel in person. Instead, as we saw in the last chapter, 'a commission under the privy seal, 22 April 1485, empowered lord Maltravers to keep the feast in the Sovereign's absence'.[9] This very late appointment of Maltravers (Richard III's first cousin once removed on his mother's side, and the son and heir of the Earl of Arundel) as the king's deputy for the occasion suggests a rather hurried and last-minute change of plans. This may in some way have been connected with the execution of Sir Roger Clifford, for reasons unknown, on 2 May 1485.

On Thursday 12 May (the Feast of the Ascension) the king rode out of Westminster to return to Windsor Castle. He was never to see London or Westminster again. There may perhaps have been a particular reason why Richard III chose to return to Windsor Castle at this time. The anniversary of the death of the last Lancastrian king, Henry VI, was fast approaching. Henry VI was already popularly regarded as a saint and martyr, and the feast days of martyred saints are normally celebrated on the anniversaries of their deaths.

King Henry is usually said to have died, or been killed, on the night of 21 May 1471.[10] This date is derived from John Warkworth's account, which states that Henry 'was putt to dethe the xxj day of Maij, on a tywesday night, betwyx xj and xij of the cloke'.[11] This date has, however, been questioned. Betram Wolffe, in his biography of Henry VI, suggested that the death may actually have occurred early on the morning of Wednesday 22 May,[12] and Vergil's account, while giving no specific date, assigns Henry's demise to the period *after* Edward IV had pacified Kent and dealt with Fauconberg, which would suggest very late May or possibly even early June.[13] Sir Clements Markham 'made use of the Exchequer *Issue Rolls* (detailing expenditure during Henry's final days in residence in the Tower), to demonstrate that the deposed king was still alive up to 24 May at least',[14] though other writers have suggested that this merely represents a convenient date at which to end the accounting period. But the *Arrival of Edward IV* gives the date of Henry's demise as Thursday 'the xxiij day of the monithe of May' and claims he died from natural causes.[15] There is also the poem of Dafydd Llwyd of Mathafarn, apparently written shortly after Bosworth and rejoicing at the death of Richard III, which likewise implies that Thursday 23 May was the day on which Henry VI died.[16] Therefore, although most modern accounts continue to state baldly that Henry died on 21 May, it is possible that the real date was slightly later. However, apart from drawing attention to that fact that divergent accounts exist, we need not dwell upon this point here, other than to observe that even in 1485 there may possibly have been some doubt as to the precise date of Henry VI's death. Nevertheless, it must have been well known that he had died towards the end of May, and some date in that vicinity – possibly 21 May – had probably already begun to be thought of as representing 'the Feast of St Henry VI'.

The saintly cult of Henry VI must have begun very soon after his demise, and certainly within a year or so of his death, for as early as 1473 'Richard Latoner was paid for his work in writing the testimonies of certain persons offering at the image of Henry VI in the Cathedral of York'.[17] It may also have been at about the same time that the wild spinach plant, also known as 'Mercury', or 'Poor Man's Asparagus' (*Chenopodium bonus-henricus*), acquired in England its now usual name of 'Good King Henry' – presumably in honour of the last Lancastrian monarch.[18]

Curiously, while later ages – on the basis of no evidence whatever – would see fit to impute Henry VI's martyrdom to Richard himself,[19] the reality is that if the last Lancastrian monarch had died from unnatural causes, it must have been King Edward IV who ordered his death. Indeed, his younger brother Richard may well have disapproved of this action, as he certainly did in the case of the subsequent execution of his own brother, the Duke of Clarence. At all events, Richard III seems to have regretted Henry VI's death, and to have evinced a curious personal devotion to Henry's cause as a putative saint. Thus it is an interesting fact that in 1484, Richard himself had ordered and paid for the translation of the remains of this erstwhile Lancastrian king and budding saint from the obscure grave at Chertsey Abbey, to which Edward IV had originally consigned them, to a royal tomb in St George's Chapel at Windsor Castle, on the opposite side of the sanctuary from the burial site of Edward IV himself.

There may have been practical motives underlying Richard III's action, and Griffiths, for one, considers that he 'was wise to harness the dead king's reputation rather than try to suppress it as his brother had done, in view of the growing popular veneration and the miracles associated with Henry's name which are recorded from 1481'.[20] On the other hand, it is also perfectly possible that Richard's decision is attributable to a genuinely religious motive. He was a sincerely religious man, and human beings are not invariably motivated solely by cynical self-interest, whatever historians may say.

The choice of the chapel royal at Windsor as the site for the new tomb may have been in part determined by practical considerations. The traditional royal burial area around the shrine of King St Edward the Confessor at Westminster Abbey was more or less full. King Henry VII would later find himself obliged to construct a large new Lady Chapel at the eastern end of the abbey to accommodate his own burial and that of Elizabeth of York. Richard III must have been well aware of the shortage of space at Westminster, since his brother, Edward IV, had been interred at Windsor, while Queen Anne Neville's tomb at Westminster had been squeezed into a site in front of the sedilia, to the right of the high altar, where no funeral monument was possible other than a brass set into the pavement.

'In the absence of known copies of Richard III's will his intentions concerning his own burial remain unknown … [but] Richard may have shared Edward [IV]'s concept of the new foundation [of St George's Chapel at Windsor Castle] as the mausoleum of the Yorkist dynasty … The suggestion has been made that he had Henry [VI] interred in the second bay of the south choir aisle because he had reserved the first bay as his own place of burial.'[21] The fact that Richard chose to bury Queen Anne Neville at Westminster rather than at Windsor is probably not significant. We have already seen that Richard was well aware of the fact that he would have to marry again and produce new heirs. If he did intend his own burial to be in St George's Chapel, no doubt it would have been his second queen – the mother of the new Prince of Wales – who would have shared this tomb.

Henry VI's new tomb, towards the east end of the south aisle, was sited – apparently quite deliberately – in a part of St George's Chapel, which was already strongly associated with two other pilgrimage cults: those of the popularly canonised John Schorne (a Buckinghamshire parish priest whose supposedly miraculous remains were translated to St George's Chapel in 1481) and of the Cross Gneth (the captured Welsh reliquary containing a fragment of the True Cross, which had been presented to the chapel by Edward III). Richard III had Henry VI's new tomb created in the second bay of the south aisle of the choir, 'and the whole of it was formerly decorated in his honour with colour and gilding, traces of which may still be seen'.[22] The space beneath the archway was arranged as a chantry chapel, with the king's tomb and a small altar, as described in the will of King Henry VIII.[23] It was therefore clearly a tomb, and not yet a saint's shrine, to which Richard III transferred Henry VI's remains. Nevertheless, there seems to be little reason to doubt that Richard III's intention was to encourage the growth of Henry VI's cult, and thereby attract additional funds to St George's Chapel in the form of pilgrim offerings. The fifteenth-century offering box marked with a large 'H' which stands by the tomb was made by John Tresilian in the 1480s, and is quite possibly contemporary with the 1484 reburial.[24]

Richard III's reburial of Henry VI – curiously presaging the ultimate fate of Richard's own remains – can be tentatively reconstructed by means of the evidence found when the Windsor tomb vault of 1484 was opened in 1910. Clearly, when the remains of Henry VI were exhumed from their tomb at Chertsey Abbey the body had already partly decayed.[25] The decomposed remains were therefore reverently collected. They were then wrapped in fabric as a small parcel, which was placed in a box made of a dark wood, 3 feet 3½ inches in length, 10 inches wide, and 9 inches deep. This wooden box was closed by a sliding top panel. The box was then sealed into a neat but plain lead casket, 3 feet 5 inches in length, 15 inches wide and 12 inches deep, the top of which was soldered into place so that it could not be opened without cutting the lead. The lead casket was in turn enclosed in a full-sized wooden coffin, surrounded by bands of iron.[26] The full-sized coffin was clearly a cosmetic feature. The intention was obviously that at the formal reburial it would appear to those present that an intact body reposed within.[27]

The account roll for the treasurer of the College of Windsor for 1483–84 records expenses of £5 10s. 2d. incurred for the translation of the remains, and the fifteenth-century antiquary John Rous recorded that the exhumation from Chertsey Abbey took place in August 1484, and that the body was then transported to Windsor, where 'it was honourably received and with very great solemnity buried again on the south part of the high altar'.[28] It is not impossible that Richard III had personally been present at the reburial, for he was certainly at Windsor Castle on Thursday 19 August 1484.[29] Subsequently, in May 1485 Richard may have wished to mark the coming anniversary of Henry's death – the first since the previous year's 'translation' of his remains to Windsor – by offering his own prayers at the new graveside in St George's Chapel as the 'feast day' of this saint-by-acclamation approached.

The king was not, however, at St George's Chapel for the actual anniversary of his predecessor's putative martyrdom (whether that fell on 21 May or later). As we have already seen, on Tuesday 17 May he left Windsor and rode on to Berkhamsted Castle, where he visited his now semi-reclusive mother, Cecily Neville, Duchess of York. Two weeks earlier (Tuesday 3 May) Cecily had celebrated her seventieth birthday. Probably her son wanted to talk to her about his future remarriage with a Portuguese princess. Perhaps he also took the opportunity to discuss suitable arrangements for the future housing of his niece, Elizabeth, and her preparation for her forthcoming role as a Portuguese royal duchess. At all events, two or three weeks after seeing his mother Richard would make arrangements for Elizabeth, and possibly also her unmarried younger sisters, to join the Earls of Lincoln and Warwick at Sheriff Hutton Castle in Yorkshire.[30] Following the visit to Berkhamsted, Richard was not to meet his mother again. He took his leave of her on or about 20 May, when he rode north to the castle of Kenilworth.[31]

It was probably at about the end of May, or perhaps very early in June, either at Kenilworth Castle or in Coventry, that Richard III received a formal letter of condolence upon the death of Queen Anne Neville from the Doge and the Senate of the Most Serene Republic of Venice.[32] The usual diplomatic wheels were turning at the somewhat slow rate enforced by the length of time it took, in the fifteenth century, for news to travel backwards and forwards between England and Italy.

In his letter on behalf of *La Serenissima*, penned on Monday 2 May, the Doge wrote in Latin:

> a few days ago we received the sad news that Queen Anne, your beloved consort, had deceased. We, together with our Senate, mourn greatly, for we bear Your Majesty such love and good will that, as we rejoice at any prosperous event that befalls you, so we are partakers of your sorrows. We exhort Your Majesty, endowed with consummate equanimity and marvellous virtues, of your wisdom and grandeur of mind to bear the disaster calmly and resign yourself to the divine will; and be it Your Majesty's consolation that your consort led so religious and catholic a life, and was so adorned with goodness, prudence and excellent morality as to leave a name immortal.[33]

By this time it is probable that Queen Anne Neville's funerary monument had been completed at Westminster Abbey. It comprised a slab of dark marble (perhaps Purbeck 'marble') let into the pavement on the south side of the nave altar, directly above the burial site. This slab was a matrix for a funeral brass which, had it survived, would have been unique: the only English brass monument to a queen. Unfortunately, 'today all that remains of her tomb is a bluish-grey marble slab in the pavement … brass nails can still be found, showing that a "brass" marked [her] last resting place'.[34]

5

'Þe Castel of Care'[1]

Thursday 2 June 1485 – the Thursday after Trinity Sunday – was the Feast of
Corpus Christi.[2] This was a relatively recent feast day of the western Church,
which had been officially approved by Rome only in the fourteenth century.
It was very popular, and was universally celebrated with great enthusiasm. The
feast celebrates the sacramental 'Real Presence' of Christ in the elements of
Holy Communion. Thus the principal liturgical focus of the celebration was
and is the 'Host', or wafer of bread consecrated by the priest at mass. On the
Feast of Corpus Christi a large consecrated Host is traditionally displayed in
a monstrance.[3] This is then borne aloft by a priest richly robed in a cope. In
modern celebrations the priest also wears a humeral veil over his shoulders
and arms, so that his hands are not in direct contact with the sacred vessel, but
medieval depictions of Corpus Christi celebrations do not show this veil, the
wearing of which may not have been the practice in the fifteenth century. In
other respects, however, fifteenth-century Corpus Christi processions were
clearly very similar to those that may still be seen today. Preceded by thurif-
ers with incense-burners and an acolyte ringing a *sanctus* bell, accompanied
by burning torches, and walking beneath a canopy of rich fabric, the priest
would process out of the church into the village streets. In country districts
the procession then made its way to the local fields, where, holding the monstrance aloft, the priest would trace the sign of the cross with the consecrated
wafer in blessing. Towns and cities likewise had their Corpus Christi processions, often accompanied in the Middle Ages by dramatic interludes, enacted
at various pausing places or 'stations' where the Host and its bearers could rest
on their way.

In 1485, on the vigil or eve of this feast day, the king and his attendants
rode out from Kenilworth Castle heading for the city of Coventry, a few
miles to the north-east. This short royal visit was obviously undertaken

to allow Richard the opportunity of celebrating the coming feast day in Coventry. There, every year, as the king and his court knew well, one of the greatest medieval drama cycles in all England was mounted in honour of this holy day. 'In its fullest form the cycle comprised at least ten plays, though only two have survived to the present day. Of these two, the Shearmen and Tailors' Pageant was a nativity play portraying events from the Annunciation to the Massacre of the Innocents, and the Weavers' Pageant dealt with the Purification and the Doctors in the Temple.'[4] By the sixteenth century the Shearmen and Tailors' play included the famous 'Coventry Carol' for the scene of the massacre of the Innocents, and although the earliest known text of this carol dates only from 1534, it is very probable that Richard III heard it sung at the Corpus Christi celebrations in Coventry just two months before his death.[5] If so, the words of this song (which laments the fate of innocent children murdered by a wicked king) apparently carried no special significance to Richard's ears, nor to those of the citizens of Coventry who watched the pageant with him that summer.

Richard III was already familiar with the lavish Corpus Christi celebrations held annually in the city of York, which he had attended on various occasions prior to his accession, and again with Queen Anne Neville in 1484.[6] It seems the king was now eager to see how the feast was celebrated in Coventry. Richard had visited Coventry on previous occasions – but not, so far as is known, on the Feast of Corpus Christi. Nor was he the first fifteenth-century monarch to stay in Coventry. Henry VI and his queen, Margaret of Anjou, had been earlier royal visitors. The Lancastrian sovereigns had based their Coventry court on St Mary's Guildhall, a building which, though damaged during the Second World War, nevertheless survives (see figures 13 and 14). It was probably also at this guildhall, and beneath its carved, painted and gilded wooden ceiling of angel musicians, that Richard III was entertained during his 1485 visit to Coventry.

The royal visit lasted a few days. By Monday 6 June at the latest, the king had returned to Kenilworth Castle. Later that week, probably on or about Thursday 9 June, Richard III and his suite set off again in a northerly direction, riding to Nottingham Castle, which they would have entered by means of the surviving gateway on the eastern side of the castle bailey (see figure 18). This castle was centrally located in Richard's kingdom and was strongly defended, and these may have been among the reasons why he now decided to make Nottingham his base. Indeed, most previous writers have assumed that the king's choice of Nottingham as his residence at this juncture was motivated by military considerations. However, we should not necessarily take too grim a view of the factors underlying Richard's decision. One must also remember that Nottingham Castle had consistently been a favourite residence of the Yorkist kings.[7] Nor need this visit be seen as a sign of gloomy prognostications on the part of the king – though many historians have chosen to so interpret it. The king had last been at Nottingham Castle the previous summer, and this in itself may indicate that it would have become a habitual port of call for him at about this time of year had his reign continued. In 1484 he had been accompanied by his consort, and it had been at Nottingham Castle that the royal couple had received news of the death of their young son. Large parts of the medieval castle that Richard knew were demolished and rebuilt in the seventeenth century, and 'we have no authentic drawing of the Castle as it existed when in its complete state [but] … we can get a good general idea of its appearance from the plan made by an architect named John Smithson in 1617'.[8]

Nottingham Castle had been a favourite with the late King Edward IV, who enlarged it:

> carrying almost to completion the work of his predecessors, and made it his chief residence and military stronghold. In addition to the Norman fortress on the highest part of the plateau (the site of the present Art Museum), the whole of the space now known as the Castle Green formed at this time the inner ballium, surrounded by beautiful buildings, protected by a dry moat, with portcullis and drawbridge, with fantastically sculptured 'beasts' and 'giants' on the parapet, and all the recognized means of defence; in fact, it was now looked upon as one of the largest and most magnificent castles in the land, and a secure retreat in time of danger. Edward's love for the place was perhaps only exceeded by that of his brother Richard, who completed with loving care what little remained to be done at the time of Edward's death. The great tower at the N.W. angle – 'the most beautiful part and gallant building for lodging,' as Leland termed it – had been carried up for three storeys in stone, and Richard completed it by erecting 'a loft of tymbre with round windows (*i.e.* bow windows) also of tymbre, to the proportion of the aforesaid windows of stone, which were a good foundation for the new tymbre windows.' … Thereafter the great tower which he had completed was known as 'Richard's Tower'.[9]

From Nottingham Castle, on Tuesday 21 June, Richard sent instructions to Bishop John Russell, the Chancellor, to reissue a royal proclamation against Henry 'Tudor' and his allies, which had first been published the previous December. Two alterations were now made to the text. The name of Elizabeth Woodville's son, the Marquess of Dorset, was removed from the list of 'rebels and traitors'. At the same time, details were supplied carefully chronicling Henry 'Tudor''s bastard royal descent.[10] The omission of Thomas Grey's name was no mere oversight. First, it was part of Richard's ongoing attempt at a rapprochement with the Woodville family – and particularly with Elizabeth Woodville and her children – of which we have already noted signs in connection with his Portuguese marriage plans. Second, it was a clear indication of the fact that Richard III was well aware that the marquess (who had fled into self-imposed exile after his involvement in the so-called 'Buckingham Rebellion', and taken refuge with Henry 'Tudor') had subsequently been strongly encouraged by his mother, the erstwhile queen, to put his trust in Richard and return to England. Indeed, Dorset had actually sought to escape from the 'Tudor' 'court' in Paris by night, making for the French coast and for England beyond. However, he had been overtaken by Henry 'Tudor''s men at Compiègne and 'persuaded' to return to Paris. Thus in June 1485 Richard III knew that Dorset was an unwilling 'Tudor' supporter.[11]

As for the details which Richard published of Henry 'Tudor''s illegitimate descent, this accords well with his recorded actions on other key occasions. In 1483, for example, faced suddenly and unexpectedly with Bishop Stillington's revelation of Edward IV's marriage to Eleanor Talbot (in consequence of which Edward's Woodville marriage was bigamous, and the children of it bastards), Richard's immediate reaction was to bring all the evidence out into the open and make it publicly accessible, so that people could see and judge for themselves. It was not, apparently, in Richard's nature to 'hush things up'. In the same way, he now set out the facts of the very dubious royal descent of Henry 'Tudor', no doubt in the conviction that these would speak for themselves. Obviously, Henry 'Tudor''s false claim to be a younger son of Henry VI was well known in English court circles to be ridiculous, and could not be left unchallenged. Richard was an honest man, but perhaps politically somewhat naive. He seems not to have realised that not everyone was as concerned as he was that the sovereign's claim to the throne should be unimpeachable.

On Wednesday 22 June instructions were sent out to the commissioners of array for every county in the realm:

> For asmoche as certain informacion is made unto us that oure Rebelles and traytors associate with oure auncyent ennemyes of Fraunce and other straungiers entende hastely to invade this oure Royaulme purposing the distruccion of us, the subversion of this oure Royaulme and disheriting of al oure true subgiettes We therefore wol and straitly commaunde you that in alle haste possible after the Receipt hereof ye doo put oure Commission heretofore directed unto you for the mustering and ordering of oure subgiettes in new execucion according to oure instruccions whiche we sende unto you at this tyme with thise oure lettres. And that this be doon with alle diligence. As ye tender oure suertie the wele of youre self and of alle this oure Royaulme.[12]

The specific instructions appended to this letter were that the commissioners of array should first pass on to the king's subjects his thanks for their past services in resisting traitors and rebels, urging them to renew their efforts now. Second, they were to check that all men already mustered were properly equipped, and that their wages had been paid up to date. Third, they were to notify all knights, esquires and gentlemen to appear in person at the king's array, assigning each of them to the command of suitable captains. Fourth, all men were to be warned to be ready to serve the king at an hour's notice, and last, all lords, noblemen and captains likewise were commanded to present themselves, ready to serve the king, and setting aside any private quarrels.

Despite this last injunction, on or about Friday 24 June Richard's Chamberlain, and Constable of England, Thomas, Lord Stanley requested leave of absence from the court and from attendance upon his sovereign. In May, Lord Stanley had ridden out of London to Windsor Castle at Richard's side, and he had been in continuous attendance on the king throughout the following weeks. Nevertheless, his overall record was equivocal. At various times during the succession disputes, Stanley had supported both York and Lancaster. Although, in the immediate aftermath of Edward IV's death, he seems to have sided with Lords Howard and Hastings, supporting Richard as Lord Protector and opposing the ambitions of the Woodville family, like Lord Hastings he seems to have baulked at the notion of disinheriting Edward IV's children.[13] When Hastings was executed, Stanley had briefly been imprisoned. His already somewhat equivocal loyalty was unquestionably further complicated by the fact that he had married as his second wife Lady Margaret Beaufort. As a result of this marriage he had become the exiled Henry 'Tudor''s stepfather. Despite all this, Richard III had been willing to employ him, and to entrust him with responsible posts in his household and government. Now, however, Stanley asked 'leave to retire for a time to his estates, from which he had been long absent, in order to rest and refresh himself. Should the invasion occur during this interval, he was quick to point out, he would be the better able, at home, to rally his men to the king's cause.'[14]

It is surely a measure of Richard III's character that, instead of refusing, dismissing Stanley from his posts, or imprisoning him as a suspected traitor, he simply acceded to the request. Ironically (given the popular picture which has been painted of him since the sixteenth century), one key feature of Richard's character was apparently a *lack* of ruthlessness. Time and again his behaviour proved too kind, too generous, too trusting. Thus Bishop John Morton and others survived to betray him. And now, in the penultimate week of June 1485, Richard repeated his mistake, and allowed Lord Stanley to depart. The king was in the strongly fortified castle of Nottingham, surrounded by his yeomen. 'He had but to move his hand and, whatever course the house of

Stanley might take, the enigma of Lord Stanley himself would be solved by simply holding him in custody until the invasion had been mastered. No doubt John Kendall, Ratcliffe, Catesby, when they learned of Stanley's desire, begged him [Richard] to refuse it.'[15] Yet Richard III granted Lord Stanley his leave of absence, and Stanley rode off into the west.

✦✦✦

On Richard III's previous visit to Nottingham Castle, the year before, he had been accompanied by his wife. And although their son, Edward of Middleham, had not been with them in Nottingham, the boy had still been alive at the time of the royal couple's arrival there. By contrast, on his visit in 1485 Richard III was alone as far as his immediate family was concerned, even though he had trusted friends and supporters with him. Possibly one of his distractions at this time was music: an art in which the king had a great interest. In 1484 a foreign visitor to Richard's court had been most impressed by the quality of the music at the royal mass.[16] It is also on record that:

> as king Richard issued a warrant to one of the gentlemen of his chapel 'to seize for the king all singing men as he can find in all the palaces, cathedrals, colleges, chapels, houses of religion and all other places except Windsor royal chapel', and some of his musicians were identifiable composers.[17]

Like many of the aristocracy Richard employed his own performers, and in the years before he ascended the throne we find mention of his trumpeters, his minstrels, and his shawm players.[18] The shawm was a robust and lively instrument from which the rather more genteel modern oboe and clarinet are descended. As Duke of Gloucester, Richard also had his own 'players', and there were more than four of these in his troupe.[19] The players in question were probably actors rather than musicians, though the English word could have either meaning.[20] We know that within a year of Richard's death, Henry VII was maintaining a company of four actors who were called *lusores regis* ('the King's Players'), and there is no reason to suppose that this was an innovation at court. 'Since these men were specialists in the presentation of stage-plays they needed both a repertoire of scripted plays and certain minimum physical conveniences for their performance.'[21] Although medieval plays are best known today from religious contexts, this is largely an accident due to the survival of texts of miracle and mystery plays. Secular dramas certainly existed too, though little trace of them has survived.[22]

During his stay at Nottingham Castle, Richard III also had time to remember his interest in the University of Cambridge, and specifically in Queens'

College, which he and Queen Anne had already conspicuously patronised. In July 1485 the king granted to the president of the college – his friend, Master Andrew Dockett – a selection of lands in Buckinghamshire, Lincolnshire, Suffolk and Berkshire, the combined value of which, in terms of yearly income, amounted to £329 3s. 8d.[23]

❦❦✕✕❦❦

Yet even amongst his varied interests and activities in the summer of 1485, Richard could not completely forget the threat posed by Henry 'Tudor', the self-styled 'earl of Richmond', whose French-financed expedition was now poised at Harfleur for the invasion of England. On Sunday 24 July the king sent to his Chancellor in London asking for the Great Seal. It was not that Bishop Russell was being dismissed from his post, merely that the king was aware he might need rapid personal access to the seal during the coming days and weeks. It was on Friday 29 July, at the Old Temple, that Chancellor Russell surrendered this solemn object into the hands of the royal messenger. Two days later, across the Channel in Harfleur, Henry 'Tudor' embarked his expedition and set sail. He landed at Milford Haven in Wales a week later (Sunday 7 August). His first intention was said to be to make straight for London. It took just four days for the news of his landing to be brought to the king at Nottingham. Richard III at once summoned his array. The king was seen to be publicly rejoicing at the news of 'Tudor''s landing, since he fully expected to defeat him.[24]

He then did something which may now, in retrospect, seem quite extraordinary, but which nevertheless tells us a great deal about his mood at the time, and which also speaks volumes as to his opinion of the 'Tudor' invasion force. Having summoned his array, the king left Nottingham Castle with some of his close friends. This little company then rode a few miles into nearby Sherwood Forest.[25] There, at the royal hunting lodge in the deer park of Bestwood, the king planned to give himself a short holiday.[26] Most previous writers have painted a dramatic picture of a Richard III obsessively preoccupied at this time by pessimistic thoughts of the coming fight for the throne. Yet, as we have seen already, contemporary sources contradict this, telling us that Richard rejoiced at Henry 'Tudor''s coming because he was confident that he would defeat him. The medieval nobility certainly considered hunting a very suitable preparation for war, but Richard III's hunting holiday also appears to confirm that at this juncture the king felt optimistic and completely in control of the situation.

6

Bucks at Bestwood

While the queen had lain dying at the Palace of Westminster, and also in the miserable period following her death, King Richard had sought some small distraction from his grief in making plans for the traditional royal sport of hunting.[1] As has already been indicated, on 8 March a commission was issued to John Montyguy [Montigue?], Sergeant of the Hawkes, to purchase 'at price reasonable in any place within this Royaulme fawcons, laverettes, goshaukes, tircelles and almaner othere haukes as by him shalbe thoughte convenient for the kinges disportes'.[2] On 11 March a similar commission was given to John Gaynes, who was to travel abroad with four companions in quest of more hawks for the king.[3] On 27 March Waltier Bothnam [*sic*] was charged with the same commission in respect of Wales and the Marches.[4]

Hawking was a costly sport of middle-eastern origin, restricted to the elite by the expense involved. It was certainly indulged in by the upper ranks of fifteenth-century society, and evidence of expenditure on hawking is to be found in the surviving accounts of Richard III's great friend and supporter, John Howard, Duke of Norfolk.[5] The birds of prey used for this purpose were of various kinds, ranging from the large peregrine falcon, used by men, to the little merlin, a lady's hawk.[6] Hawks were highly prized,[7] and their prey was very varied, including larger birds: mallard, partridge, woodcock, heron; and small song-birds such as blackbirds, starling and larks. Hare were also hunted in this way. However, one wonders whether, in the short time left to him, King Richard ever had the opportunity to enjoy riding out with any of his newly acquired birds to try out their prowess in the field. Training a hawk was a long and slow process, and even if the commissions of March 1485 did succeed in producing new stock for the royal mews, the hawks may not have been ready for the king's use before he was obliged to take the field for another purpose entirely.

Hawking was only one form of hunting, an activity which Richard III (in common with others of his period and social background) had enjoyed in all its forms from the days of his youth. On his first independent excursion as a teenaged royal duke to the eastern counties, as the guest of Sir John Howard (as he then was), Richard had almost certainly been taken hunting at the Earl of Oxford's park at Lavenham.[8] Hunting was the universal pastime of the aristocracy, and since ancient times the hunt had been regarded as reflecting the prowess required in military service. Although the fifteenth century had seen a reduction in the proportion of English land reserved for deer, both in open forest and in enclosed parks, large tracts of forest were still set aside as hunting parks for the enjoyment of this elite activity, and they were vigorously protected. Fifteenth-century commentators continued to see hunting both as an important training for war and as a genteel activity.[9]

The royal hunting park to which, in the second week of August 1485, Richard now made his way, accompanied by a few friends, was that of Bestwood, a little to the north of Nottingham, in Sherwood Forest. This park comprised some 3,000 acres, centred around a royal hunting lodge. It had been a royal hunting preserve since at least the twelfth century, 'where King John and his brother Richard stayed to get away from Nottingham … Bestwood Country Park was [then] a royal deer park – one of the best parks in Sherwood Forest. It was very strongly guarded and kept very well stocked.'[10]

The building in which Richard III stayed, however, did not date back to the days of the earliest Plantagenet kings of England. It was of rather more recent construction, having been built by his ancestor, Edward III. 'Prior to his visit to Nottingham in 1363 King Edward III sent instruction to Robert Maule of Linby, the custodian of Bestwood to fell sufficient timber to enclose the park in order to build a suitable lodge on the most attractive part of the enclosure, somewhere for the King to stay whenever he wished.'[11] Subsequent English monarchs, including Richard's brother, the late King Edward IV, had likewise stayed at Bestwood Lodge and hunted the deer in the park. When Bestwood Lodge was repaired, just over a hundred years after Richard's visit, in 1593, it was described as a timber-framed building of lath and plaster construction, with a tiled roof. At that time it seems to have contained thirty-eight rooms, and it had outbuildings comprising cottages and barns.

One of the closest approximations to such a medieval royal hunting lodge to survive today is perhaps 'Queen Elizabeth's Hunting Lodge' in Epping Forest, near London. Despite its popular name, this structure was actually built in 1543 for King Henry VIII, and was originally known as 'The Great Standing'. In fact, it was built in part to function as a grandstand from which guests could both view the royal hunt, and also participate by shooting at the game with bows and arrows as beaters drove the animals past the lodge. However, this building, like the royal hunting lodge at Bestwood, also contained extensive kitchens, together with facilities for entertaining visitors. Like the hunting lodge at Bestwood park, 'Queen Elizabeth's Hunting Lodge' is a timber-framed building with laths and plaster and a tiled roof. But the lodge at Bestwood was probably a somewhat more extensive building, albeit one which probably lacked the 'grandstand facility' of the lodge in Epping Forest, being designed rather for the overnight accommodation of royal hunting parties than as an actual venue for the hunt itself.

Beneath its ceremonial trappings, hunting served two practical functions: the provision of meat, and the control of animals regarded as vermin. In fifteenth-century England possible quarry included deer,[12] boar, hare and game birds (as sources of meat).[13] Otter were hunted as vermin.[14] Heron were both a kind of vermin (as a threat to the fish ponds) and also a source of meat. Bear were still hunted on the European mainland, but wild bear – once a native species – had finally become extinct in England during the fourteenth century. Richard III's great uncle, Edward, Duke of York, who wrote an English hunting text based upon a French treatise, also refers to wolf-hunting, but wolves were certainly very rare in England by the fifteenth century, if not already extinct. In fact, wolves may have figured in the Duke of York's text merely because he was working from a French original.[15] York had also referred to hunting foxes. Foxes and wolves were classified as vermin, hence they were certainly destroyed as and when occasion arose. They could be killed with traps, snares and poison. The supposedly 'traditional' English 'sport' of foxhunting with horses and hounds is a much more recent invention which in Richard III's day had yet to be thought of. In the fifteenth century the fox was considered an unsuitable quarry for a gentleman, and far beneath the notice of aristocratic huntsmen.[16] The Duke of York also utterly despised the hunting of rabbits, an unspeakably plebeian activity, which was carried out with nets and ferrets.

Richard III's quarry at Bestwood was that favourite quarry of aristocratic fifteenth-century English huntsmen: the deer. Both red deer and fallow deer lived in the park at Bestwood. The former were a native species, whereas the latter had been introduced to England by the Norman kings. However, by the fifteenth century fallow deer were naturalised in England and had become quite numerous. Later, in 1607, a survey was undertaken, and at that time the deer stock at Bestwood was reported to consist mainly of fallow deer: 'We find that there are in the park at least three hundred fallow-deer, and four-and-twenty red deer.'[17] The respective numbers in the fifteenth century are not on record.

Whether he was hunting red deer, fallow deer, or both, during the month of August, Richard III's quarry can only have been the male animals of these species.[18]

> Deer were best hunted on a seasonal basis. Males were at their best in summer when they were 'in grease', that is, had built up fat in preparation for the rut. The fattest harts and bucks were to be caught in the relatively brief period between mid-June and early September, though they were often hunted earlier. By Michaelmas, the season was over. Hinds and does, conversely, were best hunted in autumn and winter, their season lasting until February or Lent. Fresh venison could be obtained for much of the year.[19]

Both horses and dogs were employed in hunting. During the fifteenth century the main role of horses was as transport. In pursuing animals such as boar, otter and the slower-moving game birds, once the huntsmen had reached the hunting site they dismounted and proceeded on foot. However, the hunting of swift-moving prey, such as deer and some birds, was pursued on horseback. 'Scent-hounds', such as the famous (and now extinct) white Talbot breed, were used to track prey by smell,[20] while swift 'sight-hounds', such as greyhounds, were for the pursuit of deer. The large and powerful alaunt was a hunting dog which resembled the greyhound, but was both bigger and endowed with a broader head and wider jaws. It was employed for tackling the dangerous wild boar.[21] Smaller dogs, such as terriers and spaniels,[22] were for flushing out prey for the hawks, while retrievers and other spaniels were of assistance in collecting the birds once the hawks had brought them down.

Not only deer hunting, but all medieval hunting was strictly seasonal, taking due account of the breeding cycle of the prey animal in order to preserve the game for the future. The prime season for deer hunting was summer and early autumn. As previously mentioned, when Richard had been a mere teenaged royal duke, Sir John Howard had apparently taken him deer hunting at Lavenham in Suffolk.[23] Many years later, as Duke of Norfolk, Howard was created master forester of Desenyng and Hemgrave [Hengrave] by Richard III, following the execution of the Duke of Buckingham, who had previously held these posts.[24] He also received similar appointments in the county of Norfolk.[25] Information survives relating to some of John Howard's dogs, but the names of the king's own hounds are not on record.[26]

❦❧

While Richard and his friends were hunting the deer in Sherwood Forest, Henry 'Tudor' and his small invasion force made their way through Wales, and on Friday 12 August they entered the town of Shrewsbury unopposed. It was about two days later, probably on the vigil of the Feast of the Assumption, that John Howard, Duke of Norfolk, received his summons to the king's array. Howard's precise whereabouts at this time are unknown. He was not with the royal hunting party at Bestwood, but somewhere in the East Anglian region, which comprised the heartland of his territory. Quite possibly he was at Sudbury, not far from his ancestral manor house of Tendring Hall at Stoke-by-Nayland. During the fifteenth century the Feast of the Assumption was kept with special solemnity in Sudbury, where the celebrations are believed to have included a procession, bearing from its shrine in St Gregory's church the miraculous image of Our Lady of Sudbury. Reportedly, the statue was first carried through the streets and then out into the countryside to bless the fields around the town. It then seems to have spent the night at the town's Dominican Friary, the gatehouse of which still survives, before being returned to its shrine chapel the following day in an even grander procession known as 'Our Lady's Homecoming'.[27] John Howard was a patron of the Sudbury shrine,[28] which also enjoyed the patronage of members of the royal house of York.[29] Moreover, Sudbury was not far from Bury St Edmunds, and we know that it was at Bury that the Duke of Norfolk commanded his own men to assemble when he received the royal summons.[30]

It was certainly on the Feast of the Assumption itself (Monday 15 August) that the royal summons reached the city of York. Somewhat surprisingly, perhaps, this city of supposedly loyal and devoted supporters of Richard III did nothing whatever on the actual feast day. On the following day, when they did get around to discussing the most appropriate response to the king's message, they finally decided not to send the men they had been asked for, but instead to ask the king for further information!

It was also on the feast day that Richard III, still at the Bestwood Park hunting lodge, received a messenger from Lord Stanley, who regretted that he would be unable to attend the royal array in accordance with the royal summons, which he also had received, since unfortunately he was suffering from the sweating sickness.[31] Lord Stanley seems to have been running true to form, and the king probably concluded that his polite excuses were merely a pretext. However, it is conceivable that Stanley really was ill, and it is even possible that his messenger carried the contagion to Bestwood (see below). In either case, Richard probably took comfort from the fact that the doubtful lord had sent his excuses – thus indicating that he was unwilling (for the time being, at least) to disobey the king openly.

The king requested that Lord Stanley send in his place his son George, Lord Strange, and Stanley complied. Lord Strange seems to have been regarded as a hostage for his father's good behaviour. The Crowland chronicler goes on to tell us that Lord Strange subsequently tried to escape to rejoin his father, but was captured, whereupon he revealed a plot involving his uncle, Sir William Stanley, and Sir John Savage. According to the chronicler, Richard III then had both men publicly denounced as traitors at Coventry and elsewhere.[32]

On the afternoon of Wednesday 17 August, the messengers dispatched in quest of further information by the city fathers of York reached the royal hunting lodge at Bestwood Park. There they were received in audience by the king. Subsequently, Richard brought his hunting holiday to an end, and returned to Nottingham Castle. One of the messengers from York rode home with the king's answer, in response to which, on Friday 19 August, the city of York finally committed itself to sending eighty men to the royal array. It was probably also on 19 August that Richard III rode out of the gates of Nottingham Castle for the last time, making for Leicester.

On Saturday 20 August the Earl of Northumberland and his men arrived to swell the royal host, the muster of which was being supervised by the Duke of Norfolk who, in the meanwhile, had reached Leicester with his own East Anglian forces. These latter probably included his trumpeter from Harwich, Richard Lullay, together with men from John Howard's home village of Stoke-by-Nayland, and men from Colchester, Ipswich and the surrounding villages, at least some of whose names can be tentatively listed.[33]

By Sunday 21 August the assembled royal army had reached its full strength (allowing for the known absence of the Stanley contingent), and both the Crowland Chronicle and Vergil's *History* agree that it comprised a very large force.[34] Indeed, Vergil states that it was twice as big as Henry 'Tudor''s army.[35] The royal force was assembled outside Leicester, and on Sunday 21 August, with great pomp, wearing a crown,[36] and accompanied by the Duke of Norfolk, the Earl of Northumberland and the whole of his great army, Richard III marched westwards out of the city, preparing to meet Henry 'Tudor' and his rebel forces. He and his men camped for the night near Market Bosworth.

7

Crossing the River

On the evening of Saturday 20 August 1485, when Richard had ridden into Leicester at the head of his army, Hall's sixteenth-century chronicle tells us that the king was 'mounted on a great white courser'.[1] There seems to be no earlier source now surviving for this information. However, Shakespeare apparently believed that Richard rode this same horse again the following day, when he left Leicester for the battlefield of Bosworth, accompanied by the Duke of Norfolk, the Earl of Surrey, the Earl of Northumberland, Sir Robert Brackenbury and the royal army. Shakespeare thought that this same white horse was subsequently the royal charger ridden by the king in the battle itself, and he gave the horse's name as 'White Surrey' or 'White Syrie'.

It used to be thought that a horse called 'White Syrie' – Syria being a major source for horses of what we should now call 'arab stock', and of the finest quality – was listed among King Richard's horses in a contemporary manuscript.[2] However, this reading of the manuscript proved to be in error. Thus there is, in fact, no surviving indication of the name of the horse that Richard rode into his last battle, nor do we know for certain that he used the same white (or grey) horse which he had reportedly ridden into Leicester on Saturday 20 August. It is true that evidence exists that both noble stables in the second half of the fifteenth century, and the royal stable of Richard III, did contain horses whose names included a reference to their colour,[3] so that, despite the lack of firm written evidence to support it, the oral tradition that Richard III owned a horse called 'White Syrie' is plausible.

The story of 'White Syrie' is just one of a number of traditions associated with the final three days of Richard III's life. While widely reported, these traditions lack contemporary written authority. They may all be worthless. On the other hand, some of them, at least, may be accurate. We shall therefore explore them as far as possible, while bearing in mind their unsubstantiated nature.

One such tradition comprises a cycle associated with Richard III's supposed bed and the Leicester inn at which he slept. There is a popular legend that Richard spent the night of 20–21 August at an inn, which was then called the White Boar in Northgate Street, a fine timbered building in the town centre, which supposedly bore his own personal badge as its sign, and which may therefore have had some pre-existing connection with Richard. Some medieval inns did have established connections with aristocratic patrons, being either owned by them and run by a tenant 'landlord' on their behalf, or enjoying the patronage of a particular nobleman on a regular basis.[4] The claim that Leicester's Blue Boar Inn – which unquestionably existed under that name in the sixteenth century – was called the 'White Boar' prior to 22 August 1485, is traceable as far back as John Speede.[5] However, no contemporary evidence survives to substantiate the existence of a Leicester inn called the 'White Boar' in the fifteenth century. Indeed, even the earliest surviving mention of the 'Blue Boar' dates only from the 1570s.

Nevertheless, Richard III is reputed to have slept at this inn 'in a large gloomy chamber, whose beams bore conventional representations of vine-tendrils executed in vermilion, which could still be seen when the old building was pulled down' in 1836.[6] Here the king is supposed to have had his own bed set up – having brought it with him from Nottingham Castle in his baggage train. On departing in the direction of the eventual battlefield the following morning, the story recounts that Richard left this bed at the inn. Perhaps it was too large and cumbersome to use in the royal tent, where he would doubtless have to sleep during the coming night, and where he would have to make do with a smaller but more easily transportable camp bed of some kind (see below). Perhaps Richard contemplated returning to the Leicester inn after the battle, and sleeping there again. Alternatively, he may have simply planned to send for the bed later.

This account of Richard transporting his own bed from Nottingham to Leicester has an intriguing sequel, which we shall explore presently. It has also been claimed (once again, without written authority) that Richard happened to be one of those people who 'slept ill in strange beds'.[7] Possibly it was for this reason – rather than as a simple matter of ostentation – that he preferred to avail himself of his own familiar sleeping arrangements whenever possible. In the event, of course, Richard neither slept again in Leicester, nor had any opportunity to send for his bed. We may here digress briefly to trace the supposed subsequent fates of both inn and bed.

When the news of the outcome of the battle reached Leicester, together with the intimation that Henry 'Tudor' and his victorious forces were already approaching the city, the innkeeper of the White Boar reportedly thought it wise to remove rapidly the inn sign that linked him so visibly with the defeated Richard. But time was short, and there was no opportunity to commission something new. Instead, he simply availed himself of some blue paint, by means of which he effected a speedy transformation in the colour of his boar. Blue boars were perfectly safe in the new, post-Bosworth world, since they comprised the badge of John de Vere, a supporter of Henry 'Tudor' (by whose decree John was now at last legally entitled to call himself 'Earl of Oxford'). Thus the old White Boar inn reputedly became the Blue Boar overnight in the aftermath of the Battle of Bosworth.[8] While this story is not implausible, we have already seen that there is absolutely no evidence to support it.

The royal bed, never sent for, reportedly remained at the inn. According to local legend, almost a century later Agnes Clarke (*née* Davy), whose husband was then the innkeeper at the Blue Boar, was making up this bed one day when she was surprised by a medieval gold coin dropping down onto the floor beneath it. A subsequent search supposedly revealed a whole hoard of such coins hidden in a false bottom under the bed. This was assumed to be Richard III's money. The legend suggests that it was as a result of their lucky find that the Clarkes became prosperous citizens, and that Thomas Clarke went on to become Mayor of Leicester. In fact, however, Thomas had been involved in civic affairs since his late twenties – years before he became land-lord of the Blue Boar.[9]

As for the reputed royal bed, it allegedly still exists, and is now exhibited at Donington-le-Heath Manor House, Leicestershire (figure 20). Unfortunately, the Donington bed appears, for the most part, to be a seventeenth-century construction. Moreover, it also differs in detail from an engraving of Richard III's supposed bed published by John Throsby in 1777. The differences between the eighteenth-century engraving and the surviving bed appear greater than can be accounted for by Throsby's report, which claimed the bed had been lowered by the removal of its feet.[10] It is, therefore, questionable whether any part of the Donington bed has a genuine connection with the king. Moreover, there are other contenders for the role of Richard III's bed.[11] Thus, in the final analysis, it is impossible to ascertain whether any part of the Blue (White) Boar bed story is based upon fact.

⚜

Richard III rode out of Leicester on Sunday 21 August, reportedly crossing the little River Soar by means of Bow Bridge, which was then a stone-built structure with a humped back, supported on four low arches (figure 22). This stone bridge survived until the 1860s, when it was replaced by the present cast-iron construction. The old bridge was quite narrow, with a low stone parapet on either side. According to folklore, as he rode across the bridge the king's heel struck the stone parapet and an elderly pauper woman, whose cries for alms the king had ignored, foretold that 'where his spurre strucke, his head should be broken'.[12] This may well be a prophecy invented with the benefit of hindsight – though medieval fortune tellers certainly did exist.[13]

There is no surviving source which tells us that on the eve of the Battle of Bosworth Richard III made his will, but this was the common practice, just before an important conflict, and it is therefore highly probable that he did so. He was a king about to embark upon an important battle, with no direct heir in prospect. This last point, at least, may have required Richard to make some written provision detailing who should succeed to his Crown in the event of his death. It would be extremely interesting to be able to read Richard III's will, but unfortunately no such document has come down to us. Surviving medieval wills are generally copies made when the wills were proved – a process which Richard III's will never underwent.

It is often reported that Richard III's tent the night before the Battle of Bosworth was a very unquiet place, as the king tossed and turned in a troubled sleep; the prey of visions and nightmares. This account is based on two early sources for the battle: the Crowland Chronicle continuation (1486) and Polydore Vergil (early sixteenth century). The former says that 'the king, so it was reported, had seen that night, in a terrible dream, a multitude of demons apparently surrounding him, just as he attested in the morning when he presented a countenance which was always drawn, but was then even more pale and deathly'.[14] Vergil tells us:

> yt ys reported that king Rycherd had that night a terrible dreame; for he thowght in his slepe that he saw horrible ymages as yt wer of evell spyrytes haunting evidently abowt him, as yt wer before his eyes, and that they wold not let him rest; which vision trewly dyd not so muche stryke into his brest a suddane feare, as replenyshe the same with heavy cares: for forthwith after, being troublyd in mynde, his hart gave him theruppon that thevent of the battale folowing wold be grievous, and he dyd not buckle himself to the conflict with such lyvelyness of corage and countenance as before, which hevynes that yt showld not be sayd he shewyd as appallyd with feare of his enemyes, he reportyd his dreame to many in the morning.[15]

The problem with these accounts is that, naturally, neither the Crowland chronicler nor Polydore Vergil had actually been present in the royal camp during the night of 21/22 August, and they therefore had no personal knowledge of this matter. Thus, at best, we are dealing with hearsay evidence. In fact, we may be dealing with nothing more than the deliberate invention of early 'Tudor' propagandists.

It is nevertheless interesting to extract from Vergil's mass of hearsay the point that, up until 21 August, at least, Richard III was considered, even by his enemies, to have been preparing for the forthcoming conflict with 'lyvelness of corage and countenance'. In addition, it is reasonable to conclude that, since both the Crowland text and Vergil report that Richard had a troubled night, there may have been a fairly early tradition to this effect, and that this story was not simply invented either by the chronicler or by Vergil. Nor should we discount the possibility that Richard III's reported lack of sleep contains a kernel of truth at its heart. Earlier, the suggestion was made that Richard III may have been one of those people who find it difficult to sleep comfortably in an unfamiliar bed. Given the fact that Richard had reportedly left his particular bed – no doubt a large and cumbersome piece of furniture – at the inn in Leicester, and was therefore obliged to make do with a smaller camp bed for the night of 21/22 August, this may be sufficient to explain why the king passed a somewhat uncomfortable and sleepless night. Incidentally, parts of his royal camp bed are also reputed to survive, in the form of a chair preserved at Coughton Court in Warwickshire (see figure 21).[16]

There is one other conceivable (but novel, and probably controversial) explanation of Richard III's troubled night, which would involve neither ghosts nor a guilty conscience. In chapter 6 we saw that early in August 1485 the sweating sickness struck England. If Richard had happened to fall victim to this unpleasant – but not necessarily fatal – complaint, its symptoms might perhaps account for the fact that the king passed a restless night.[17] Since the main course of this malady lasted typically for about twenty-four hours, such an illness might also arguably correspond with certain aspects of the king's conduct on the battlefield the following morning.[18] Richard III is reported to have been thirsty, and to have stopped to drink from a local well. There would have been no opportunity to do this once the king had initiated his final and fatal charge, so the incident must have occurred at an early stage of the battle, and, therefore, at a time when he had not personally undertaken any strenuous activity (other than wearing full armour on a possibly warm morning) to account for his thirst. Subsequently, Vergil reports that Richard, 'inflamyd with ire … strick his horse with the spurres' and initiated a charge which may have been an unwise move, in that it carried the king down from what was possibly a commanding position. This charge certainly led ultimately to Richard's own death. It led also to the defeat of the royal army, despite the fact that the royal forces are generally acknowledged to have been far superior, numerically, to those of Richard's rival.[19] We shall return to the subject of the battle of

22 August presently. First, however, let us conclude our review of Richard III's reported experiences during the night before the conflict.

Both the Crowland chronicler and Vergil, in reporting Richard III's disturbed sleep and the reasons for it, state that the king himself was the ultimate source of their information. Frankly, this sounds inherently improbable. A far more likely source for any such report would have been the royal servants (who, unlike Richard himself, were still around after the battle). Clearly, at a period when dreams and portents were still taken seriously, it would ill have become a military commander who happened to experience a bad night's sleep on the eve of a battle to broadcast the fact to all and sundry the following morning. A far more likely response would surely have been to do everything possible to conceal the fact. Thus, if Richard III did behave in the manner reported, this was extraordinary conduct on his part and seems inexplicable.

The excuse given by both writers – that Richard looked drawn and wished to make it clear that this was not because he feared the enemy – really will not do, since Richard's reported solution was as bad as (if not worse than) the problem which he was supposedly seeking to resolve. If he looked drawn and wished to attribute this to something other than fear of his foes, he could simply have told his companions that he had been suffering from toothache.[20] Moreover, the picture that emerges of a reluctant and lacklustre Richard on the morning of the battle, does not accord at all well either with the accounts of his evident courage during the preceding days, or with the subsequent reports of his bravery and determination on the battlefield itself. In the final analysis we have no possible way of knowing whether Richard III slept well or badly on the night of 21/22 August. However, even if we accept that his sleep was disturbed, there nevertheless seem to be sound reasons for doubting the *cause* alleged by both the Crowland author and Polydore Vergil.

One sentence from these narratives which is of some possible interest is the remark from the Crowland chronicler that Richard III 'presented a countenance which was always drawn'. This sounds like the report of someone who had actually seen King Richard on a fairly regular basis, and it may, therefore, be accurate.[21] This detail is not essential to the story of Richard's troubled night (within which context it coincidentally occurs) since our other source, Polydore Vergil (who certainly had not seen Richard on a regular basis), omits it. However, it appears to accord quite well with the physical evidence of the earliest surviving copy of the portrait of Richard, the original of which, as we have already seen, was probably painted in 1485.

There are a number of possible explanations as to why Richard may have looked drawn, and the choice between them can be nothing more than guesswork. We know that Richard had suffered intimate bereavements during the course of 1484/85. He had also been catapulted into the role of king, a position which he had never expected to occupy, and which he may well have assumed more from a sense of duty than from any strong desire to do so. Having attained that exalted and lonely eminence, he had then learnt the hard way that those who protest their friendship and support are not always sincere. It is doubtful whether Richard III considered the throne a bed of roses.

'He has now Departed from Amongst the Living'[1]

As we have seen, there are two important early written sources for the Battle of Bosworth: the Crowland Chronicle continuation and Vergil's history. Based upon these and upon the recent battlefield site excavations, we shall now attempt to reconstruct this much discussed battle.[2]

Richard III is traditionally thought to have camped upon Ambion Hill the night before the battle. However, it is perhaps more likely that the large royal army camped in and around Sutton Cheney. Henry 'Tudor' had spent the night of 21/22 August at Merevale. Like Richard, he was apparently wakeful. Before dawn, he is reported to have had a secret conference with Sir William Stanley. A conference which possibly included William's brother – and Henry's stepfather – Thomas, Lord Stanley. According to Vergil, Lord Stanley was present, though this has been disputed and Stanley himself later implied otherwise.[3] It is difficult to judge whether Stanley or Vergil was telling the truth. Our understanding of what Lord Stanley did – or did not do – is complicated by his own subsequent editing of history.

We shall presently summarise the events of King Richard's last morning on earth. Before we can do so, however, there are three important elements of our story which are somewhat contentious, and which therefore need to be reviewed in specific detail, in order that we can integrate them correctly into the broader picture of events. The three points in question are reports relating to Richard's last mass, to his breakfast on the morning of the 22 August, and to an object often referred to as the *Bosworth Cross* – but which should more accurately be called the *Bosworth Crucifix*.

Whether he slept well or badly during the night of 21/22 August 1485, Richard III probably awoke early and we know that he rose at dawn (6 a.m. BST or 5 a.m. GMT on 22 August – see appendix 3). This was traditional on the morning of a battle, for the fighting itself often started at an early hour, and there were personal preparations and military dispositions to be dealt with first. There is no reason whatever to countenance the unfortunate and quite incredible twentieth-century invention that was added to the Bosworth legend in the 1920s,[4] which would have us believe that on the morning of the battle Richard III walked up to the parish church at Sutton Cheney to attend mass there. There is certainly no contemporary authority for this nonsense.[5] As we shall see later, when we explore the question of Richard's burial, in attempting to rediscover the *real* Richard III it is very important to deal ruthlessly with all the later mythology. Therefore, in view of recent attempts to defend the utterly improbable story that Richard heard his last mass in Sutton Cheney church, perhaps a little more needs to be said about this.

First, no parish church would have celebrated its regular daily mass at dawn! If Richard had walked to Sutton Cheney when he arose on the morning of 22 August, he would have found the door locked and no priest in attendance. If he took his own chaplains with him they would have needed to break in to the church and then into the sacristy to obtain the essentials for celebrating mass. There are no possible grounds for believing that they would have done this when they had all the necessary equipment for celebrating the liturgy with them in Richard's camp, and when mass could easily have been celebrated in the king's tent, using a travelling altar.

Our evidence for the presence in Richard's camp of his own clergy comes from the Crowland Chronicle, which specifically tells us that – just as one would expect – Richard III was accompanied in the royal camp by chaplains of the royal household. Like every Catholic priest, these royal servitors were under a religious obligation to celebrate mass on a daily basis. Thus there can be no possible doubt that all of them celebrated mass both on the eve of the battle (Sunday 21 August), and again on Monday 22 August.

Normally, one would simply have assumed that one or more of these chaplains celebrated mass for the king soon after he arose on Monday morning, and before he had breakfast. However, the Crowland chronicler reports that 'at dawn on Monday morning the chaplains were not ready to celebrate mass for King Richard'.[6] Since, as we have already noted, the chronicler himself was almost certainly not present in the royal camp that morning, the source for his information on this point remains unknown. Thus it amounts merely to another piece of hearsay. Nevertheless, the statement as it stands may be literally correct. There is some evidence that the reports which imply there was a degree of confusion surrounding the preparations for the royal mass on the morning of 22 August may have originated with members of Richard III's own immediate entourage. In his *Account of Miracles Performed by the Holy Eucharist*, which Henry Parker, Lord Morley, presented to Queen Mary I in 1554, Morley – himself the son of a Yorkist who fought for Richard III at Bosworth – ascribed this information to a servant of Richard's called Bygoff (now usually identified as Sir Ralph Bigod). This man 'sayd that Kyng Richard callyd in the morning for to have had mass sayd before hym, but when his chapeleyne had one thing ready, evermore & they wanted another, when they had wyne they lacked breade, And ever one thing was myssing'.[7]

The preparations required for saying a low weekday mass, which would have been of quite short duration, were so basic and routine that any priest should have been able to accomplish them in a good deal less than half an hour, even with his eyes blindfolded. Since we know the chaplains were present, even if they were not ready the instant the king arose, it seems highly unlikely that they would not have been given rapid instructions to prepare themselves as soon as they knew that Richard was up. If bread and wine were not immediately on hand these could easily and promptly have been procured. Add to this the certain fact that the chaplains *had* to celebrate mass on a daily basis and one cannot but conclude that mass must have been celebrated in the royal tent as soon as the preparations for it were complete.

The fact that the Crowland writer also reports that breakfast was not ready when the king first got up can likewise be dismissed as relatively insignificant. As we have already seen, medieval breakfast was usually a very simple meal, probably comprising bread and wine. How long can this have taken to prepare? And since the king could not break his fast until after mass in any case, there would have been ample time to make the necessary preparations while mass was being said. In short, the reports of the Crowland chronicler may suggest either that Richard III got up earlier than expected, or that his servants overslept, but they certainly prove neither that no mass was celebrated for Richard III on the last morning of his life, nor that the king went into battle on an empty stomach. It may nevertheless be the case that, for his own ends, the chronicler deliberately wished to leave his readers with the impression that Richard III died in a godless and ravenous state.

Until recently, relatively few archaeological finds relating to the Battle of Bosworth had ever been discovered. There is one eighteenth century find, however, which tends to confirm that Richard III's camp was properly staffed by chaplains, equipped with all the necessary items for fulfilling their religious function. In the collection of the Society of Antiquaries of London there is a fifteenth-century crucifix 23 inches tall and 11 inches wide (585mm x 280mm).[8] It is generally known from its find location as the 'Bosworth Cross', although it is in fact not a cross but a crucifix, since it bears an effigy of the crucified Christ. This object has an outer frame forming a foliated border (damaged at either extremity of the transverse limb of the cross).[9] The frame surrounds an inner cross formed of strips of decorated metal and bearing a *Corpus* (figure of Christ crucified) somewhat crudely cast in a bronze alloy. A knop on the crown of the head probably indicates that a nimbus was once attached. The whole object was originally gilded. Substantial traces of the gilding remain.

The arms of the crucifix end in roundels, which are decorated on the front with symbols of the four evangelists. The backs of these roundels display suns or stars with many rays, which have been interpreted as Yorkist emblems; the sunburst badge of Edward IV and, by extension, of the house of York.[10]

The limbs of the inner cross which bears the *Corpus* are formed, both front and back, of strips of gilded metal, engraved with a foliate design. In the case of some other, similar crucifixes, such strips are of *champlevé* enamel, typically with the background coloured blue, but the Bosworth example was never decorated in that way. It is made throughout of a yellow bronze alloy, now darkened, and originally overlaid with gold. Presumably the evangelists' emblems on the roundels once had enamelled backgrounds such as are seen on other examples of this type of cross, but no trace of the enamel is now visible.

As now preserved, the item is mounted on a modern base for display purposes. It was originally designed to be used either as an altar crucifix, mounted on a base, and with the addition of side brackets supporting figures of the Virgin and St John, or as a processional cross, mounted on a staff. From the evidence of other, more complete specimens of the type, when mounted as an altar cross it would have had a six-lobed base surmounted by a dome, upon which a small open crown would have acted as the seating for the shaft of the cross. For processional use it would have been mounted on a long wooden stave, possibly covered by brass tubing.

Nineteenth-century speculation that this crucifix might have come not from the vicinity of the battlefield but from Husbands Bosworth has been shown by the present writer to be baseless.[11] Although its precise find location cannot now be identified, the crucifix is an object of the correct period, and may well be a relic of the battle of 1485. A connection with the travelling chapel royal of Richard III, if unproven, is very plausible. In fact, the crucifix is described in a note in its file at the Society of Antiquaries as belonging to a class of objects 'intended for use in minor churches and in private chapels'. It is, therefore, precisely the kind of artefact which one would expect to have figured amongst the church plate in use by those royal chaplains who, as we have already seen, undoubtedly accompanied Richard III to Bosworth.

There has been some confusion about the name of Richard III's last battle. However, there seems no particular reason to reject the traditional 'Bosworth Field', since Henry VIII so referred to it in 1511.[12] In addition, 'there have been as many different accounts of Bosworth as there have been historians, and even today it is hard to produce a reconstruction of the battle which will command general acceptance'.[13] Ross and other modern writers continue to stress the numerical superiority of Richard III's army over 'the mixed force of French and Welsh levies which was all Henry "Tudor" could command'.[14] While the smallness of the 'Tudor' force may later have been exaggerated to point up the scale and miraculous nature of Henry VII's victory, superficially the respective numbers appear to suggest that Henry 'Tudor' had not succeeded in attracting any significant English support, and that the only English on his side were probably the small number of exiled noblemen who had formed his entourage in France.

As we have already observed, Richard III's army probably camped in and around Sutton Cheney. Let us now attempt to reconstruct the events of the last few hours of Richard III's life.

In the royal camp, the king probably arose soon after monastery and convent bells had sounded the hour of Prime, at about ten minutes past six (BST) on the morning of Monday 22 August.[15] As we have already seen, reportedly there were slight delays in the preparations for his morning mass and his breakfast. Let us assume that these delays took up some thirty minutes. The celebration of low mass in the royal tent will then have begun at about 6.40 am. The Bosworth Crucifix (a standard gilt and enamelled piece of royal travelling chapel equipment) mounted upon its lobed base, and with its side brackets in place, bearing figures of the Blessed Virgin and St John, stood, perhaps, on the portable altar, flanked by candlesticks. One of the royal chaplains began intoning the opening words of the mass for the feast day of SS Timothy and Symphorian. He was probably vested in the blood-red chasuble appropriate for the commemoration of martyrs.[16] The Latin words of the introit may have reminded the king of his coronation, and of the crown that he had worn the previous day, and would shortly put on again.[17]

The service will not have taken more than half an hour. Thus, by ten past seven, Richard will have been consuming his modest breakfast, probably comprising bread and wine. While he did so his esquires no doubt began to put his armour on him. At the same time, the royal chaplains were dismantling their portable altar in the royal tent. For the last time ever, the Bosworth Crucifix was taken off its lobed base, its side brackets were removed, and it was remounted upon a tall processional stave. A hinged ring of iron was clipped into place at the foot of the crucifix, just above the socket where the latter was now attached to its wooden shaft. To this the chaplains may then have tied ribbons or tassels in the Yorkist royal livery colours of murrey and blue.[18]

It was perhaps just after half past seven in the morning when the king finally donned an open crown, probably of gilded metal, set with jewels or paste, which he put on around the brow of his helmet. Richard III then left the royal tent to address his army. His chaplains, bearing the Bosworth Crucifix (now mounted as a processional cross), accompanied him to bless the royal forces.

It seems to have been a bright, sunny morning.[19] The enemy army had spent the night about 5 miles away at Merevale, which is located on Watling Street – a direct route to London. Richard, therefore, left his camp and marched his own forces westwards. The king's aim was to block Henry Tudor's route to London. However, Richard did not march as far as Watling Street. This was possibly because a Stanley banner was already visible to the south-west of Dadlington, near Stoke Golding. The Stanleys' precise intentions were still unclear, but it would have been wise to treat them with caution, and Richard would not have wanted to position his army confronting Henry 'Tudor', but with the Stanley forces lurking behind him.

Richard, therefore, positioned himself to the north-west of Crown Hill (as it would later be called). There, he arranged his force in an extended line on high ground, with the Duke of Norfolk's forces to the north-west, and the Earl of Northumberland's men to the south-east of the central contingent, which was commanded by Richard himself. Probably by seven fifty or thereabouts, the royal host had taken up its position on a low ridge. According to the Crowland Chronicle, Richard then ordered the execution of George Stanley, Lord Strange, but this execution was certainly not carried out, and

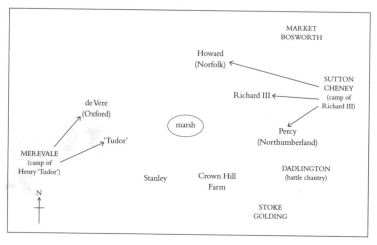

MAP 1: The Battle of Bosworth.

the order may never have been given, since the Stanleys had so far taken no overtly hostile action.[20]

On the lower ground in front of Richard's army some of the terrain was marshy.[21] As the king and his men gazed down they saw Henry 'Tudor''s much smaller force mustered beyond this marshland. Towards eight o'clock this smaller rebel force slowly began to advance towards the royal army, skirting the boggy ground. For a time the king took no action, but eventually, seeing that the rebel forces were clearing the marshland, he gave orders to oppose their further advance.

When John de Vere (*soi-disant* Earl of Oxford, and one of Henry 'Tudor''s most experienced commanders) saw men of the royal army advancing to oppose them, he swiftly ordered his men to hold back and maintain close contact with their standard bearers. In consequence, the rebel advance may have more or less ground to a halt, but by maintaining a fairly tight formation Henry 'Tudor''s men effectively prevented any serious incursion into their ranks by the royal army. In total, all this slow manoeuvring may have taken up as much as an hour.

It was apparently at this point – when in religious houses throughout the land monks and nuns, canons and friars were beginning to sing the office of Terce[22] – that the king suddenly caught sight of his second cousin, Henry 'Tudor', amongst the rebel forces.[23] Perhaps out of bravado; or from a sense of *noblesse oblige*; from fury at seeing 'Tudor' displaying the undifferenced royal arms, or possibly because he was suffering from a fever and not in full possession of all his faculties, Richard called his men around him and set off with them in person, at the gallop, to settle Henry's fate once and for all. An eyewitness account reports that 'he came with all his division, which was estimated at more than 15,000 men, crying, "These French traitors are today the cause of our realm's ruin"'.[24] The king's action could be seen as a risky move, and one which suggests that Richard may not have been thinking very clearly. In some ways it recalls his father's *sortie* from Sandal Castle, which had led to the Duke of York's death in December 1460. But unlike his father, Richard was in command of a large army and he should have had every chance of winning his battle. Jones prefers to see his charge as 'the final act of Richard's ritual affirmation of himself as rightful king', and it was certainly an action fully in accord with the late medieval chivalric literary tradition.[25] Whichever interpretation is correct, the king's dramatic charge did come very close to succeeding. The force of his charge cut through the 'Tudor' army, and Richard engaged his rival's standard bearer, William Brandon, whom he swiftly cut down. The 'Tudor' standard fell to the ground, and at this point Richard's hopes must have been high indeed, since probably only Sir John Cheney now stood between him and his adversary.

But Henry 'Tudor''s foreign mercenaries now suddenly deployed themselves in a defensive manoeuvre never hitherto witnessed in England. They fell back, enclosing Henry in a square formation of pikemen, through which the mounted warriors of the king's army could not penetrate.[26] The forefront of Richard's charging cavalry suddenly stalled, and the men riding behind cannoned into them. Many must have been unhorsed as a result. Seeing the royal charge thus broken in confusion against the wall of pikemen, the treacherous Stanley now took a swift decision and committed his forces on the 'Tudor' side.[27] His army cut more or less unopposed through the muddled *mêlée* of the royal cavalry, and in minutes the balance of the field was reversed. Richard III's horse was killed beneath him, and the king fell to the ground, losing his helmet in the process. He was struck on the head. As he struggled to his feet, one of his men offered him his own mount and shouted to Richard to flee, so that he could regroup and fight again. But the king refused. Surrounded now by enemies, he received further blows to his exposed head. His body, still protected by plate armour, was safe, but one hefty blow to the back of his unprotected skull was fatal. Given that in one sense his defeat and death clearly lay at Stanley's door, the report that Richard III's dying words were 'Treason – treason' may well be true.

The king had died some six weeks short of his thirty-third birthday. Polydore Vergil's account of his death recorded simply that 'king Richerd, alone, was killyd fyghting manfully in the thickkest presse of his enemyes'.[28] Although this account was written by and for Richard's enemies, it is a fitting tribute. Interestingly, it is also one which, in the final analysis, acknowledges without question the one key point which Richard himself was defending, namely his kingship.

Meanwhile, the rest of the vast royal army, most of whom had as yet done no fighting whatever, watched aghast as their sovereign fell. The quick-thinking John de Vere now seized the initiative. Taking rapid advantage of the new situation he hurled himself and his men at the position defended by his cousin, the Duke of Norfolk (who was in command of the royal archers). As de Vere grappled with his cousin, the latter unluckily lost his helmet. It was in that instant that an arrow, loosed at a venture, pierced the Duke of Norfolk's skull and he too fell dead.[29]

The vast royal army was now, in effect, a leaderless rabble. As the great host began to disintegrate, and its individual men-at-arms started to flee in the direction of Dadlington, the men of the smaller Tudor army began to pursue them and cut them down. The premise that the final stages of the combat were located in the vicinity of Dadlington is based upon the known fact that Henry VIII later established a perpetual chantry at Dadlington parish church for the souls of those who had been killed in the battle.[30]

By about ten o'clock in the morning the fighting was over. It was only from this point onwards that Henry 'Tudor' would have had the leisure to detail a search for Richard III's body, which had been left lying where it fell, somewhere near Henry's position at the outset of the battle. We shall explore in detail what happened to the king's remains in the next chapter.

⁂

Ironically, it was apparently in the month of August 1485 that Richard III's marriage negotiations in Portugal finally came to fruition. We have seen already that the Portuguese Council of State, meeting in Alcobaça, had urged both their king and their infanta in the strongest possible terms to accede to Richard III's marriage proposals, for they feared that otherwise the English court would turn its attention to Castile and Aragon, in which case the 'Catholic Kings' were only too likely to agree to a marriage between King Richard and the Infanta Doña Isabel de Aragón.

Duly impressed by his councillors' arguments and prognostications:

> King John bullied and brow-beat his sister, but also employed their aunt, Philippa, to try more feminine means of persuasion. A dramatic dénoûment [sic] followed. Joanna [sic] retired for a night of prayer and meditation. She had either a vision or a dream of a 'beautiful young man' who told her that Richard 'had gone from among the living'. Next morning, she gave her brother a firm answer: If Richard were still alive, she would go to England and marry him. If he were indeed dead, the King was not to press her again to marry.[31]

Apparently the infanta had been granted supernatural help in resolving her (and her country's) dilemma. The earliest extant written account of her vision dates from 1621, by which time Joana was, of course, also dead, and indeed, well advanced upon the path to sainthood. She was finally canonised in 1693 by Pope Innocent XII, and it is as St Joana of Portugal, Princess, that the Catholic Church remembers her today. Her mortal remains now lie splendidly enshrined at the Dominican monastery to which this princess, who came so close to being Queen of England, finally and definitively retired after Richard III's death in order to cultivate the religious life.

9

'A Sorry Spectacle'[1]

After Richard III's death, his body, stripped and slung over a horse's back, was carried back to Leicester: a distance of some 15 miles.[2] This journey was accomplished during the afternoon of 22 August, for it was the evening of that day when Henry VII and his army reached the city with their 'bag and baggage',[3] which now included Richard III's remains. If we assume the new king and his entourage set out from the battlefield at about two o'clock in the afternoon, the tail end of Henry VII's baggage train would probably have reached the city by about six in the evening, an hour or two before sunset.[4] Thus, it may well be the case that the arrival of Richard's corpse was greeted by the sound of bells from the city's churches. But these would not have been the 'great bells', which were traditionally tolled solemnly for the passing of a soul.[5] Rather, the sound would have been the bright chiming of little *Sanctus* bells, sounding from the parish churches for the evening *Angelus*, combined with the bells of Leicester Abbey and of the various Leicester friary churches, calling their respective communities to the evening office of Vespers.

The basic facts of the transportation of Richard's corpse to Leicester, and the manner of it, are fairly well known, and the interpretation usually applied to this event is to see it as a major example of Henry VII's vindictive nastiness. Thus Kendall, writing in the 1950s, chose to amplify the very basic information available from contemporary sources as follows:

> Stark naked, despoiled and derided, with a felon's halter about the neck, the bloody body was slung contemptuously across the back of a horse, which one of the king's heralds was forced to ride. As it was borne across the west bridge of the Soar, the head was carelessly battered against the stone parapet. For two days

the body lay exposed to view in the house of the Grey Friars close to the river. It was then rolled into a grave without stone or epitaph.[6]

The adjectives, of course, are Kendall's own. Moreover, his highly coloured account certainly contains errors. The Franciscan (Greyfriars) Priory was not close to the River Soar.[7] Nor is there any evidence that it was at that priory that Richard's body was exposed to public gaze.[8] Indeed, a religious house, parts of which were certainly closed to public access, would not have been a very suitable location for such a public display of the dead king's body. Kendall's account also contains other errors and misinterpretations, as we shall see in due course.[9]

The whole thesis that the treatment accorded to Richard's body represents gratuitous horror, personally inflicted upon Richard's corpse by his successor, is open to question. We must not forget that, whether or not he was held to be the *rightful* king, Richard III was certainly the *de facto* king in August 1485, and it was a political necessity for Henry VII to acknowledge that fact, since his claim to the throne, as subsequently embodied in an act of Parliament, was based first and foremost on conquest, which implied defeat of the previous *de facto* sovereign.

Henry VII is often portrayed by Richard III's defenders as an innately unpleasant character. One piece of evidence adduced in support of this portrayal is Henry's reported cynical attempt to date his reign from the day *before* the Battle of Bosworth (21 August).[10] Another is his supposedly barbaric treatment of Richard III's body. In fact, there is no evidence that Henry VII antedated his succession. Certainly it was subsequently 22 August, not 21, which was counted as the new king's accession day for the purpose of calculating his regnal years.[11] Nor was there, from Henry VII's point of view, any possible political or financial advantage to be gained from gratuitous nastiness in respect of Richard III's corpse – indeed, rather the reverse, since Henry needed to try to conciliate the defeated Yorkists if he was to reign in peace. In this context, it is significant to note that our two main written sources for the battle – Vergil's account and that of the Crowland Chronicle – are in complete agreement in consistently referring to Richard III as 'the king' up to, and indeed beyond, the point of his death. At the same time both sources consistently call Henry 'Tudor' 'the earl' until *after* his victory.[12] Bearing this important evidence in mind, let us now carefully re-examine the facts in this case.

Vergil offers an early sixteenth-century account of the sorry spectacle of Richard III's return to Leicester after the battle:

Interea Ricardi corpus, cuncto nudatum vestitu, ac dorso equi impositum, capite et brachiis et cruribus utrimque pendentibus, Leicestriam ad coenobium Franciscorum deportant, spectaculum mehercule miserabile, sed hominis vita dignum, ibique sine ullo funeris honore biduo post terra humatur.

[Meanwhile, they took Richard's body to the Franciscan Priory in Leicester, stripped of all clothing and placed on a horse's back with the head, arms and legs hanging down on either side; a sorry sight by Hercules, but one worthy of the man's life; and there, after two days, he was buried in the ground without any funerary honours.][13]

An earlier but briefer statement is supplied by the Crowland Chronicle:

Inventa inter alios mortuos corpora dicto Richardi regis … multasque alias contumelias illatas ipsoque non satis humaniter propter funem in collum adjectum usque Leicestriam deportato.

[King Richard's body having been discovered among the dead … many other insults were offered and after the body had been carried to Leicester with insufficient humanity (a rope being placed around the neck)].[14]

Although there are no other contemporary or near contemporary written accounts, attempts to flesh out this basic story begin with the later sixteenth-century writer Holinshed. His authority (if any) is unknown, and parts of his fuller account may very well have been based upon nothing more than his own imagination. However, for what it may be worth, he tells us that Richard's body 'was naked and despoiled to the very skin, and nothing left about him, not so much as a clout to cover his privy parts: and [he] was trussed behind a pursevant of arms, one Blanch Senglier, or White-boar, like a hog or calf; his head and arms hanging on one side of the horse, with his legs on the other side; and all besprinkled with mire and bloud'.

Since they are based upon no known contemporary source, Holinshed's details cannot be relied upon. Nevertheless, it is interesting to note that, while in general he apparently sets out to depict disgraceful treatment of the corpse – trussed like a dead animal, soiled with blood and mire (details absent from Vergil's account) – he also adds one snippet which may tend in a different direction: he informs us that Richard's naked body was transported to Leicester accompanied by the dead king's pursuivant of arms. We shall return to this point presently.

On arrival in Leicester the corpse seems to have been exposed to the public gaze in the Newark so that all might know for certain that the king was dead.[15] This can only have been done on Henry VII's instructions, and it is certainly probable that Henry VII would have wished as many people as possible to see for themselves that Richard III was indeed dead. We have no account of what preparation might have been accorded the remains before their public display. However, from Henry VII's point of view it would have been important that the body should be recognisable. It is likely, therefore, that the corpse was washed and that the cuts to the face and head were pressed shut rather than being left as gaping wounds.

Since it was late August and the weather was probably hot, one might suppose that some preservative measures would have been taken in order to retard the natural process of decomposition. In similar circumstances the body of James IV of Scotland was embalmed in 1516 by the enemies who had vanquished him. Incidentally, the treatment of the dead body of James IV, and the light which this may throw on the events of August 1485 and how we should judge them, will be considered in fuller detail below.

Against embalming, however, we have two pieces of evidence. First, there is the fact that the body of Richard's friend and supporter, John Howard, Duke of Norfolk (which must have been brought to Leicester at about the same time as the king's), seems not to have been embalmed. Howard's body cannot currently be identified for certain, but it seems possible to narrow it down to one of two sets of remains now interred at Framlingham church in Suffolk. Although we cannot be sure which of these two possible bodies belongs to John Howard, both were found to be preserved only as skeletons, and no traces of cere cloth were reported when the vaults containing these remains were opened in 1841.[16] The second piece of evidence is that, when Richard III's own grave was open in August 2012, as in the case of John Howard, no signs of cere cloth were found.

⚜

First, let us return to the treatment that is reported to have been accorded to Richard's body immediately after the battle. We have seen that, based on the Crowland chronicler (who was almost certainly not present in Leicester in August 1485), followed by Holinshed and other later accounts, this treatment has generally been categorised as barbarous. But perhaps we need to pause at this point and consider carefully what happened. We shall then be in a position to observe that, in terms of the burial arrangements for expelled English medieval monarchs, only in two respects does the treatment of Richard's remains appear to have been unique, and that is the stripping of his body and its transport from the battlefield slung over a horse. The funeral arrangements made for other deposed medieval English monarchs by their conquerors are considered in greater detail at the end of this chapter. For the moment, let us concentrate on the unique features: the stripping and transportation of Richard III's corpse. We need to remember that amongst the displaced medieval monarchs of England, the *manner* of Richard's death was in itself unique, a fact which cannot fail to be significant when we consider how his remains were handled.

Richard III is often described as the *last* English king to die in battle, but in point of fact he is the *only* English king to die in battle after the Norman Conquest, so the circumstances surrounding his burial were bound to be unique in some respects. It is also a well-known fact that bodies on battlefields were routinely stripped – not by their conquerors in person, but by looters (see below). It is highly improbable that Henry 'Tudor''s men would have stopped to strip Richard's body in mid-battle. It is far more likely that the stripping was carried out by local people routinely picking over the field in the wake of the victorious army. The king's body, which was probably more richly attired than most, would have been particularly susceptible to the attentions of such looters as soon as the tide of battle moved on in pursuit of his retreating army. In this context it is interesting to note that the crown from Richard's helmet (which was made of gold or gilded metal, perhaps set with jewels or paste) was reportedly found in a thorn bush after the battle. Had it perhaps been pushed there by a looter, intending to conceal it for later retrieval when things had quietened down? The fact that in the aftermath of the battle Richard's corpse was naked is probably not to be attributed to the innate nastiness of Henry 'Tudor' and his men, but was rather the normal and inevitable concomitant of battlefield death. Thus we know, for example, that when the first Earl of Shrewsbury was killed at the battle of Castillon, his corpse could subsequently only be identified by his missing left molar. Clearly, like Richard's, his body after the battle was heavily disfigured by blood and mire, and had been stripped of every particle of armour and clothing that might have been recognisable.[17] Further apposite examples of this common battlefield phenomenon will be cited presently.

Meanwhile, Vergil tells us that the battle itself lasted for two hours, in the course of which time the tide of the fighting will have swept on to areas far distant from the spot where Richard's battered remains were lying, thus allowing ample opportunity for looters to make off with the king's ruined but rich attire. Later, Henry 'Tudor' – now acclaimed as Henry VII – will have had to send a search party in quest of Richard III's corpse, which was eventually 'discovered among the dead'.[18] When it was found the corpse had almost certainly already been stripped. It is at *this point* that the body was subjected to post mortem injuries and obscenity, as reported by the Crowland chronicler. Naked, undefended, and in the hands of a group of fighting men who may well have been foreigners, vulgar jokes were probably made and wounds were inflicted on the face, chest and buttocks, before the body was carelessly hauled off to the new king.[19] This was probably when a rope was tied around the corpse's neck. Had Henry VII been present, he would surely have prevented the infliction of post mortem facial injuries, since he needed Richard's face to be recognisable.

As for the fact that Richard's body was reported by Virgil to have been transported from the field to Leicester slung over the back of a horse, this also requires careful evaluation. For those who wished to remove bodies from medieval battlefields the available resources were probably somewhat limited, and we know that in most cases such bodies were not removed at all, but were simply interred on or very near the spot where they fell. Medieval warlords would not routinely have taken with them into battle such items as coffins and hearses – the presence of which might have been liable to misinterpretation by one's supporters! Thus the obvious possible ways of transporting a body from the field would have been to have it dragged by men or by beasts, to throw it into a wheeled vehicle of some kind, or to drape it across the back of a horse. Where, on a battlefield, would anyone have chanced upon a stray coffin, a hearse, or mourners?

The very fact that Richard III's body was removed from the field at all, and carried back to Leicester, is a clear sign that it was being accorded quite special treatment. As for the means of its transportation, it may well have been considered by Henry 'Tudor' that the back of a horse was actually the most honourable of the limited available options – and fitting for a vanquished warrior of royal blood. This brings us back to the interesting point that, according to Holinshed's later account, Henry also ordered that Richard's body should be accompanied by the dead king's *Blanc Sanglier* pursuivant of arms.[20] Perhaps, in his own way, and within the limits of the resources available to him on the battlefield, Henry VII was, in fact, treating Richard's body as a royal corpse.[21] And if a rope remained around Richard's dead neck from its earlier hauling across the battlefield by Henry's search party, this may now simply have been used to help tie the body in place on the horse's back, thereby avoiding accidents.[22]

At this point it will, perhaps, be instructive to introduce two further kinds of evidence, which may throw light on what we know of the fate of Richard's remains in the immediate aftermath of the Battle of Bosworth. The second such category of evidence (which we shall come to in a moment) is literary and cultural evidence bearing on fifteenth-century attitudes to such matters as death in battle. First, however, let us examine late fifteenth- and early sixteenth-century evidence from beyond the boundaries of England, which relates to the deaths of two other European leaders who were likewise defeated and killed.

Richard III's brother-in-law, Charles the Bold, Duke of Burgundy, was vanquished and slain at the Battle of Nancy in 1477, eight years prior to the Battle of Bosworth. 'Refusing to fly, and fighting desperately to cover the retreat of his scattered forces, [he] was surrounded and was cleft through helmet and skull by the tremendous blow of a Swiss halberd ... all his face was one gash from temple to teeth.'[23] Subsequently, 'it took two days to find his body and then only after a patient and macabre search over the battlefield. It appeared that his horse had fallen while trying to jump a frozen stream and the duke had been killed by a mighty blow to the head, which left him totally unrecognisable except to his Italian valet who knew him by his long fingernails, and to his Portuguese doctor who identified him by the old battle scars on his stripped and frozen corpse.'[24] Thus, like Richard III's remains, Charles' body was found naked, having likewise been stripped by looters. It was clearly in much more of a mess than Richard's when it was finally removed for burial, for in Richard's case it does not seem to have been unduly difficult to identify his remains once they were found, and this suggests that Richard's features had not been heavily disfigured.

About thirty years later, in 1513, King James IV of Scotland was defeated and killed by English forces at the Battle of Flodden. After the battle James' body was recovered, carried initially to Berwick,[25] and embalmed. It was then sent to London with the intention that it should be buried there, but initially the body remained above ground because James had been excommunicated before his death, so a religious burial was not possible. Later, Henry VIII arranged for it 'to be given honourable burial by the monks at Sheen, after he had persuaded the Pope to assume that James had given some sign of repentance as he lay dying on the battlefield, which enabled the Pope to release him from excommunication and to allow him to be buried in a church'.[26] It is not absolutely clear whether James' body had also been stripped on the battlefield, but this seems probable, because afterwards there was considerable debate as to whether the correct body had really been recovered, and it seems unlikely that this would have been the case if the remains were still clothed in their royal garb. James IV's bloodstained plaid or tunic, at least, seems to have been separated from his corpse after his death but before the body was recovered, for this garment was later delivered to the queen regent, Catherine of Aragon, who then sent it as a token of victory to Henry VIII in France.[27]

The second category of external evidence, which may be illuminating in relation to the treatment of Richard III's corpse, is the general evidence of the late medieval chivalric literary and cultural tradition. Late medieval warriors did not exist in a vacuum. They had behind them a whole gamut of written and oral tradition which informed their attitudes. The military heroes of their literature and history were exemplars for their own conduct. Thus, both Richard III and Henry 'Tudor' will have known stories of Greek and Roman heroes. They will have been familiar with the fact that Achilles had tied the dead body of the vanquished Hector behind his chariot and dragged it round the walls of Troy before eventually surrendering the mangled remains to King Priam for burial.[28] They will also have been familiar with the quasi-historical, quasi-mythological tales of the great Alexander, whose treatment of the dead body of his defeated enemy, Darius III of Persia, was considered quite exceptional and remarkable (Alexander accorded the dead Darius a full royal funeral). As for the typical aftermath of a battle, that had been graphically described in the previous century by the English poet Chaucer:

Whan that this worthy duc, the Theseus,
Hath Creon slayn and wonne Thebes thus,
Stille in that feeld he took al nyght his reste,
And dide with al the contree as hym leste.
To ransake in the taas of bodyes dede,
Hem for to strepe of harneys and of wede,
The pilours diden bisynesse and cure
After the bataille and discomfiture.[29]

We have already remarked that Richard III was not the only English king to have been violently deprived of his crown and his life. It is now time to consider briefly the other medieval examples of this phenomenon: Edward II, Richard II and Henry VI. In all three cases, the king's dead body was exposed to the public gaze, before being buried with little funeral pomp in a monastic church: Gloucester Abbey in the case of Edward II; the Dominican Priory at King's Langley for Richard II; and Chertsey Abbey for Henry VI.[30] It therefore seems that we may have evidence of a consistent pattern of what might be described as 'alternative royal burial' for ousted kings. This pattern consists of exposure of the corpse (to demonstrate publicly that the former monarch is dead), followed by a basic funeral, with discreet burial in a priory or abbey church, which would not be readily accessible to the general public, and where the body would be out of sight and hopefully, for the time being, out of mind.[31]

In all three cases we find also that after a suitable lapse of time the burial arrangements were subsequently upgraded. Thus Edward III later provided a splendid tomb for his father at Gloucester Abbey. Henry V, soon after his accession, transferred Richard II's remains from King's Langley to the tomb at Westminster Abbey, which Richard had prepared for himself during his lifetime, and, as we have already seen (in chapter 5), Richard III, when he came to the throne, transferred Henry VI's remains to a new royal tomb in St George's Chapel, Windsor. We shall explore the later upgrading of Richard III's tomb in chapter 11, but let us begin by looking first at what arrangements were made for his interment in August 1485.

10

The Franciscan Priory

Precise and detailed information as to the arrangements made for the final disposal of Richard's remains is not recorded by any contemporary source. Writing more than one hundred years after the event, George Buck (*c.* 1563–1622?), the descendant of a Yorkist family, and the first writer to attempt a re-evaluation of the 'Tudor' image of Richard III, states that 'they gave his corpse a bed of earth, which was done *by commandment and order of King Henry VII*, and honourably in the chief church of Leicester, called St Mary's, belonging to the order and society of the Greyfriars'. It is clear at once that Buck's account is somewhat muddled. A dedication to the Blessed Virgin Mary was quite common for medieval priory churches of the Franciscan Order, so it would not be surprising if the Leicester Greyfriars had been so dedicated. Nevertheless, in the case of the Leicester priory, a dedication to St Francis himself has also been alleged. Surviving impressions of the priory seal, however, actually depict St Mary Magdalene in the scene *noli me tangere.*[1] This strongly suggests that the Greyfriars church may indeed have been dedicated to St Mary – but to St Mary Magdalene rather than to the Blessed Virgin Mary. Even so, it was certainly not 'the chief church' of Leicester. Leicester Abbey (which was indeed dedicated to the Blessed Virgin) had a better claim to pre-eminence, and would arguably have been a more prestigious place of interment for Richard's corpse. This, together with the fact that there is no contemporary evidence that Henry VII took any initiative whatsoever in the matter of Richard's burial, means that Buck's account leaves us with certain questions.

Nonetheless, Richard's burial location is confirmed as the Franciscan Priory Church by the fifteenth-century Warwickshire antiquary, John Rous.

Moreover, Rous states specifically that, as one would expect for a person of such rank, the interment took place in the choir of the church. However, he has been perceived by some authorities as complicating the issue somewhat by his use of the word *finaliter* (ultimately) to describe the friary burial. Based on this evidence, and on the account given in the Frowyk Chronicle, Anne Sutton and Livia Visser-Fuchs have suggested that Richard's body was initially interred elsewhere (possibly in the church of St Mary-in-the-Newark) and was only moved to the Franciscan Priory Church at a later date. Yet it seems difficult to account for such a change of location. Why should Richard's body have subsequently been moved in this way? In the case of the other deposed kings, whose remains were later reburied (Richard II and Henry VI), these were taken *from* a priory church to a more publicly accessible place of burial. The removal of Richard III's body from the Newark to the Greyfriars would have run counter to this trend. It seems more likely, therefore, that the burial took place directly at the friary, and that the word *finaliter* refers simply to the brief delay representing the time during which Richard's body had been exposed to public view. The wording of a document referring to the construction of Richard's tomb at the Greyfriars certainly appears to imply that his body was already buried there at the time when the tomb was commissioned.[2]

It is known that 'Henry stayed two days at Leicester, and then pursued his course to London'. The new king's stay in Leicester presumably coincided with the period during which Richard's dead body was on public show. On the morning of Thursday 25 August, having formally been proclaimed king before the army, the nobility and representatives of Leicester, Henry VII prepared to ride away in the direction of the capital.

Without actually giving a precise date for the interment, Polydore Vergil indicates that Richard's burial took place on the same day as Henry VII's departure from Leicester, namely Thursday 25 August. Coincidentally, this happened to be the feast day of Richard's (and Henry's) sainted ancestor, King Louis IX of France. The English translation of Vergil's text reports the burial to have been 'without any pompe or solemn funerall … in thabbay [*sic*] of monks [*sic*] Franciscanes at Leycester'.[3] Vergil's account is in several respects remiss, and we can discern in it the seeds of George Buck's later confusion between the Franciscan Priory and Leicester Abbey. As we have already seen, the Franciscan house in Leicester was in fact a priory, not an abbey, and of course members of the Franciscan Order are friars, not monks.[4]

Bearing in mind that some of his wording regarding Richard's burial is rather careless, we can now review the rest of Vergil's very brief account. His reported lack of 'pompe' and solemnity may imply that Richard's remains were simply tipped into a grave with no religious rites at all.[5] Everything will have depended upon who made the decision to inter Richard at the

Franciscan Priory, and upon who exactly carried out the burial. There are two possible scenarios. In the first, the friars themselves would have requested the new king's leave to inter the body of his predecessor, and carried out his burial. However, it is also possible that the burial was carried out by servants of the new king. In that case, the arrangements are likely to have been less respectful.

If the friars were in charge, surely no fifteenth-century religious community of friars, carrying out a private burial, well away from the eyes of the public,[6] would have failed to pray for the soul of the deceased person whom they were burying, whoever this might have been. Such prayers are an important part of Catholic tradition, and were considered extremely important at this particular period, when the cult of the dead was very strong. Moreover, late fifteenth-century evidence suggests that friars were considered by the general public to be particularly reliable and assiduous in carrying out this religious duty.[7]

In this case, the reported lack of ceremonial would not mean that the offices of the dead and Requiem Mass were never celebrated for Richard. It would merely mean that the liturgies which were celebrated were accomplished without 'solemnity' – a word which, in a religious context, has quite specific connotations. In 'solemn' celebrations the officiating priest is supported by assistants and a full range of vestments is worn. Music and tapers are also extensively employed in solemn liturgies, and incense is offered.

Of course, not one of the trappings of a 'solemn celebration' is essential. Clearly, based upon Vergil's account, we would have to imagine that some – and perhaps all – of these ceremonial trappings were lacking in the case of Richard's burial. This would not be surprising. However, while Speede's account emphasises the lack of 'funeral *solemnity*', and Baker, later in the seventeenth century, says that Richard was buried 'with *small* funeral pomp', in the case of burial by the friars this could hardly mean that there were no religious rites.[8]

If the friars buried the body, representatives of the priory must have called upon the new king, probably on Wednesday 24 August. Either the friars requested leave to bury Richard's remains, or King Henry VII ordered them to take on this task.[9] Buck's later account speaks of a royal command, but it may be that the initiative actually came from the friars, whose order had enjoyed the patronage of the royal house of York.[10] These friars certainly had a Yorkist history. Earlier, their Leicester priory had opposed the accession of Henry IV, and two of its friars had been hanged as a result![11] In either event, it must have been Henry VII who made the final decision about the disposal of Richard's remains.

Early on the morning of Henry VII's departure a small group of friars would then have gone to collect Richard's remains. The body had not been coffined.[12] It had probably been displayed at the Newark on a kind of hurdle or stretcher, possibly partly covered by a cloth. The friars who went to collect the corpse will have merely covered the body completely or placed it in a shroud, and lifted the hurdle between them. Then, without any of the usual royal funerary pomp their simple little cortege will have made its way through the streets of Leicester on foot, at an hour when most of the citizens were probably still in bed. There will have been few, if any, witnesses in the streets or at the windows from whom Vergil or others could later have obtained the essential information for any detailed account of what took place.

Likewise, what happened at the priory church would have been private, unseen by any but the friars themselves. We can be certain of this because Rous reports that the burial took place in the choir, and the recent excavation at the Leicester Greyfriars site confirms this. The choir was an enclosed part of the church, which was not usually accessible to lay people. No great royal hearse with mountains of candles will have been prepared before the high altar, and the stretcher bearing Richard's body must just have been placed on trestles before the altar, perhaps with tapers burning on either side.

There may have been a brief period of vigil after the reception of the body, with one or two friars watching over the corpse and praying silently. At some time during the morning, Requiem Mass will have been celebrated. There will have been no mourners in attendance with torches: only the friars themselves, standing in their choirstalls. At the end of the funeral mass, the body will have been lowered into a new grave, which had been opened in the floor the day before near the centre of the western end of the choir, close to the point where an archway gave access to the walkway and the nave beyond it. Here some of the coloured, glazed floor tiles had been lifted up and a shallow hole had been dug in the earth beneath. There, Richard III's shrouded body was laid. It proved a tight fit. The body had not been measured, and the grave was barely long enough for it.

But we must also consider the alternative possibility: that Richard III's remains were not buried by the friars but by servants of Henry VII. In this case, the friars may not even have been warned in advance of the plans. On the morning of 25 August, as the new king was preparing to leave Leicester, some of his servants would simply have been sent to pick up the body from the Newark and cart it to the Fanciscan Priory. The friars may only have become aware of these arrangements when they were summoned by the banging on their door. The king's servants would then have dragged the body into the choir and rapidly dug a simple pit to receive it. Into this they would have thrust the body, shovelled the earth back on top of it, and then left the astonished and probably appalled friars to deal with the sequel in whatever way they saw fit. Unfortunately, there is some evidence from the excavation of the grave site that this kind of burial may have been accorded to Richard's remains. Even so, it is hard to imagine that the religious community would not have offered prayers for the dead once the new king's servants had departed.

Certainly no coffin was employed for Richard's burial. This was confirmed by the excavation of August 2012. A little more needs to be said about coffins, because unfortunately a seventeenth- and eighteenth-century tradition in Leicester ascribed to Richard III a stone coffin, which was displayed to visitors at that period, at a Leicester inn. The normal pattern for royal and aristocratic burials in the fifteenth century was to use either a lead coffin (as attested by the cases of Edward IV and Lady Anne Mowbray) or a wooden coffin (as in the cases of Eleanor Talbot and Elizabeth Woodville). In Richard III's case, however, it is clear that no coffin was used.

The supposed 'stone coffin of Richard III' was a much later red herring, pressed into service by a canny innkeeper simply to generate tourist interest. Stone coffins had certainly been used in the *early* Middle Ages, but they were not used in the fifteenth century. The one displayed at the Leicester inn in the eighteenth century very probably came from a genuine priory site – perhaps even from the Greyfriars. No doubt it was unearthed by chance during the redevelopment of the site after the Dissolution, and was then immediately seized on by a quick-thinking entrepreneur with an eye to business as a potential 'tourist attraction'. Unfortunately, this story has recently resurfaced with the discovery of a similar stone coffin in the Leicester area, in use as a garden water feature. This 'new' stone coffin has subsequently been transported to, and placed on display at, the Bosworth Battlefield Centre, where it is now apparently playing a very similar tourist role to that of its eighteenth-century predecessor. The 'new' coffin probably also came originally from a priory site. However, the recently discovered coffin is certainly not identical to the one which was displayed in Leicester as 'King Richard's' in the eighteenth century, for we know that by the end of the eighteenth century that one had been broken into fragments which later disappeared – probably used as rubble in the foundations of later buildings. On the other hand, the 'new' coffin is more or less intact. It is also important to stress that it is absolutely certain that neither the old stone coffin nor the new ever had any genuine connection with Richard III.

෴

We can summarise and conclude our review of the burial arrangements made (or at least approved) for Richard by Henry VII in August 1485 by observing that they present no surprising or unexpected features. Henry exposed the corpse to public view, and then had it buried with basic funeral rites in a priory church. As we have already seen, this corresponds very closely to the treatment accorded to the corpses of England's other displaced monarchs. Based upon those earlier examples we might then anticipate that at some convenient later date – possibly after the accession of Henry VIII – a royal tomb for Richard would have been commissioned. As we shall see in the next chapter, this is more or less exactly what happened. The reburial of Henry VI at Windsor had taken place twelve years after the king's death and original burial, and it had to wait for the death of Edward IV and the accession of Richard III. The upgrading of Richard II's burial had taken about fourteen years, and also had to wait for Henry V to succeed his father. However, in Richard III's case the provision of his new royal tomb took only nine years, and Richard did not have to wait for the accession of the second 'Tudor' king.

Meanwhile, in the aftermath of Bosworth, the news of Richard III's death slowly crept its way around the courts of Europe. On 20 October 1485, the Bishop of Imola wrote, in a letter to Pope Innocent VIII:

> According to common report as heard by me on my way, the King of England has been killed in battle.[14]

11

'King Richard's Tombe' [1]

As has just been noted, the one slightly unusual feature which we encounter in the upgrading of the burial of Richard III, is the fact that he did not have to wait quite so long for his royal tomb as his dethroned predecessors. We shall explore possible reasons for this shortly.

As a matter of fact, although it has usually been assumed that Richard's burial place was initially left unmarked, we actually have no surviving evidence on this point. It is possible that, once the earth had settled and it was possible to reinstate the paving at the western end of their choir, the friars themselves marked King Richard's burial site in some way. In any case, the lapse of time was relatively short, so that knowledge of the precise burial location would certainly not have been lost when the time came to install the new royal monument.

It seems to have been in about the summer of 1494, nine years after the Battle of Bosworth, that King Henry VII initiated the creation of a fitting tomb for his erstwhile rival.[2] The king delegated the responsibility for this project to Sir Reynold Bray and Sir Thomas Lovell, committed 'Tudor' adherents and well-established servants of the new king. Nevertheless, Richard III's mother, Cecily Neville, dowager Duchess of York, seems to have considered both men trustworthy, since in April–May 1495 – within a year of their being charged by Henry VII with supervising the construction of her son's tomb – she named them amongst the executors of her will.[3] Since one of Cecily's motives was a wish to ensure her own proper entombment at Fotheringhaye, it is reasonable to suppose that Bray and Lovell had dutifully fulfilled their task in respect of Richard III and had commemorated him in a fitting manner.

In fact, they commissioned a Nottingham alabaster man, Walter Hylton, to erect a monument 'in the Church of Friers in the town of leycestr where the bonys of Kyng Richard the iij[de] reste'.[4] This was probably that same Walter Hylton who served as Mayor of Nottingham in 1489/90 and again in 1496/97.[5] We are aware of his commission only because it subsequently gave rise to a legal dispute. The case was presented to the chancellor, Cardinal Morton (though it was not, of course, heard by him in person), at some date between 1493 and 1500, and the plea is dated on the reverse 1 July 11 Henry VII [1496]. Following Hylton's commission, an alabaster tomb monument for Richard III was made in Nottingham and subsequently installed at the Greyfriars church in Leicester. As we shall see, Richard's epitaph appears to date the commissioning of this monument to 1494. The sum paid to Hylton for his work on the tomb is usually reported to have been £50, though in fact the reading of this figure is problematic.[6]

It is virtually certain that the payment to Hylton (whatever the sum involved) did not represent Henry VII's total expenditure on Richard's tomb. BL, Add. MS 7099 contains extracts from the household accounts of Henry VII in the form of manuscript copies in the handwriting of the antiquarian Craven Ord (c. 1755–1832).[7] On folio 126 Ord notes that the original documents which he transcribed were then 'in the Exchequer, every leaf signed by the king'. However, those original fifteenth-century records are now lost. Ord's surviving copies in the British Library contain tentative attempts at regnal year dating, although these have been subsequently erased, and appear to have been in error. We shall return to the question of dating presently.

Folio 129 (in the modern, pencil enumeration) includes the entry '11 Sept. – to James Keyley for King Rich. Tombe – £10. 0s. 12d.'. Superficially the sum specified may appear odd, but the extracts contain other entries where the figure in the pence column is 12 or above, or where the figure in the shillings column is 20 or above. Presumably, therefore, the sum paid to James Keyley was in fact £10. 1s. 0d.

The unequivocal use of the title of king in relation to Richard in both the Hylton and Keyley texts is interesting, since it appears to confirm that there was absolutely no question as to his status. The Keyley reference includes no royal numeral, but it could not possibly relate to Richard I (who lay buried in France). Some might wish to argue that Keyley's payment could refer to some repair to the tomb of Richard II in Westminster Abbey. In that case, the fact that the date of the payment corresponds with the period at which Henry VII is known to have been arranging a tomb for Richard III would be a remarkable coincidence – for although the payment to James Keyley mentions no year, the precise date can be ascertained. The preceding folio records the payment of £10 to Sir William Stanley 'at his execution'. This entry is dated 20 February, and Stanley was executed in February 1495. Thus the payment to Keyley was clearly made on 11 September 1495. This, in turn, suggests that the inauguration of Richard III's new tomb may well have taken place on the tenth anniversary either of Richard's death or his burial (22 or 25 August 1495). Moreover, the occasion might perhaps have been marked by some royal ceremonial, since this would have been in Henry VII's interest at that time, as we shall see.

It is not stated what exactly Keyley did in respect of Richard III's tomb, but one possible clue is provided by another entry dated 20 January [1501?] recording the payment of £10 to Master Estfield 'for conveying of the King's [Henry VII's] Toumbe from Windesor to Westmr'. In a similar way Richard III's tomb may have been made in Nottingham in Walter Hylton's workshop, and then transported to (and set up in?) Leicester by James Keyley. Certainly the payment of £10. 1s. 0d. cannot possibly refer to Richard III's actual burial. First, the date is far too late, and second, the Add. MS 7099 accounts also record a payment 'for burying of a man that was slayn in my Lady Grey's chamber' on 27 May 1495, and the sum involved on that occasion was merely one gold angel (6s. 8d.).

Assuming that the money paid to Keyley was not part of the sum of ?£50 mentioned in connection with Walter Hylton's indenture, but was additional to it, this would bring the total cost of the tomb to not less than (perhaps) £60. Nor can we assume that these two payments to Hylton and Keyley represent the total cost of the tomb. The records which have come down to us, mentioning Hylton and Keyley and their connection with Richard's monument, survived by chance. Had there been no litigation in respect of the Hylton contract, and had Craven Ord not transcribed the reference to the Keyley payment, we should have no knowledge of either. There may well have been other payments of which nothing is now known. No other records referring to Richard III's tomb in Leicester and dating from the period 1490–1500 are currently extant, either at The National Archives or at any other English repository. The total sum expended by Henry VII on Richard III's tomb, therefore, remains unknown.

For the purposes of comparison, we may note that in the 1450s an alabaster retable for an altar (roughly the equivalent in size of one side of a table tomb) cost £1. 17s. 3d., while in 1462 an alabaster image of the Virgin Mary (size unspecified) could be purchased for £2.[8] A contract, drawn up in 1508, for a fine alabaster table tomb for Henry Foljambe of Chesterfield, Derbyshire, survives. This specifies a cost of £10 for the tomb table, decorated with small effigies and shields bearing arms on the side panels. In this case the table was to be topped off with gilt copper effigies which are presumed not to have been included in the price of £10.[9] By comparison, a tomb costing in total more than ?£60 for Richard III – even given that this sum may have included

an alabaster recumbant figure of the king – should therefore have been a mag-
nificent specimen of the alabaster men's craft. Tombs made of harder stone,
and with bronze gilt effigies, were a good deal more costly of course. Thus
the tomb of Richard Beauchamp, Earl of Warwick (d. 1439), had cost £715.
Yet the only recorded expenditure for the original tomb of Cecily Neville,
Richard III's mother, was 100 marks (roughly £66).[10]

No detailed description of Richard III's tomb exists, but it was made by
workers in alabaster, and although Richard's epitaph describes its stone as
'marble', this was a very common late medieval synonym for alabaster. The
tomb was surmounted by an effigy or image of Richard, which was certainly
of alabaster. In the words of Holinshed, 'King Henry the Seventh caused a
tomb to be made and set up over the place where he [Richard] was buried,
with a picture of alabaster representing his person'. The word 'picture' in
sixteenth-century texts can mean 'statue'. Whether Richard's alabaster 'picture' actually comprised a statue or a flat engraved slab is uncertain, but
alabaster tomb effigies were two-a-penny at this period, and were almost
mass-produced. Surviving incised alabaster slabs from the end of the fifteenth
century are much rarer – though not unknown.[11] On balance, a recumbent
alabaster effigy seems the more likely alternative.

Richard III's new tomb remained in place in the Greyfriars church for the
next forty-three years. During this period, at least seven times a day, as they
entered and left their choir for the 'Hours' of their daily Office, the Franciscan
friars of Leicester would have passed by Richard's tomb as they made their
way to their choirstalls.

For an idea of the possible appearance of the tomb, see figure 25. Near-
contemporary English tombs of members of the royal family, such as the
bronze gilt tomb of Henry VII himself in Westminster Abbey, or the alabaster
tombs of Richard's sister, Elizabeth of York, Duchess of Suffolk, and her husband, John de la Pole, at Wingfield Church, provide possible guidance as to
the likely design of Richard's monument. Both are also table tombs topped
by recumbent effigies, lying with their feet towards the east end of the sanctuary. In the case of Henry VII the tomb is centrally placed in the specially
built new Lady Chapel, which bears his name. Likewise, Richard's tomb was
centrally located in the choir of the priory church, with his feet towards the
high altar – not placed against one of the side walls of the choir, like that of
his sister and brother-in-law at Wingfield Church. However, Richard's burial
was towards the western end of the choir, presumably for the simple reason
that all the available sites closer to the high altar were already occupied by
earlier tombs.

The text of an epitaph associated with Richard III's tomb in Leicester has
been preserved. This first appeared in print in the seventeenth century as an

appendix to the posthumously published life of Richard III by George Buck. Until recently this epitaph had been little studied. Moreover, discussion of it focused on a seventeenth-century English 'translation' (possibly by Buck himself) rather than on the original Latin text – leading to a tendency to dismiss the epitaph as a seventeenth-century invention. However, even a glance at the Latin text is sufficient to disprove this notion. The currently available Latin versions of the epitaph, together with the seventeenth-century English translation, are supplied below in Appendix 6. A modern English translation by the present writer will be given presently.

The epitaph displays overt connections with the monument erected for Richard III in Leicester in the 1490s. Clearly the writer was aware of Henry VII's commemorative arrangements, for the wording refers to the honours paid by Henry to Richard's corpse and (apparently) to 1494. The epitaph must have been written after Richard's death in 1485, and before 1619, when it was reproduced by Buck. On religious grounds it is unlikely to have been written later than about 1535, since it concludes with a request for prayers for Richard's soul: something unlikely to have been written after the Reformation had begun.

As for the style and structure of the epitaph, very close parallels, both in verse form and in length, are to be found among the recorded memorials of medieval English royalty. Among the closest parallel inscriptions are the epitaphs of Queen Catherine (widow of Henry V, mother of Henry VI and grandmother of Henry VII), and one of the epitaphs from the tomb of Henry VII himself.[12] Thus, stylistically, Richard III's epitaph could easily have been written in about 1495.

Another important factor in favour of the authenticity of the epitaph is the fact that there are two independent seventeenth-century published sources for it: Buck and Sandford. The text was first reported by Sir George Buck in 1619 at the end of his *History of the Life and Reigne of Richard the Third* (published posthumously by his nephew in 1647). But it was printed again, in a slightly different version, by Francis Sandford in his *Genealogical History of the Kings of England* (London, 1677). Sandford was aware of the 1647 publication of Buck's *History*, and he noted specifically that its version of Richard's epitaph differed in minor respects from his own text. Clearly, therefore, Sandford's source for the epitaph was different from that of Buck – and possibly closer to the original inscription.

Francis Sandford was Lancaster Herald, and derived his text from a manuscript at the College of Arms (figure 27). This manuscript is in the handwriting of Thomas Hawley, who became a herald in 1509 and died in 1557. Hawley's text of the epitaph and the compilation in which it figures comprise copies of reference material, made by Hawley for his own use. The existence of this manuscript in Hawley's hand proves conclusively that the epitaph must have been written before 1557.

The whole of the Hawley MS, in which Richard's epitaph figures, was copied from an earlier compilation in the handwriting of Sir Thomas Wriothesley (d. 1534). Wriothesley's manuscript is now at the British Library (figure 26). Thomas Wriothesley was one of the sons of John Wrythe, who was a herald during the reigns of Edward IV, Richard III and Henry VII. Thomas became a pursuivant in the private service of Arthur 'Tudor', Prince of Wales (1489), and subsequently (1503) Garter King of Arms. In the days of Thomas Wriothesley, the heralds kept their own libraries of reference material. The inclusion of a copy of Richard's epitaph in Wriothesley's collection securely dates the epitaph before 1534. Indeed, its context within the collection suggests a date for Wriothesley's copy prior to 1531, and possibly much earlier. It is, therefore, absolutely certain that Wriothesley's text of the epitaph was written down at a time when Richard III's tomb in Leicester was still extant and undamaged. Although no record of a visit by Thomas Wriothesley to Leicester now survives, such a visit, either by Thomas himself or by one of his colleagues, may well have taken place. Wriothesley's version of the epitaph could thus have been copied directly from the tomb. The fact that the writer changed his mind about some of the readings suggests that he might well have been working directly from an inscription.

As for Buck's text, that apparently belongs to a separate line of transmission, distinct from the Wriothesley–Hawley–Sandford tradition. Buck gave his source for the epitaph as a manuscript at the Guildhall in London. Small differences in the texts show that Buck's Guildhall source was not identical with Sandford's source at the College of Arms.

Buck not only recorded his interpretation of the original Latin inscription, but seems also to have produced the versified English 'translation' from which most previous commentators have worked. This was the only version of the epitaph available in English until now, and the fact that its English verse forms are clearly of the seventeenth century was the major factor that encouraged earlier writers to dismiss the epitaph as a fabrication. This latter judgement was certainly incorrect. The epitaph was unquestionably written at about the time when Henry VII commissioned a tomb for Richard, and it may well have been inscribed upon the tomb itself, though we shall return to that point presently.

First, however, we should also note that Buck's English version is an approximate – and sometimes inaccurate – rendering of the rather complex Latin of the original. Here is a new, more direct and literal translation of Buck's Latin text:

I, here, whom the earth encloses under various coloured marble,[13]
Was justly called Richard the Third.[14]
I was Protector of my country, an uncle ruling on behalf of his nephew.
I held the British kingdoms in trust, [although] they were disunited.
Then for just[15] sixty days less two,
And two summers, I held my sceptres.
Fighting bravely in war, deserted by the English,
I succumbed to you, King Henry VII.
But you yourself, piously, at your expense, thus honoured my bones
And caused a former king to be revered with the honour of a king[16]
When [in] twice five years less four[17]
Three hundred five-year periods of our salvation had passed.[18]
And eleven days before the Kalends of September[19]
I surrendered to the red rose the power it desired.[20]
Whoever you are, pray for my offences,
That my punishment may be lessened by your prayers.

While the manuscript texts and Sandford's publication contain slightly different readings at some points, the major part of the text is identical in all the currently extant versions.

So was this epitaph actually inscribed on the tomb of *c.* 1494? This point cannot be absolutely proved either way, since there was a well-authenticated fifteenth-century tradition of epitaphs inscribed on tablets of wood, or on parchment, and hung by admirers around the tombs of the famous. It is therefore possible that Richard III's epitaph was not directly inscribed on the tomb, but hung up nearby. Even so, the text remains interesting. It is generally favourable to Richard, and certainly not overtly hostile. It seems highly improbable that any writer of the 'Tudor' period would have dared to pen a valedictory text on Richard III without the authorisation of the reigning monarch. Thus we must assume that the text reflects the 'official viewpoint' of Henry VII's regime on Richard III in about 1494.

If the epitaph may be regarded as an 'official statement' by the government of Henry VII on Richard III, it is certainly of interest. Unsurprisingly, perhaps – for this is a theme encountered in other 'Tudor' sources – it pays tribute to Richard's bravery. The final couplet has sometimes been seen as implying that Richard was evil (and Buck's verse translation, which employs the word 'crimes', certainly carries that flavour). In fact, however, the closing lines merely reflect the standard late medieval preoccupation with purgatory, common to all believers at the time when Richard's tomb was erected. It was normal in tomb inscriptions to request prayers for the deceased, and the fact that this epitaph does so need not imply that Richard III was more in need of such prayers than other people.

The text of the epitaph, together with the fact that it is not overtly hostile to Richard, raises a broader question. Why did Henry VII decide, nine or ten years after Richard's death, to create a monument for him? Had Henry simply mellowed as time passed? Did he come to feel sorry for Richard? Was it that sufficient time had elapsed for him to feel that a memorial to Richard would now be safe?

Early in 1493, having already survived an attempt on his crown by the Earl of Lincoln and the young pretender generally known as 'Lambert Simnel',[21] Henry had become aware of a new Yorkist conspiracy against him. He knew that Margaret of York, Duchess of Burgundy, had under her wing a young man reputed to be his brother-in-law, Richard of Shrewsbury, Duke of York.[22] During 1493 and 1494, Yorkists at home in England were known to be plotting against Henry, and in the interests of Margaret's *protégé*. This was the background against which Henry took the decision to erect a tomb for Richard III, and it is interesting to note in passing that 1494 (the year apparently mentioned in the epitaph text as the date of the tomb's commissioning) was also the year in which Henry VII issued a silver medallic token possibly intended to contest the claims of the new Yorkist pretender.[23] Was the commissioning of Richard III's tomb a calculated move on Henry's part, designed to curry favour with Yorkist opinion? The epitaph rather cleverly exploited Yorkist divisions. Logic decreed that the sons of Edward IV on the one hand, and Richard III on the other, could not *both* simultaneously have legitimate Yorkist claims to the throne. Their claims were mutually exclusive: if Edward V was a legitimate king, then Richard III was a usurper, and *vice versa*. Previously it had suited Henry to treat Edward IV's sons as legitimate claimants. However, now that one of those sons was reputedly moving against him, it may have seemed preferable to reassert Richard III's claim. After all, King Richard was safely dead.

12

'Here Lies the Body'[1]

When Henry VIII dissolved the religious houses of England, the fate of the burials within the monastic and conventual churches varied. Occasionally, surviving relatives took steps to rescue their loved ones. In such rare instances coffined bodies – or even entire tombs – were moved elsewhere. In other cases, empty tomb superstructures alone may have been salvaged without their accompanying bodies, and re-erected as cenotaphs. This seems to have occurred in the case of three tombs from Earls Colne Priory, which once housed the de Veres (Earls of Oxford). As we shall see in greater detail below, King Henry VIII himself had the body of his sister, Mary, moved from Bury St Edmunds Abbey to St Mary's church in the same town. The Earl of Essex had the monuments and remains of his father and grandparents moved from Beeleigh Abbey to the parish church at Little Easton in Essex. Later, following the death of the third Howard Duke of Norfolk, his heirs transferred the remains of his father and grandfather (the two preceding Howard dukes) from Thetford Priory to Framlingham church. The bodies and tombs of the Howards' Mowbray forebears, however, were left behind in the ruins of Thetford Priory, and theirs was the more common fate by far. The superstructure of their tombs subsequently pillaged and lost, the mortal remains of the Mowbrays still lie buried where they were originally interred.

In the case of Richard III there were no close relatives on hand to rescue his remains when the Leicester Greyfriars were expelled in 1538. The superstructure of his tomb probably remained for a while in the roofless ruin of the choir. Indeed, it is even remotely possible that Richard's tomb effigy survives to this day, having eventually been salvaged and relocated in another church, like the de Vere tombs from Earls Colne.[2] As for Richard's body, as recent excavation at the Greyfriars site has proved, it simply remained lying where the friars had buried it in 1485. Even before the excavation, the available evidence strongly suggested that this was so. In due course the friary site was acquired by the Herrick family. Robert Herrick, one-time mayor of Leicester, constructed a house and laid out a garden on the eastern part of the site, where once the choir of the priory church had stood. Here in 1612 Christopher Wren (future dean of Windsor and father of the architect of St Paul's Cathedral), who was then tutor to Robert Herrick's nephew, saw 'a handsome stone pillar, three foot high', bearing the inscription: 'Here lies the body of Richard III, some time King of England'.[3] This pillar had been erected by Robert Herrick when he redeveloped the site in order to preserve the location of Richard's grave. What subsequently happened to this 'handsome stone pillar' is unknown. 'It may not have survived the taking of Leicester by the Royalists [during the English Civil War], when desperate fighting took place near St Martin's Church [Cathedral] which was immediately north of the Grey Friars' grounds.'[4] Part of Robert Herrick's former garden now comprises three Leicester car parks. Indeed, remains of Herrick's garden paths were discovered just to the south of the church choir ruins, in trench 3, during the recent excavation of the Greyfriars site. Until 25 August 2012, Richard's bones remained lying a short distance to the noth-west of this paved area. In the alderman's garden their location had been pinpointed by Herrick's pillar. More recently, they were concealed beneath the modern tarmac. But for more than 500 years they simply remained lying in the very spot where they had been buried in August 1485.[5]

Despite the fact that the site of Richard's grave was both known and clearly marked in the early seventeenth century, that same century was to witness the growth of an extraordinary and macabre fantasy which we must pause briefly to consider, since until very recently it continued to mislead incautious historians. The earliest recorded hint of this farrago was published in 1611 by Speede, whose text is reproduced in appendix 4 (below). This version stated that following the Dissolution, Richard's tomb was completely destroyed, and that his remains were then dug up and reburied at one end of Bow Bridge. Speede cites no source for his curious account other than 'tradition' and, as we shall see in due course, quite apart from the fact that it is very difficult to see how *any* burial would have been possible under the low stone arches of the old Bow Bridge (see illustration) there were also other excellent reasons for doubting Speede's accuracy.

Subsequently, Speede's story grew vastly and luridly in the telling. In its fully developed, modern form, the tale related that at the time of the Dissolution, Richard's body was dug up and dragged through the streets of Leicester by a jeering mob, being finally hurled into the River Soar near Bow Bridge. It is worth noting that this later version of the story does not at all accord with Speede's original report. Nor was there a single shred of contemporary (that is to say, mid-sixteenth-century) evidence in support either of Speede's account, or of the later version of the exhumation story. On the other hand, there *was* evidence that, even as late as the 1620s, Leicester inhabitants and visitors were unaware of these accounts.[6] This strongly suggested that the story of Richard III's exhumation was far from being a matter of universal 'common knowledge'. It is also relevant to remark that there seem to be no recorded instances, at the time of the Dissolution, of dead remains being treated in the sacrilegious way which the tale purported to describe.[7] Nor was there any reason to suppose that Richard III was the target of popular hatred in Leicester (or anywhere else for that matter) in the 1530s. In fact, it is a matter of record that the House of Commons *defended* Richard's reputation at this very period before a bemused Cardinal Wolsey.[8]

But the lurid tale was colourful and memorable. It appeared to accord with later perceptions of Richard III's reputation. Moreover, as we have already seen, it was apparently backed up in the eighteenth century by the existence and display in Leicester of the old stone coffin, reputed to be Richard's, and then in use as a horse trough. Despite the obvious fact that this object dated from many centuries earlier than King Richard's time, it was displayed to eighteenth-century tourists as 'Richard III's coffin'. This improbable but visible relic, combined with the fact that an existing tradition linked Richard III with Bow Bridge (see chapter 7), helped to popularise the post-Speede story that Richard's body had been thrown into the river close by the bridge. Both coffin and legend were widely reported in the late seventeenth and eighteenth centuries. Implicitly reinforced in the nineteenth century by the erection of a prominent and well-meaning (if regrettable) commemorative stone plaque, the tale of 'the body in the river' became so widely accepted that a skull of unknown age, dredged up from the Soar, and exhibiting damage which was thought to be attributable to sword cuts, could not fail to be hailed, on its appearance, as 'King Richard's skull'.[9] Meanwhile, as redevelopment took place in Leicester, the king's authentic gravesite, once well known and clearly marked, became quietly lost to view.

⁂

The Dissolution of the English religious houses led inevitably to the secularisation of the Franciscan Priory site in Leicester. The last guardian, William Gyllys, together with the six remaining friars, surrendered the priory to the king in 1538.[10] Henry VIII had already granted the site to John Bellowe esquire and John Broxholme, gentleman. The general practice in such cases was that the lead and timbers from the church roof and other materials of value were removed and sold for the benefit of the crown before the site was handed over to its new owners, so although some of the domestic buildings of the priory may have been left intact, the former church probably changed hands as a ruin. The surviving ruins of Franciscan priories in other parts of the country give some idea of what the Leicester Greyfriars might have looked like in about 1540.[11]

Writing in the early seventeenth century, Weever reports that following the Dissolution and Reformation there was widespread destruction of funeral monuments in those churches which continued in use, where the main targets were inscriptions inviting prayers for the dead. Since this defacing of monuments was chiefly motivated by religious considerations, the monuments left behind in the ruins of monastic and conventual churches were probably less of a target for the zeal of reformers (as they did not offend the gaze of the reformed faithful during worship). Moreover, such monuments now stood on private property, and indeed, were themselves part of that private property. They may thus have escaped the iconoclasts. Nevertheless, they will inevitably have suffered from the elements now that their church buildings were roofless, and in most cases they will gradually have had their materials sold off for the profit of the new owners. Gradually their tomb superstructures will have disappeared.

What exactly happened at the Leicester Greyfriars is unknown. John Speede (widely followed by incautious later writers) stated that Richard's tomb 'was pulled downe and utterly defaced'.[12] For reasons which will emerge presently, Speede's account was completely unreliable and despite the fact that it enjoyed widespread credence, it had no evidential value whatever. Nevertheless, by 1612 Richard III's 1495 tomb superstructure had certainly gone, for by that date, as we have seen, it had been replaced by a new monument: the commemorative pillar set up by Robert Herrick, a former mayor of Leicester, who had acquired the Greyfriars site and laid out a house and garden there. Our informant in this matter is Sir Christopher Wren's father and namesake, who was an eye-witness.

At the dissolution [of the Greyfriars] the place of his [Richard III's] burial happened to fall into the bounds of a citizen's garden, which being (after) purchased by Mr Robert Herrick (some time mayor of Leicester) was by him covered with a handsome stone pillar, three foot high, with this inscription, 'Here lies the body of Richard III, some time King of England'. This he shewed me walking in the garden, Anno 1612.[13]

When precisely Herrick's pillar was erected is unknown, but in all probability it was set up immediately after the clearance of the final remains of

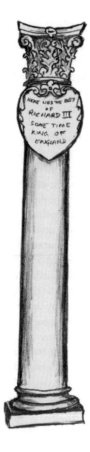

IMAGE 1: Conjectural reconstruction of Herrick's pillar, based on an architectural engraving of 1596.

Richard's ruined tomb of *c.* 1494. Thus there was probably no time-gap during which the grave's location was unmarked.

As for John Speede's unreliability, he reported that at the beginning of the seventeenth century the gravesite was 'overgrowne with nettles and weedes … very obscure and not to be found'.[14] Many subsequent writers uncritically repeated Speede's account. Nevertheless, it was worthless, because Speede's 1610 map of Leicester wrongly labelled a site well to the north-west of St Martin's church (now Cathedral) as 'Graye fryers'. This site had actually belonged not to the Grey friars but to Leicester's Black (Dominican) friars. The real site of the Franciscan Priory lies to the south of St Martin's church (Cathedral) (see figure 28). On Speede's map the authentic Greyfriars site is not labelled at all, but it can still be easily identified. This fundamental error on Speede's map – which completely misled many subsequent researchers – proves that John Speede sought Richard III's grave in entirely the wrong location. His nettles and weeds grew not on the site of the Franciscan Priory, but amongst the ruins of the former Dominican Priory. Small wonder, then, that Speed was unable to find any trace of Richard's tomb. He was looking amongst the wrong priory ruins!

Even if Richard's grave was unmarked for a time, this can only have been for a very short period. We may guess that Herrick's commemorative pillar at the former Greyfriars site was put in place by the year 1610 at the latest. Herrick had been born in 1540 – only two years after the dissolution of the Greyfriars priory – and he may well have seen Richard III's 1495 tomb as a boy, since it is probable that this monument (or the remains of it) had remained standing in the priory ruins until at least the last quarter of the sixteenth century. We know that many other monastic and collegiate church tombs survived until about that time. John Weever – author of *Ancient Funeral Monuments* – went round in the early years of the seventeenth century and recorded their existence, while only a decade or two earlier, Queen Elizabeth I had found and rescued the remains of her Yorkist ancestors amongst the ruins of the east end of the collegiate church at Fotheringhaye.

It is just possible that by about 1550 the superstructure of Richard's tomb had been vandalised, though we have no actual evidence to this effect. Even if this was the case, however, it would certainly not imply that Richard's remains were disturbed, and in this context it is worth noting in passing that the short text carved on Alderman Herrick's new monument indicated plainly that Herrick's inscribed column was not a cenotaph. His deliberate choice of the words 'Here lies the body ...' shows that Herrick was not only certain that his column marked Richard's burial site, but also that Richard's physical remains *still lay buried* beneath it.

Thus, while the Greyfriars' church may have been gradually demolished, and parts of the priory site may have been redeveloped, the ground where Richard III lay was never built over. Only some building work in the nine-teenth century came dangerously close to destroying the original burial. A narrow trench cut by the nineteenth-century workmen cut across the east-ern end of the king's grave, depriving posterity of the bones of Richard III's feet. Apart from this, the king lay quietly where he had been buried, while above him Alderman Herrick's garden was eventually transformed into a council car park.

13

'The Honour of a King'[1]

While Richard III lay undisturbed in his grave in Leicester, his reputation was changing. Some of the change may have been natural, but many aspects of it were orchestrated by the regime and dynasty which had replaced his rule. As a result Richard III became, and remains, one of the most controversial figures in English history. Some contemporary writers certainly character-ised him as a good king.[2] He appears to have been for many years a loyal son, brother and husband.[3] Yet – unsurprisingly perhaps – after his defeat and death at the battle known as Bosworth Field he became the subject of vili-fication under the 'Tudor' regime which replaced his own Yorkist dynasty. It may be worth emphasising at this point that the unsupported word of Henry VII is not invariably trustworthy, since clear evidence exists that on occasions the first 'Tudor' monarch told lies or rewrote history. Thus, as we saw earlier, during his exile in France he represented himself as a son of Henry VI in order to enhance his dubious 'Lancastrian' credentials. Once on the throne he ruthlessly wrote Lady Eleanor Talbot out of history, and falsified Richard III's claim to the throne. These are not matters of opinion, but of fact.

However, Henry VII's position on his predecessor was complex, and was apparently subject to a degree of evolution. Henry purported to cham-pion the cause of the house of Lancaster, and this inevitably implied overall opposition to the claims of the house of York. But at the same time, Henry claimed to be reuniting the rival Yorkist and Lancastrian claims (just as Richard himself had been planning to do in 1485). In Henry's case this aim was furthered by means of his marriage to Elizabeth of York, eldest daugh-ter of Richard III's elder brother, Edward IV, by Elizabeth Woodville. In general, therefore, Henry had no choice other than to accept the legitimacy of Edward IV as King of England. He is even on record as having referred to Edward as his 'father'.[4] This in itself was a somewhat anomalous position for the 'Tudor' monarch to take, since there can be no question that King Edward had deposed and replaced Henry VII's 'uncle', Henry VI, for whose subsequent death Edward IV may also have been responsible. The political correctness of the new 'Tudor' regime in 1485 certainly stressed that Edward IV had been a lawful and (on the whole) good king. It also suggested that Edward V would have been a lawful – and probably good – king had circumstances allowed him the opportunity. On the other hand, Richard III was initially presented as an evil usurper, from whose illegal tyranny Henry VII had rescued England. Even in 1485, however, the *de facto* kingship of Richard III had perforce to be acknowledged for practical reasons. Moreover, only if Richard was *de facto* king could Henry VII, by defeating him, have gained the crown. Richard had also to be publicly acknowledged as a valiant warrior, since Henry's victory over him was thereby magnified and seen to be glorious.

At a slightly later date, when a putative son of Edward IV appeared on the scene to challenge Henry's right to rule, the latter's position was inevitably subject to a degree of modification. Although not all writers on the period seem to have grasped this fundamental point, in reality it was always absolutely clear that in legal terms the respective claims to the throne of Richard III and the sons of Edward IV were mutually exclusive. Supporters of the house of York could not simultaneously claim both Edward V and Richard III as lawful monarchs. If Richard was the rightful king then Edward IV's sons were bastards with no claim to the crown. Conversely, if Edward's sons were legitimate claimants, Richard III was a usurper. Richard himself had demonstrably perceived this point with absolute clarity. Nor was it lost on Henry VII. Thus, in the 1490s, when Henry was confronted with the 'Perkin Warbeck' phenomenon, he appears to have modified his position on Richard III. As previously noted, it was at this period that Henry created a royal tomb for Richard, almost certainly furnished with a carefully worded epitaph, the text of which has fortunately survived.

Later still, when the threat of 'Perkin' had been overcome, and the pretender was safely dead, Henry largely reverted to his earlier stance on Richard. It was at this stage that – for the first time – Richard was accused of having killed Edward IV's sons. This claim seems to have been initially advanced in a posthumously published 'confession' allegedly made by Sir James Tyrell of Gipping (Suffolk), Captain of Guines.[5] This 'confession' killed two birds with one stone. It had the effect of blackening Richard's name (by attaching to it the opprobrium of what was to become his most notorious supposed crime), while at the same time also conveniently removing Edward IV's sons from the running in respect of the succession, by purporting to establish beyond question (and for the first time) that both of the boys were long dead.

Opinions about Richard III have been violently polarised ever since. Chief among the controversies associated with Richard's name remain the propriety of his accession to the throne, and the fate of his nephews, those so-called 'princes in the Tower'. Various attempts have recently been made, by means of new evidence and new approaches to existing evidence, to shed light on the matter of Richard's accession.[6] In order to try to elucidate the fate of the so-called 'princes' it will be necessary to seek new sources of information. One potential new source might be the DNA sequences of key members of the house of York, and this is an area which the author has been researching for some time. Aspects of this ongoing DNA research – what has so far been learnt from it, and what we may yet hope to learn – constitute the main subject of the chapters which follow. Finally, we shall look into the future to see what further discoveries might yet be made, and by what means.

14

Richard III's Genes part I – the Fifteenth Century and Before

Modern attempts to discern 'the real Richard III' behind the 'Tudor' and later image have certainly encompassed an astonishingly wide variety of approaches and sources. These have included the study of fifteenth-century and later written evidence, examination of Richard's portraits, and analysis of the books which comprised Richard's library. In addition, attempts have been made to analyse Richard III's handwriting, and to cast his horoscope.[1] However, prior to my research, no-one had attempted to explore Richard's genetic make-up.

Before 2012, no direct investigation of Richard III's physical remains was possible because, until the recent excavations in Leicester, Richard's body had been inaccessible. Therefore I initially sought alternative sources of appropriate genetic material. The obvious route would have been the remains of one of Richard's descendants, but this approach also appeared to be closed to us. The king's only legitimate son, Edward, Prince of Wales, died in childhood, some months before his father. What some believe to be the boy's tomb is in the church at Sheriff Hutton, in Yorkshire, but the identity of this burial is controversial, nor is it easy to obtain permission for the exhumation of royal remains. Richard's other known children, Catherine Plantagenet and John of Gloucester, were illegitimate. John was executed by Henry VII.[2] His tomb and that of his (half?) sister have not been located. Moreover, since (so far as is known) all Richard III's children died childless, the king apparently has no direct living descendants.[3] Thus, in seeking Richard III's genes I was obliged to range further afield, exploring collateral lines of descent from Richard's siblings. Of potential interest were Richard's parents, the Duke and Duchess of York; his brothers, Edward IV, Edmund, Earl of Rutland and George, Duke of Clarence; and his sisters, Anne, Duchess of Exeter, Elizabeth, Duchess of Suffolk and Margaret, Duchess of Burgundy.

The burial sites of some of these individuals were known, and their remains could very easily have been examined – had their exhumation ever been authorised. The Duke and Duchess of York, together with Richard's brother, Edmund, Earl of Rutland, lie entombed in secondary and tertiary burials at Fotheringhaye church. Earlier, their tombs were in the chancel, at the east end of the collegiate church, but when the Reformation led to the demise of the college and the ruin of the chancel, Elizabeth I had the bodies of her ancestors and relatives moved into the surviving nave of the building. The new tombs which she provided flank the present high altar.

Richard's brother, King Edward IV, still lies in his tomb in St George's Chapel, Windsor, and his eldest sister Anne of York, Duchess of Exeter, lies in a nearby side chapel, in the same building. Permission to exhume these remains is unlikely ever to be granted. Nevertheless, some genetic material from the body of Edward IV is available. This avenue has been explored, and we shall return to this point presently.

The burial site of Elizabeth of York, Duchess of Suffolk, the second surviving sister of Richard III, is also known. Elizabeth lies undisturbed in her alabaster tomb at Wingfield church in Suffolk. Apart from the king himself, she is one of the few members of Richard's immediate family whose remains had lain untouched from the time of her death in 1503 until the present day.

As for George, Duke of Clarence, he was probably buried in Tewkesbury Abbey, Gloucestershire, but the remains once thought to be his are now considered to be of doubtful authenticity.[4] These bones lie behind the high altar in what is known as the 'Clarence Vault'. The remains are contained in a glass case which was opened and examined in 1982. On that occasion a physical examination revealed the fragmentary remains of at least two individuals – at least one male and at least one female. Superficially this sounds quite promising, since the Duchess of Clarence was unquestionably buried at Tewkesbury,[5] and Clarence is believed to have been interred beside her. However, the male remains were tentatively assigned to the age range 40–60+ years, while the female remains were designated in the range 50–70+ years. This was completely incompatible with the known ages of the Duke and Duchess of Clarence at the time of their deaths (when they would have been 28 and 25 years of age respectively). It is known that in the eighteenth century the Clarence Vault was taken over for burials of members of the family of Samuel Hawling, an alderman of Tewkesbury, and it seems highly probable that at least some of the skeletal remains now in the

Clarence Vault are those of Hawling and his wife and son, who were aged respectively 72, 96 and 86 at death.[6] To date, however, no DNA testing of the bones from this vault has taken place. Osteological re-examination of the bones would be highly desirable and, depending on the results of that examination, DNA testing of them might at some stage be considered.

As for Richard's youngest sister, Margaret of York, Duchess of Burgundy, the current whereabouts of her remains present major problems of their own.[7] Nevertheless, it was the confusion regarding Margaret's burial that provided the immediate impetus for my research which finally led to the establishment of a mitochondrial DNA sequence for Richard III and his brothers and sisters.

※※※※※

At her own request, Margaret of York's body was buried in the Fransciscan Priory Church at Mechelen (Malines), in modern Belgium.[8] This building lies just to the west of Mechelen's cathedral church of St Rombout. The Priory Church, sacked during the religious conflicts of the ensuing centuries, is now a cultural centre, and all trace of Margaret's once splendid tomb has vanished. A manuscript copy of Margaret's memorial inscription tells us that she was buried 'beneath the threshold of the doorway of this chancel'.[9] This rather odd location, which now appears to reflect precisely the burial location of her brother Richard at the Franciscan Priory in Leicester, may not have been accidental. Perhaps Margaret deliberately requested burial in a priory church of the same order as her slaughtered brother, and deliberately asked for her tomb to be placed in an identical position, just inside the entry to the choir. Until Richard's burial was discovered, however, the exact meaning of the somewhat imprecise description had been debated, owing to the fact that the choir of the Mechelen priory church may have had more than one entrance. Originally, of course, the meaning had presumably been clarified by the physical location of the bronze memorial plaque within the church. Sadly, however, this vital evidence was lost to us. As a result, doubts had been expressed as to where exactly Margaret's corpse had been laid to rest.

In 2003 Dr Paul De Win published in Mechelen a paper on the multiple possible remains of Margaret of York.[10] He explained the circumstances of Margaret's burial, explored the subsequent vicissitudes of her tomb, and catalogued twentieth-century attempts to find her body. He also highlighted the problem of resolving which (if any) of the various female remains disinterred from the former Franciscan church in Mechelen might really be Margaret's bones.

As reported in Paul De Win's paper, three sets of female remains of approximately the right age were found in the former Franciscan church of Mechelen during the course of the twentieth century, and in locations which could potentially be interpreted as consistent with the approximate site of the lost tomb of Margaret of York.[11] These remains were found respectively in 1936 (excavations led by Vaast Steurs),[12] 1937 (excavations associated with the name of Maximilien Winders)[13] and 1955 (accidental discovery, subsequently examined by Professor François Twiesselmann).[14] Until recently these remains were stored in five boxes at the Mechelen Town Archives. They have recently been transferred to the Archaeology Service,[15] and are now stored in two boxes (but reportedly a record of their former numbering has been retained). The bones from the 1955 discovery were photographed at the time, and these bones were subsequently coated with varnish. As a result, they can still be relatively easily identified. It is not currently possible to distinguish for certain which of the other female remains from Mechelen's Franciscan Priory site were discovered in 1936, and which in 1937.[16]

In 2003, following discussions with Dr De Win, I began the attempt to establish a mitochondrial DNA sequence for Margaret of York and her siblings. Since mtDNA is normally inherited unchanged in the female line, the methodology adopted was to seek a living all-female-line descendant of Margaret's mother, Cecily Neville, Duchess of York, or of one of Cecily's close female relatives. We shall follow this research in a moment. First, however, it may be useful to summarise briefly what DNA is, and how it can currently be used in historical research.

⊶⊱✕⊰⊷

The letters 'DNA' are an abbreviation for 'deoxyribonucleic acid'. All living beings have DNA, which functions rather like an order pad. It lists, in coded form, the materials required to make the components of living bodies, and it specifies the order in which they must be assembled in order to create these components. In 1953 two Cambridge scientists, James D. Watson and Francis Crick, first worked out the structure of DNA, and demonstrated its significance as the basic coding material of life. 'Watson and Crick had discovered that each molecule of DNA is made up of two very long coils, like two intertwined spiral staircases – a "double helix". When the time comes for copies to be made, the two spiral staircases of the double helix disengage.'[17]

DNA has a very complicated molecular structure, but four principal components are the heterocyclic bases which are known by their initial letters: A for adenine, C for cytosine, G for guanine and T for thymine. In 1988, thirty-five years after the original discovery of DNA by Watson and Crick, an Oxford University team discovered that it was sometimes possible to extract, replicate and analyse DNA from ancient bones.[18]

While our present focus is on human DNA, the same basic rules apply to animals and plants, for all living things have DNA. Their cells contain two kinds of DNA: nuclear DNA, which resides in the cell nucleus, and mitochondrial DNA (mtDNA). Self-evidently, the latter is the DNA of the mitochondria: tiny structures which reside outside the cell nucleus in the surrounding cushion of cytoplasm and which help the cell to use oxygen in order to produce energy. The division in our cells between the two kinds of DNA is by no means equal. Each cell contains far more nuclear DNA than mitochondrial DNA. The latter represents a mere 0.5 per cent of our total.[19]

Nuclear DNA is a mixture, fifty per cent of which is inherited from each parent. Conversely, mitochondrial DNA is inherited from the mother, and is normally transmitted unchanged to the child. In addition, 'mitochondrial DNA mutates at a much higher rate than nuclear DNA … Two organisms will therefore be far more similar in their nuclear DNA than in their mtDNA'.[20] For both of these reasons mtDNA is generally more useful than nuclear DNA in tracing genetic relationships in historical contexts. With one exception, nuclear DNA is at present useless for genealogical research over a wide time-gap, because there is currently no way of determining which components of the nuclear DNA are derived from which ancestor. In fact, many ancestors may be represented by no nuclear DNA components in their living descendants. The one certain exception to this rule is the Y-chromosome – and we shall return to this point later, because it is of potential interest in the attempt to establish an overall picture of the DNA of the Yorkist princes.

For the moment, however, let us consider only mitochondrial DNA. Occasional spontaneous mutations occur in mtDNA, and these are then passed on to descendants, though they may take up to six generations to become firmly established. Such mutation occurs on average once every 10,000 years. Thus it is possible, by comparing the mitochondrial DNA of two individuals, to establish roughly how much time has elapsed since the lifetime of their last common ancestress in the female line. It has been calculated that all human beings now living are descended in the exclusively female line from one single woman, known as Mitochondrial Eve, who lived in Africa about 150,000 years ago. It is argued that every human being now living on the planet can trace his or her mitochondrial DNA back to Mitochondrial Eve. Of course, the latter was not the only living woman of her time and place. What is unique about her is the fact that she is the only one of her contemporaries to have living descendants in the female line.

It is likewise posited that most of the historic native population of Europe can trace their female line ancestry back to one of only seven 'clan mothers' who lived between 45,000 and 10,000 years ago. Each of these clan mothers was a descendant of Mitochondrial Eve. The seven clan mothers of Europe are usually referred to by letters, or names, as follows:[21]

U ('Ursula') – ancestress of about eleven per cent of the European population. She probably lived in Greece about 45,000 years ago. Her descendants are especially to be found in western Britain.

X ('Xenia') – probably lived in Russia about 25,000 years ago. Her descendants (about six per cent of the population) are to be found today mostly in central and Eastern Europe.

H ('Helena') – lived in the Bordeaux region of France about 20,000 years ago. Hers is the most widespread European clan, with about forty-seven per cent of the modern population descending from her in the female line.

V ('Velda') – probably lived 17,000 years ago in northern Spain, near Santander. About five per cent of native Europeans belong to this clan, which is found mainly in Western Europe.

T ('Tara') was more or less a contemporary of Velda. She probably lived in Tuscany. Her descendants, who account for about nine per cent of the modern population of Europe, live mostly along the Mediterranean coast or the western edge of the continent, including western Britain and Ireland.

K ('Katrine') – probably lived 15,000 years ago, in the Venice region. She is the clan mother of six per cent of modern Europeans who are most likely to be found around the Mediterranean. 'Ötzi' the 'iceman' was one of her descendants.

J ('Jasmine') – thought to have lived in Syria about 10,000 years ago. Her people were the ones who introduced farming to Europe. Her descendants are found today either in Spain, Portugal and western Britain, or in central Europe. They seem to represent about seventeen per cent of the European native population.

When DNA is being used to attempt to identify long-dead bones, the first thing to note is that it cannot *prove* the identity of an individual. Mitochondrial DNA has to be compared with a sample from a known relative, as was done recently in the case of the bones thought to be those of the Russian Imperial family. A mismatch proves for certain that the bones cannot be the person sought, but a match does not prove identity, merely that the bones are those of a person with similar mitochondrial DNA to – and thus a relative in some degree of – the person being searched for. Depending on factors such as how widespread the resulting mitochondrial DNA sequence is in the modern European population, and on the precise set of mutations present, that information will be of greater or lesser significance.

However, the final decision about the identity of archaeologically recovered remains will also depend on a variety of other factors: such as location, age at death, the era from which the remains date, and other evidence suggesting identity. Thus, for example, in the case of the Russian Imperial

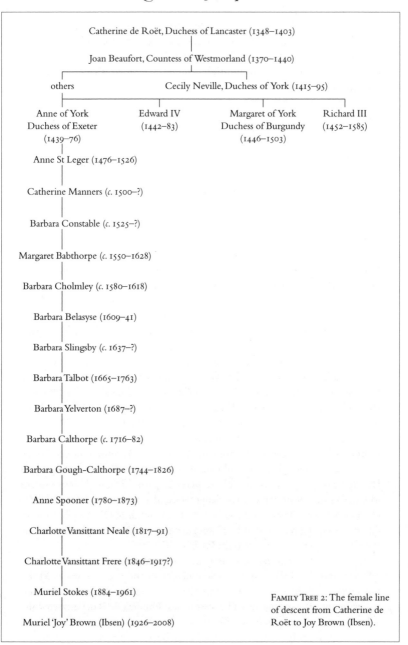

Catherine de Roët, Duchess of Lancaster (1348–1403)

Joan Beaufort, Countess of Westmorland (1370–1440)

others

Anne of York
Duchess of Exeter
(1439–76)

Edward IV
(1442–83)

Cecily Neville, Duchess of York (1415–95)

Margaret of York
Duchess of Burgundy
(1446–1503)

Richard III
(1452–1585)

Anne St Leger (1476–1526)

Catherine Manners (*c.* 1500–?)

Barbara Constable (*c.* 1525–?)

Margaret Babthorpe (*c.* 1550–1628)

Barbara Cholmley (*c.* 1580–1618)

Barbara Belasyse (1609–41)

Barbara Slingsby (*c.* 1637–?)

Barbara Talbot (1665–1763)

Barbara Yelverton (1687–?)

Barbara Calthorpe (*c.* 1716–82)

Barbara Gough-Calthorpe (1744–1826)

Anne Spooner (1780–1873)

Charlotte Vansittant Neale (1817–91)

Charlotte Vansittant Frere (1846–1917?)

Muriel Stokes (1884–1961)

Muriel 'Joy' Brown (Ibsen) (1926–2008)

FAMILY TREE 2: The female line
of descent from Catherine de
Roët to Joy Brown (Ibsen).

bones, evidence of ages at death, the location of the remains, how the individuals had died, and how their bodies had been treated after death, all
supported the identification of the bones as Romanov remains, in addition
to the DNA evidence from multiple sources, which confirmed their possible identification.

The mitochondrial DNA of Margaret of York and of all her siblings,
including Richard III, was that of her mother, Cecily Neville. Cecily received
it from her mother, Joan Beaufort, who in turn had received it from her
mother, Catherine de Roët. Rather unfortunately, the beautiful Catherine is
very widely referred to by her first husband's surname, 'Catherine Swynford'.
Genealogically, however, it is always preferable to refer to women by their
birth surnames, and in the present instance this is particularly essential, since
Richard III and his family were *not* the descendants of Sir Hugh Swynford,
but of Catherine de Roët's second husband, John of Gaunt. For our purposes
it is Catherine's *birth* family which is important.

Catherine's mitochondrial DNA may have come from the mainland of
Europe; perhaps from the area we now call Belgium, from the Netherlands,
or possibly from Germany or France. Catherine's father was a knight from
Hainault. He is usually named as Sir Payne (or Paon) de Roët (or Roelt), and
is often said to have come to England from Hainault with Edward III's wife,
Queen Philippa, of whom he was probably a relative. In fact, his real first
name seems to have been Gilles. 'Paon' ('Peacock'?) was merely a nickname.[22]
Perhaps he liked to look his best. There appears to be no real record surviving
of his having served in England. However, he did serve Queen Philippa's sister,
Margaret, the Holy Roman Empress, in Germany, and he also served Edward
III as a herald and as Guienne King of Arms in the Aquitaine. Ultimately he
died in England, and was buried at old St Paul's Cathedral.[23]

But it was not Catherine's father, but her unknown mother who was the
source of her daughter's (and thus of Richard III's) mitochondrial DNA.
In modern terms this lady might have been French, German, Belgian or
Dutch.[24] She seems unlikely to have been English.[25] Dame de Roët seems
to have borne her husband three daughters, and at least one son. All of these
children inherited from their mother the mitochondrial DNA which was in
due course to be transmitted by Catherine, the youngest daughter of the de
Roët family, to her great-grandson Richard III.

The eldest de Roët daughter, Isabelle (or Elizabeth), seems never to have
left her homeland. She entered the convent of the Canonesses at Mons,
where she lived, died and was buried. Gilles' two younger daughters, like their
father, lie interred in England. The aristocratic Philippa de Roët attracted the
attention of the young poet Geoffrey Chaucer, who was the son of mere merchant stock from Ipswich. 'It may well have been to highborn, theoretically

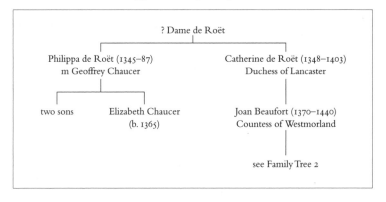

```
                        ? Dame de Roët
       ┌──────────────────────┴──────────────────────┐
 Philippa de Roët (1345–87)          Catherine de Roët (1348–1403)
    m Geoffrey Chaucer                    Duchess of Lancaster
  ┌──────────┴──────────┐                          │
 two sons      Elizabeth Chaucer          Joan Beaufort (1370–1440)
                   (b. 1365)                Countess of Westmorland
                                                   │
                                           see Family Tree 2
```

FAMILY TREE 3: The Chaucer connection.

unreachable Philippa that Chaucer wrote some of his love songs.'[26] Chaucer did eventually marry Philippa and had children by her. Philippa died in the late summer or autumn of 1387 and lies buried in the chancel of the church of St Mary the Virgin, East Worldham in Hampshire.[27]

Her younger sister, Catherine de Roët, was a member of the household of John of Gaunt, where she was employed since at least 1365 as one of the ladies attending on his first wife, Blanche of Lancaster. Soon after entering Blanche's service, Catherine de Roët married Sir Hugh Swynford of Coleby and Kettlethorpe in Lincolnshire, by whom she had a son, Thomas, and a daughter, Blanche. In 1371 Sir Hugh Swynford died while serving abroad, leaving Catherine a young widow. She was then in her early twenties, and despite his second marriage to Constance of Castile, John of Gaunt soon made Catherine his mistress. Meanwhile, her official position in his household was now that of governess to his children. There have been allegations that Catherine became John's mistress while her first husband was still alive, but this appears unlikely. Their liaison probably began in 1372, after Hugh Swynford's death, and Catherine's first child by John of Gaunt was born in 1373.[28] The affair was viewed askance at the time, and Catherine was denounced as a seductress. Nevertheless, the couple's relationship proved enduring.

After various vicissitudes (and following the death of Constance of Castile), on 13 December 1396 John of Gaunt finally married Catherine in Lincoln Cathedral. This marriage, which made Catherine the second lady in the land, after the queen, caused universal astonishment. It has been described as a *mésalliance*, but that seems hardly just. Catherine was, after all, probably a relative of John of Gaunt's mother, the late queen, Philippa of Hainault, and thus a distant cousin of her new husband. One important outcome of their marriage was that Catherine's illegitimate children by John of Gaunt, all of whom had been given the surname 'Beaufort', were legitimised by the Pope in 1396 and by King Richard II in 1397.

Mitochondrial DNA identical to that of Richard III would have been found in all four of Catherine de Roët's sons: Sir Thomas Swynford, John Beaufort, first Earl of Somerset,[29] Henry, Cardinal Beaufort, Bishop of Winchester, and Thomas Beaufort, Duke of Exeter. However, as males none of these was able to pass on this mitochondrial DNA. Nevertheless, in the following generation the same DNA would have been found in all of the numerous Neville and Ferrers children of their sister, Joan Beaufort. Richard III also shared his mitochondrial DNA with the three children of the poet, Geoffrey Chaucer, since Chaucer's wife Philippa was Catherine de Roët's sister. Although this relationship with the Chaucers has sometimes been questioned, it was explicitly acknowledged by Cardinal Beaufort, who, in a letter, referred to the poet's son, Thomas Chaucer, as his cousin.[30]

Unfortunately, no mitochondrial DNA line of descent from Philippa de Roët (Chaucer) survives to the present day, for Philippa had only one daughter and she became a nun (see Family Tree 3). From Catherine de Roët, Duchess of Lancaster, however, the mtDNA line continues through her daughter, Joan Beaufort, Countess of Westmorland. The latter had many daughters, including Cecily, Duchess of York. I traced female lines of descent from Cecily and all her sisters, producing a huge family tree resembling a spider's web on my computer. It was necessary to attempt to trace all the possible female lines of descent, because there was no way at the outset of knowing which line (if any) would prove to be continuous down to the present day. In the event, none of the lines from Cecily's sisters proved to continue to the present.

Of Cecily Neville's own daughters, two produced children: Anne of York, Duchess of Exeter, and Elizabeth of York, Duchess of Suffolk. At first, Elizabeth looked the most hopeful candidate to have living female line descendants because she had a number of children including several daughters. However, her female lines of descent soon petered out. Anne of York, on the other hand, looked less hopeful initially. She had only two children – both daughters – and the elder of these two had no descendants. Nevertheless, it was the line of Anne of York which was to preserve the mtDNA of Cecily Neville's children until the present day. I traced an unbroken line of descent, mother to daughter, from Cecily Neville's eldest daughter, Anne of York, Duchess of Exeter, to Mrs Joy Ibsen in Canada.[31] This line of descent has a number of interesting features, and in the next chapter we shall follow its history in some detail.

15

Richard III's Genes part II – the mtDNA line

Anne of York died in 1476, leaving her surviving new-born daughter and namesake to be brought up by her second husband, Sir Thomas St Leger (who was the baby's father). But seven years later, in September 1483, St Leger found himself caught up in the Duke of Buckingham's rebellion against Richard III. In the aftermath of the rebellion Sir Thomas St Leger was captured, and 'though large sums of money were offered to ransom St Leger's life, Richard saw no reason to spare the second husband of his eldest sister'.[1] Thomas was duly executed. The fact that we have just told *Thomas'* story sets a precedent for the greater part of this chapter. For, rightly or wrongly, in the past men were much more important in the world than women. Thus, although we are tracing a *female* line of descent, on the whole little is known about most of the girls descended from Anne of York, beyond their names. It is the stories of the husbands and fathers and brothers of these girls that tend to have been preserved.

Several years after Richard's fall at Bosworth the orphaned Anne St Leger was married, at the age of 14, to George Manners of Belvoir and Helmsley, the 20-year-old son of Sir Robert Manners. Young George was the grandson on his mother's side of Thomas, tenth Lord Roos, and was eventually to fall heir to his maternal grandfather's title. At the time of his marriage, however, George had no titles at all. In 1497 he was knighted by Thomas Howard, Earl of Surrey, for his service in the expedition against the Scots. Sir George attended Henry VII to his meeting with the Archduke Philip, just outside Calais, in 1500, and in 1501 he was one of those appointed to receive the Infanta Catherine of

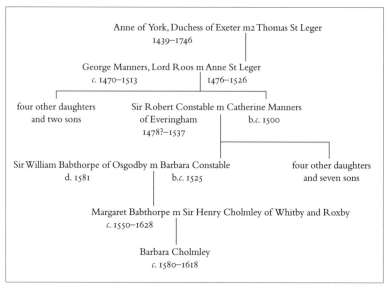

Anne of York, Duchess of Exeter m2 Thomas St Leger
1439–1746

George Manners, Lord Roos m Anne St Leger
c. 1470–1513   1476–1526

four other daughters   Sir Robert Constable m Catherine Manners
and two sons   of Everingham   b.c. 1500
1478?–1537

Sir William Babthorpe of Osgodby m Barbara Constable   four other daughters
d. 1581   b.c. 1525   and seven sons

Margaret Babthorpe m Sir Henry Cholmley of Whitby and Roxby
c. 1550–1628

Barbara Cholmley
c. 1580–1618

FAMILY TREE 4: The first six generations of Anne of York's line of descent.

Aragon, bride of Henry VII's eldest son, Prince Arthur. In 1512 George became Lord Roos, but did not enjoy the title for long, dying the following year of a sickness he had taken while on military service in France. Lord Roos was buried in St George's Chapel, Windsor, near the tomb of his mother-in-law, Anne of York, and subsequently his wife was buried beside him.

Anne St Leger was the first cousin of Henry VII's queen, Elizabeth of York, a relationship sufficiently close to the new reigning dynasty to carry some prestige – and some potential danger. However, being female, Anne was not perceived as too much of a threat. Unlike most of the other descendants of the House of York, therefore, Anne St Leger and her children were suffered to live in peace. Anne bore George Manners two sons and five daughters. Only the line of her daughter, Catherine, concerns us here, as only Catherine has living all-female-line descendants.

Catherine Manners married Sir Robert Constable, a member of the well-known Yorkshire family of Constable, and the eldest son and heir of Sir Marmaduke Constable of Flamborough in the East Riding. Sir Robert is thought to have been born only two years after Catherine's mother, so he must have been a good deal older than his young bride – who would eventually bear her husband a numerous progeny: seven sons and five daughters. Catherine and Robert were probably married before 1518, in which year Sir Marmaduke Constable died, leaving Robert his estates.

A soldier by nature, Robert Constable had taken part in the defeat of the Cornish supporters of the second Yorkist pretender, generally known as 'Perkin Warbeck', in 1497. For this service he was knighted. As a member of the Yorkshire gentry he also served as a justice of the peace and a member of the king's council of the north. However, he has been described as 'volatile', as having a 'dangerous disposition', and as being involved in a number of local feuds and disputes.² This led to his being summoned before the court of Star Chamber on more than one occasion.

Royal authority in the north of England, always somewhat equivo-cal, was rendered the more uncertain by Henry VIII's religious policies, which alienated conservative northern opinion. Cuthbert Tunstall, Bishop of Durham (whose steward was none other than Sir Robert Constable) forfeited the king's favour by defending the cause of Queen Catherine of Aragon. Henry Percy, Earl of Northumberland, who was a distant cousin of Lady Constable (Catherine Manners), and to whose affinity Sir Robert belonged, also favoured the Catholic faith. Sir Robert Constable shared the earl's point of view. 'Along with his old friends Darcy and John Hussey, Baron Hussey, [Constable] maintained a traditional stance. In 1534 all three men had agreed upon their aversion towards heresy and their determination to die as "Christian men".'³

As a result, Sir Robert Constable found himself drawn into the move-ment known as the 'Pilgrimage of Grace'. This movement was for the defence of the Church in the face of Henry VIII's break with Rome and his attack upon the monasteries. Its supporters demanded 'that the king should suppress no more abbeys, should impose no more taxation, should surrender Cromwell to the people, and get rid of the heretical bishops'.⁴ Having been drawn into the 'Pilgrimage', Constable soon became one of its leaders. Although he accepted Henry VIII's royal pardon under the terms of the agreement reached at Doncaster in early December 1535, Constable was later summoned to London where he was imprisoned in the Tower of London. He was subsequently tried, not for his activities in the main phase of the rebellion, but for offences allegedly committed after his pardon. Condemned to death, Constable was transported to Hull for execution. On 6 July 1537, he was taken to the town's Beverley Gate and there hanged in chains.⁵

One female-line granddaughter of Sir Robert Constable and his wife, Catherine Manners, was Margaret Babthorpe. Margaret married Sir Henry Cholmley of Whitby, Yorkshire, and she bore him three sons and seven daughters.⁶ The third amongst these daughters was Barbara Cholmley. This child, who was probably born in about 1580, may have been named in honour of her grandmother, Barbara Constable.

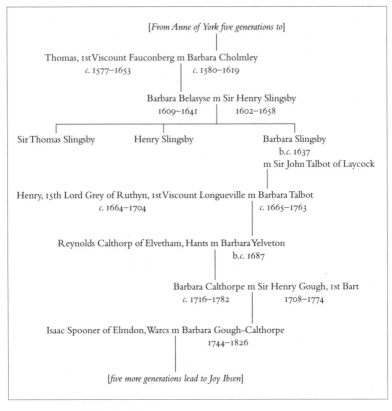

[*From Anne of York five generations to*]

Thomas, 1st Viscount Fauconberg m Barbara Cholmley
c. 1577–1653   *c.* 1580–1619

Barbara Belasyse m Sir Henry Slingsby
1609–1641   1602–1658

Sir Thomas Slingsby   Henry Slingsby   Barbara Slingsby
b.*c.* 1637
m Sir John Talbot of Laycock

Henry, 15th Lord Grey of Ruthyn, 1st Viscount Longueville m Barbara Talbot
c. 1664–1704   *c.* 1665–1763

Reynolds Calthorp of Elvetham, Hants m Barbara Yelveton
b.*c.* 1687

Barbara Calthorpe m Sir Henry Gough, 1st Bart
c. 1716–1782   1708–1774

Isaac Spooner of Elmdon, Warcs m Barbara Gough-Calthorpe
1744–1826

[*five more generations lead to Joy Ibsen*]

FAMILY TREE 5: The line of Barbaras.

When Barabara Constable had been born, in about 1525, practically everyone in England had been Catholic. The Reformation had as yet scarcely touched the land. Subsequently, however, there had been many changes, culminating in Queen Elizabeth I's establishment of the Anglican Church, which she perceived as an *aurea mediocritas*. Not all of her subjects found Elizabeth's middle way acceptable, however, and there was dissent from both Catholics and Puritans. In Yorkshire, many remained Catholics. Among them was the family of Barbara Cholmley. Thus the little girl was brought up in the old religion.

In about 1600, Barbara married Thomas Belasyse of Newborough, Yorkshire, the only son and heir of Henry Belasyse, MP for Thirsk, who was to be created a baronet in 1611. As a family, the Belasyses were not, at that time, Catholics. However, the death of Elizabeth I, and the accession of James I and his Catholic consort, Anne of Denmark, was thought at first to offer hope

1. The royal family in 1484: Queen Anne Neville, King Richard III, and Edward of Middleham, Prince of Wales. Engraving of 1844, after the Rous Roll.

Left 2. Queen Anne Neville's grave was originally marked by a brass memorial in the Abbey Church at Westminster. This lost monument – the only brass memorial to a queen in England – may once have carried a figure similar to that shown in one version of the contemporary Rous Roll.

Above 3. Nowadays Anne's place of burial is marked only by a plaque with this modern brass shield displaying her coat of arms.

4. The Gatehouse of the Priory of the Knights of St John of Jerusalem (Knights Hospitaller), Clerkenwell. Richard III came here on Wednesday 30 March 1485, possibly to perform the royal ritual of touching for the 'King's Evil', and issued a public denial of rumours that he planned to marry his illegitimate niece, Elizabeth of York.

Above 5. The seal of Richard III's nephew, John de la Pole, Earl of Lincoln. (© Colchester and Ipswich Museum Service)

Right 6. Richard III's nephew, Edward of Clarence, Earl of Warwick. Engraving of 1859, after the Rous Roll.

7. Richard III's nieces (the four eldest surviving daughters of Edward IV and Elizabeth Woodville): Elizabeth, Cecily, Anne and Catherine. Fifteenth-century stained glass from Little Malvern Priory, Worcs. (© Geoffrey Wheeler). Unlike the figures from the Royal Window at Canterbury (which have been heavily restored), these are authentic contemporary representations of Richard III's nieces.

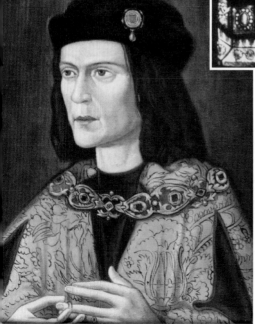

8. Copy of Richard III's earliest surviving portrait. © The Dean and Chapter of Leicester.

Left 9. Richard III's preferred prospective bride, Infanta Joana of Portugal (© Geoffrey Wheeler). Redrawn from the portrait attributed to Nuño Gonçalves in the Museu de Aveiro.

Right 10. Richard III's alternative prospective bride, Infanta Isabel of Spain (© Geoffrey Wheeler). Redrawn from 'Our Lady of Grace with the family of the Catholic Monarchs', painting of *c.* 1485, the Cistercian Monastery, Burgos.

Left 11. Henry VI as a saint, from the fifteenth-century rood screen, Eye church, Suffolk.

2. A medieval Corpus Christi procession: a bishop, walking beneath a canopy, carries the Host in a monstrance.

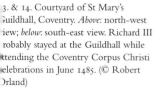

13. & 14. Courtyard of St Mary's Guildhall, Coventry. *Above*: north-west view; *below*: south-east view. Richard III probably stayed at the Guildhall while attending the Coventry Corpus Christi celebrations in June 1485. (© Robert Orland)

15. Kenilworth Castle, where Richard III stayed in May–June 1485. Engraving of 1829.

16. The approach to the hunting lodge, Bestwood Park (Sherwood Forest), where Richard III stayed for about a week in mid-August 1485. (© John Beres)

7. Deer were probably Richard III's quarry at Bestwood Park. Fifteenth-century wood carving from the Guildhall, Eye, Suffolk.

8. The outer wall and gateway of Nottingham Castle where Richard III stayed from late June to August 1485. (© Anne Ayres. Image courtesy of the Richard III Society Nottinghamshire and Derbyshire Group)

Left 19. The old Blue (White?) Boar Inn, Leicester, where Richard III reportedly spent the night of 20–21 August 1485. Engraving of 1788.

Right 20. The supposed bed of Richard III from the Blue (White?) Boar Inn, Leicester, now displayed at Donington-le-Heath Manor House. Despite its Ricardian attribution, this bed, as now preserved, appears significantly later in date. (© Sally Henshaw. Image courtesy of the Richard III Society East Midlands Branch)

Left 21. Chair from Coughton Court, Warwickshire, reputed to be made of wood from Richard III's camp bed. (© NT/Simon Pickering)

22. Old Bow Bridge, Leicester. Engraving of 1861.

Below 23. The author's tentative reconstruction of the Leicester Greyfriars church, seen from the north, in the fifteenth century.

Left 24. Tracery from a choir window of the Leicester Greyfriars church, discovered in August 2012. This tracery comes from a window similar to those shown in plate 23.

25. Alabaster tomb effigy of Richard III's brother-in-law, John de la Pole. Duke of Suffolk, Wingfield Church, Suffolk, *c.* 1495. Richard III's tomb of 1494–95 at the Leicester Greyfriars was probably very similar in appearance.

26. Richard III's epitaph from Sir Thomas Wriothesley's manuscript of *c.* 1510, BL, Add. MS 45131, f. 10v. (© British Library)

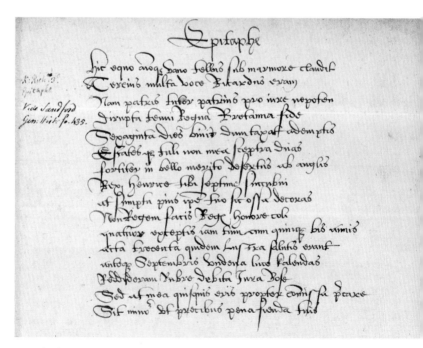

27. Richard III's epitaph from Thomas Hawley's manuscript of *c.* 1535, College of Arms, MS I 3, f. 4. (© College of Arms)

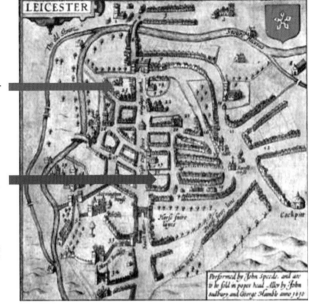

Speede's "Greyfriars" – actually the site of the Blackfriars

The *real* Greyfriars site.

8. John Speede's mistake is revealed by his plan of Leicester – proof of his unreliability regarding Richard III's gravesite.

9. Opening Trench One at the start of the excavation of Greyfriars car park in Leicester, which occupies the site of the former Greyfriars church. The white rectangle marks the site where Richard III's grave was discovered.

30. Engraving of the monument to Richard III's sister, Anne of York, Duchess of Exeter, and her second husband, in St George's Chapel, Windsor. The female-line descendants of this couple have preserved the mitochondrial DNA of Edward IV and Richard III into the twenty-first century.

31. Portrait in oils of Barbara Spooner (Mrs William Wilberforce) after the pastel portrait by John Russell. Barbara was Richard III's niece in the twelfth generation. (Private collection, reproduced by courtesy of the owner)

32. Alice Strettell (Comyns Carr), at the age of twenty-three. Alice was Richard III's niece in the fourteenth generation, the wife of an Edwardian theatre producer, a friend of Dame Ellen Terry and goddaughter of the author, Charles Kingsley. Photograph taken in 1873, at the time of her marriage.

33. Alice Strettell's only daughter, Dorothy ('Dolly') Comyns Carr, at the age of three. Dolly was Richard III's niece in the fifteenth generation. Photograph of a sketch by E.A. Abbey, published in *Mrs J. Comyns Carr's Reminiscences*, 1925.

34. Alma Strettell (Harrison), Richard III's niece in the fourteenth generation. Photograph of the portrait by John Singer Sargent published in *Mrs J. Comyns Carr's Reminiscences*, 1925. Alma was a writer, a friend of the artists Sargent and Burne Jones, and a close friend of Queen Elisabeth of Romania.

Below 35. Alma Strettell's younger daughter, Sylvia Harrison, Richard III's niece in the fifteenth generation. Photograph of the portrait by John Singer Sargent published in *Mrs J. Comyns Carr's Reminiscences*, 1925.

36. Alma Strettell's elder daughter, Margaret Harrison (Nowell; Armstrong), Richard III's niece in the fifteenth generation. Photograph courtesy of Margaret's granddaughter, Anna Lee Frohlich.

Above left 37. Charlotte Vansittart Neale (Mrs Frere), Richard III's niece in the thirteenth generation, and niece of Barbara Spooner (Wilberforce). (Photograph courtesy of Mrs J. Ibsen)

Above right 38. Charlotte Vansittart Frere (Mrs Stokes), Richard III's niece in the fourteenth generation. (Photograph courtesy of Mrs J. Ibsen)

Above left 39. Muriel Stokes (Mrs Brown), Richard III's niece in the fifteenth generation. (Photograph courtesy of Jeff Ibsen)

Above right 40. Joy Brown (Mrs Ibsen), direct descendant in the sixteenth generation (and in an all-female line) of Richard III's sister, Anne of York, Duchess of Exeter. (Photograph courtesy of Mrs J. Ibsen)

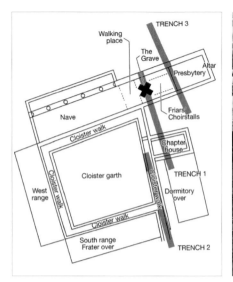

41. A tentative plan of the Franciscan Priory in Leicester, based on the excavations of August 2012, and on plans of similar priories. 'X' marks the site of Richard III's grave.

42. Richard III's grave, showing the position in which his body was found. The feet were missing, due to nineteenth-century trenching. The skeleton in this photograph is not the original.

43. Facial reconstructio based upon Richard II skull.

of renewed tolerance to Catholics, and in due course Thomas Belasyse converted to Catholicism, though he has been described as a 'church papist'.[7] He succeeded his father as the second baronet in 1624, and in 1627 he was created first Baron Fauconberg by the new king Charles I. Conspicuously loyal to Charles as the situation in England became ever more polarised and threatening, in 1643 Thomas was elevated to the rank of Viscount Fauconberg. He outlived his king, and died in 1653, in an England then ruled by Oliver Cromwell. Barbara Cholmley, however, witnessed little of this drama. She had died in January 1619 (before her husband had even succeeded to his baronetcy) having born Thomas at least two sons and two daughters.

Although the line of her elder son would inherit the title of viscount, and that of her younger son the title of baron, it is Barbara Cholmley's daughters who concern us here. It was her elder daughter, Barbara Belasyse, who maintained the female line of Richard III's mitochondrial DNA, which survives to the present day. On 7 July 1631, at the age of about 22, Barbara Belasyse married Henry Slingsby, the second son (and, since his elder brother's death in 1617, the heir) of Sir Henry Slingsby of Scriven, Yorkshire. The young Henry Slingsby was a graduate of Queens' College Cambridge, and sometime MP for Knaresborough. He succeeded to his father's estates in 1634 and was created a baronet in 1638.

Unlike her mother, Barbara Belasyse lived long enough to profit from her husband's new rank, and she became a lady. Sir Henry Slingsby's religious beliefs are somewhat difficult to disentangle. He is said to have much disliked the views of the Scottish Covenanters, and in general he appeared to be a practising Anglican of somewhat Arminian tendancy, favouring reverence in worship, while nevertheless expressing disapproval of 'bowing and adoring towards the altar' and other 'new ceremonies.'[8] At the same time, however, he opposed the clerical policies of Archbishop Laud, to the extent that he supported the exclusion of the bishops from the House of Lords. Henry Slingsby certainly married the daughter of a Catholic. Indeed, it is virtually certain that Barbara Belasyse was herself a Catholic. Moreover, although he showed no overt sign of it during his lifetime (professing himself an Anglican) Sir Henry, also, is reported to have been a Catholic, at least at the time of his death. Subsequently, Henry and Barbara's eldest son, Sir Thomas Slingsby, was a strong supporter of Charles II's overtly Catholic younger brother, the Duke of York (the future King James II), standing by him through the Exclusion crisis.

As for Sir Henry Slingsby's own politics, he was outspokenly Royalist, stating in Parliament that to refuse to pay the king ship money was tantamount to an act of rebellion. This was a point of view to which many of his fellow MPs took very vehement exception. When the Civil War started, Slingsby left London to join Charles I at York. He commanded a regiment of foot, and fought for the king at Marston Moor and at Naseby. His property was confiscated by Parliament (though relatives purchased it, to hold it in trust for his children). Barbara, his wife, was not, however, forced to endure the discomforts of this confiscation, having died in 1641.

After the execution of the king in January 1649, Sir Henry Slingsby remained in contact with the Royalist underground, and delivered a secret letter from the future Charles II to Lady Fairfax (who was a connection of his late wife's family – Barbara Belasyse (Slingsby's) paternal grandmother having been a Fairfax). Eventually, and perhaps inevitably, Sir Henry was arrested and tried at Westminster for treason against the new state. On 8 June 1658 he was beheaded on Tower Hill. His descendant, Joy Brown (Ibsen), once commented to me that she found it intriguing to have 'an ancestor, Sir Henry Slingsby, beheaded on Tower Hill in 1658 "for his loyalty". – What an interesting age.'[9]

Barbara Belasyse (Slingsby)'s daughter, Barbara Slingsby, married Sir John Talbot of Lacock, Wiltshire, thus becoming Lady Talbot. Their family home, Laycock Abbey, had originally been an Augustinian nunnery founded in the thirteenth century. John Talbot belonged to a cadet line of the descendants of the great John Talbot.

As we have seen, Barbara's family was Catholic. The main line of the Talbots of Shrewsbury also adhered to the old religion, but some cadet Talbot lines (including that which leads to the present Earl of Shrewsbury) adopted Anglicanism. The religion of Barbara Belasyse's husband is, therefore, uncertain. It is possible that he was an Anglican. Indeed, it seems to be at about this period that the family line which we are tracing finally parted company with the old religion. John Talbot and Barbara Belasyse produced two daughters: Anne and Barbara Talbot. Anne, the elder daughter, married Sir John Ivory, MP, of Wexford. As for Barbara Talbot, on 11 July 1689, at the church of St Martin-in-the-Fields, she married Henry Yelverton, Lord Grey. Henry's title carried with it the priviledge of carrying the golden spurs at coronations, and Henry had done so in 1685, at the coronation of James II.

However, Henry Yelverton deserted the Stuart king in 1688, giving his support to James' son-in-law and elder daughter, William and Mary. Henry went on to carry the spurs at the coronation of the new, Protestant sovereigns, and in 1690 the new king, William III, gave the recently married Lord Grey the title of Viscount Longueville. The new viscount once again carried the spurs at the coronation of Queen Anne, and he served as gentleman of the bedchamber to her husband, Prince George of Denmark, until his early death, in 1704. His widow (who had borne her husband two sons and one daughter) long outlived him, dying in 1763, at the age of well over 90.

The will of the Right Honourable Barbara, Viscountess Longueville, dated 13 July 1759 and proved on 5 February 1763, is preserved in the National

Archives.[10] The dowager viscountess desired to be buried beside her husband privately and without fuss. Twelve men were to attend her corpse and there was to be a coach provided for her women servants. The sum of 20s was to be paid to the minister of every village through which her body passed on its last journey, for distribution to the local poor. The bulk of her estate was divided between her surviving younger son, the Hon. Henry Yelverton, and her grandson, the second Earl of Sussex (her elder son having predecessed her). The date of death of her daughter, Barbara Yelverton (Calthorpe), is not known, but it seems virtually certain that she too had predeceased her mother, since nothing is left to her in the will. To her daughter's daughter, Lady Gough (*née* Barbara Calthorpe), however, the old lady left the sum of £100, 'and also my little japan cabinet in my chamber and my red and buff damask bed and the two leaf screen which was my daughter Yelverton's'.[11] There were various bequests to servants, and in particular 'my poor servant Elizabeth Cramp' was to have £10, together with all the viscountess' clothing (except her morning dress and the underwear which went with it). Elizabeth Cramp was also to have 'the chest of drawers in her bed chamber, a wainscot cupboard, and all the useful things in the closet by my chamber (except plate), together with my books of devotion'. As for her porcelain, her pictures and the rest of her chests and cabinets, they were to be held in trust for the young earl of Sussex by Lady Gough's husband, Sir Henry Gough, Bart. The will was signed 'B. Longueville', and was witnessed by D. Wright, by the picturesquely named John Lickorish, and by Thomas Harris.

It was Viscountess Longueville's only daughter, Barbara Yelverton, who carried on the mtDNA line of Richard III, marrying (as his second wife) Reynolds Calthorpe. The latter had acquired his seat of Elvetham from his first wife (and first cousin), the only daughter and heiress of Sir Robert Reynolds.[12] The daughter of Barbara Yelverton and Reynolds Calthorpe was Barbara Calthorpe who, as we have just seen, inherited a laquered cabinet, a damask bed and a screen from her grandmother under the terms of the latter's will. Unbeknown to her, Barbara Calthorpe had also inherited old Lady Longueville's mitochondrial DNA.

Barbara Calthorpe married Sir Henry Gough of Edgbaston, first baronet, and Barbara Gough-Calthorpe, the elder of their two daughters, was born in 1744. Barbara Gough-Calthorpe must have known her great grandmother, Lady Longueville, for she was already 19 years of age when that elderly aristocrat (then rapidly approaching her century) died at Brandon in Warwickshire.

Barbara Gough-Calthorpe came from a hybrid background. Her father, Sir Henry Gough, was a wealthy merchant while her mother was the daughter of a county family with estates in Norfolk and Suffolk. Barbara's maternal inheritance, of course, comprised more than status, for the mtDNA which her mother had inherited from Viscountess Longueville was the mtDNA of Catherine de Roët, of Cecily Neville and of Richard III. This genetic inheritance was transmitted by Lady Gough to her two daughters: Barbara Gough-Calthorpe and her younger sister, Charlotte.

Barbara Gough-Calthorpe married, according to the lights of the time, somewhat beneath her. Her husband, Isaac Spooner, was rich, but he was an ironmaster, merchant and banker from nearby Birmingham, with a pedigree which was unremarkable. His family fortune was a recent phenomenon. It had been founded by his father, Abraham, and was then extended by Isaac himself. By contrast Barbara's younger sister, Charlotte Gough-Calthorpe (1747–83) enjoyed greater marital success, acquiring as a husband a baronetted MP who conferred upon his fortunate spouse the title of Lady Palmer.

When she married Isaac Spooner in 1770, Charlotte's elder sister, Barbara, acquired no special matrimonial handle to her name. Nevertheless, Mr and Mrs Spooner ranked among the leading citizens of Birmingham. They lived at nearby Elmdon Hall, and enjoyed the luxury of a second house in fashionable Bath, though the society which surrounded them there was evidently regarded as less than brilliant, since one visitor uncharitably described their Bath house as 'the very temple of dullness'.

Barbara and Isaac Spooner had a large family. The majority of their ten children were boys. Curiously, one of these was given the name 'Richard'; a name which was in Barbara's family, for she also had a brother called Richard. Is it possible that those who named these boys had some inkling of their family connection with Richard III? Probably not. In any case, the boys were a genetic dead end. However, there were girls in the family too, and these were capable of passing on into the future the inherited DNA of Catherine de Roët and Richard III.

Barbara Ann Spooner was the third of the ten children of Isaac and Barbara Spooner, and she was born in 1777. She possessed a dark beauty, as we know both from her surviving portrait by Russell, and from contemporary descriptions of her. Those who knew her described her as pretty, pleasing and handsome. As to her character, we are told that she was a pious, sweet-tempered girl who had 'considerable humility and a mind rather highly embellished than strongly cultivated'.[13]

In the spring of 1797 the 20-year-old Barbara Spooner met a 37-year-old bachelor, the slave trade abolitionist William Wilberforce. Wilberforce, who until this point had appeared intent on remaining single (following a previous unsuccessful relationship) seems, during the winter of 1796/97 to have changed his mind. In Bath he confided his desire to find a partner to his friend Babington, who in response mentioned to him the name of Miss Spooner.

Shortly thereafter, coincidentally as it seemed to Wilberforce (though in fact Babington may have given Barbara a hint), a letter reached Wilberforce asking for his advice in spiritual matters. The letter was from Barbara Spooner.

The entries in Wilberforce's private diary chart the progress of the affair from his point of view. For a while Wilberforce agonised over what he should do, but on the Sunday after Easter he wrote Barbara a proposal of marriage. 'That night I had a formal favourable answer.'[14] On the morning of Tuesday 30 May 1797 they were married, quietly, at the parish church of Walcot, Bath. Barbara had two bridesmaids, and after the ceremony they dined at her father's house. There was no honeymoon as such, and that night Barbara asked her new husband to join her in her prayers, following which they went to bed early. The following day the couple set off on a four-day tour of the schools in the Mendips run by Wilberforce's friend Hannah More. This somewhat unusual wedding journey seems to have passed off well enough, and Wilberforce confided his opinion, at the end of the trip, that 'there seems to be entire coincidence in our intimacy and interests and pursuits'.[15]

Furneaux, one of William Wilberforce's modern biographers, has written that 'it is difficult to be fair to Barbara'.[16] Unfortunately, Furneaux seems sometimes to be naively uncritical in his evaluation of his sources. The comments that he quotes from Wilberforce's wildly jealous friend, Marianne Thornton, for example, tell us at least as much about *her* as they do about Barbara! The *facts* which emerge from these hostile comments are that Barbara idolised her husband, and was unhappy when he was away from her. (A trait which William, at least, may have rather liked, since few human beings enjoy the feeling that their presence is readily expendable.)

Probably Barbara was by nature an anxious person. As the years passed this tendency seems to have increased, and she worried a great deal about her children. However, the early deaths of her two daughters may help to make such anxieties more understandable. The Wilberforces had six children: four sons and two daughters, all of whom inherited from their mother the mitochondrial DNA of Richard III. The eldest son, another William, was born on 21 July 1798 (he lived until 1879) Robert (1802–57), Samuel (1805–73) and Henry (1807–73) followed. The two girls, Barbara (1799–1821) and Elizabeth ('Lizzie' 1801–31) fit into the family tree between William and the three youngest sons. The elder daughter, Barbara Wilberforce, died unmarried and childless in her early 20s. Lizzie's life, though also short, lasted a little longer, and when she died she left a daughter of her own.

In January 1831 Lizzie married John James who, at the time, was an impoverished young curate. Her marriage proved short-lived. She quickly became pregnant, and bore her child towards the end of the year. Subsequently she fell ill with a chest infection, and although her husband brought her from their home in Yorkshire to stay on the Isle of Wight, where it was thought the climate would suit her better, in fact her condition continued to deteriorate. Early the following year Lizzie died. Sending Lord Carrington the sad news on 23 March 1832, her father wrote: 'my poor son-in-law and his little infant are indeed much to be pitied'.[17]

The baptismal register of Rawmarsh, Yorkshire, where Rev. John James was curate, reveals that on 11 December 1831 his daughter by Lizzie Wilberforce was baptised Barbara Wilberforce James. No doubt her first name was chosen in honour of her grandmother and her deceased aunt. She grew up to marry Captain Charles Colquhoun Pye in 1860, at Avington, Berkshire, where her father John James had been the rector since the late 1830s. However, Barbara Wilberforce James left no heirs to carry forward the genetic heritage of Richard III and his family.[18] To follow the mitochondrial DNA of Richard III forward into the twentieth century we must now abandon the descendants of Barbara Spooner and William Wilberforce, and turn instead to the descendants of Barbara's younger sister, Anne Spooner.

Unlike her sister Barbara, Anne Spooner did not attract the jealous comments of other women. Her husband, an evangelical clergyman, the Rev. Edward Vansittart Neale, was never a well-known figure in the political and social world of his day, and no detailed portraits of the couple, either painted or verbal, have come down to us. Our one surviving glimpse of Anne seems to be a brief and anonymous mention of her by one of her granddaughters. It relates to a period near the end of Anne's life, when she was already more than

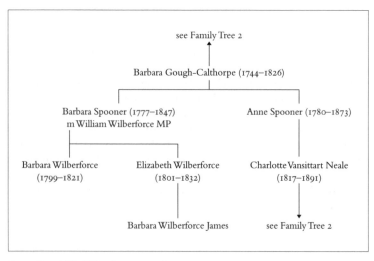

FAMILY TREE 6: The Wilberforce connection.

80 years old (for, like many members of the family which we are following, Anne Spooner was a long-lived lady). Born in 1780, in the reign of George III, she died at the age of 93, in 1873; the thirty-sixth year of Queen Victoria's reign.

Anne, it seems, remained true to her chosen *métier* as the wife of an evangelical clergyman, and perhaps true also to her upbringing at her parents' home in Bath, which we have already heard described unflatteringly as 'the very temple of dullness'. Her granddaughter, Alice Strettell, then aged about 15, found herself sent home to England by her parents (who as we shall shortly see, were then living in Italy) in order that she might attend a boarding school in Brighton. She looked forward to her holidays, when she might return to the Continent and to her parents:

> However, when the period of *congé* was short, or the weather seemed too bad for me to cross the channel, I was consigned to the care of a saintly but evangelically minded grandmother, and though her society was doubtless improving, such a holiday was, from my point of view, scarcely a relief from term-time. Many were the long Sundays I spent at the pretty satin sandalled feet of my grandmother as she sat by the green-verandahed window of her drawing room. In her cap of fluted tulle, tied under her chin with a ribbon, she taught me the Catechism and some terrifying hymns. Many, too, were the long, dull afternoons and evenings I spent sewing, or reading the Bible, until at nine o'clock the old butler appeared and my grandmother said, 'Bring in Prayers.'[19]

Alice Strettell's pen portrait of Anne Spooner is brief but vivid. However, for Anne it is perhaps unfortunate that this record of her was preserved by a teenaged granddaughter who was eager to be out in the fashionable world and living life to the full, and for whom the experience of life with the old lady felt, as Alice herself readily admits, as though 'my sprouting wings were clipped'.

Anne Spooner married a clergyman called Edward Vansittart Neale. The latter was born simply Edward Vansittart, and was not, in fact, of Neale descent. The family of Neale were seated in Staffordshire in the reign of Richard III. A descendant, John Neale, of Allesley Park, Warwick, died in 1793 without issue. At the death of his widow in 1805 the Allesley and other estates passed under her will to the Revd Edward Vansittart of Taplow, Bucks, with the provision that he should take the name and arms of Neale.[20]

Joy Ibsen, a living descendant of Anne Spooner and Edward Vansittart Neale, recalled to me:

> Edward's father owned Bisham Abbey in Berkshire, once a house of the Knights Templar and at one time owned by the Duke of Clarence and later his son, Edward [Earl of Warwick], who was beheaded in 1499 for attempting to

escape from the Tower with 'Perkin Warbeck'. In 1941 it belonged to Edward [Vansittart Neale]'s grand-daughter, Lady Vansittart Neale. There is supposed to be a curse on the place.[21]

Anne Spooner's granddaughter, Alice Strettell (Comyns Carr) also remembered 'the home of my mother's family – the beautiful Gothic Abbey of Bisham near Marlow. We were staying with my cousin, George Vansittart, who was then the owner'.[22] The latter objected to trippers along the river Thames landing on his banks and used to chase them off.

Anne Spooner and Edward Vansittart Neale produced a large family, in which daughters very much predominated – a fact which appears superficially promising for the future of the mitochondrial DNA of Richard III and his family. Unfortunately, several of the daughters remained unmarried. Alice Strettell, the granddaughter of Anne Spooner whom we have already met, was the elder daughter of one of Anne's daughters: Laura Vansittart Neale. Laura was born at Taplow (where her father held the living) in the year after the final defeat of Napoleon I at Waterloo. She died aged 62 in the year following Queen Victoria's golden jubilee.

Although Laura had clear views on what was and was not proper, and although, like her mother, she married a clergyman, her life was certainly not dull, and was open to unusually wide horizons. Her husband was Alfred Baker Strettell, who served for a time as her father's curate at Taplow, before accepting, in 1851, the rather unusual appointment as English chaplain at Genoa. The growing Strettell family (a son and two daughters) lived in Italy for many years – though in 1851, of course, no country called 'Italy' yet existed. Indeed, the Strettells were to witness the process of Italian reunification at first hand, and in 1862, after the treaty of Villafranca, the family watched from the balcony of the British Consulate, as Garibaldi accompanied King Victor-Emanuel I and the Emperor Napoleon III of France in procession through the streets of Genoa.[23]

Laura attended the royal ball at the palace later that evening and her elder daughter, Alice Laura Vansittart Strettell, has preserved for us a description of her mother's appearance on that occasion. Laura wore a crinoline with 'spreading skirts of blue gauze garlanded with tiny rosebuds. Her hair was dressed low, in the prevailing fashion, with a pink rose fastened behind her ear and a long curl falling on her neck.'[24] Some hint of Laura's appearance may be glimpsed, perhaps, in a surviving photograph of her sister, Charlotte, which must have been taken at about this period, and which shows her wearing a spreading crinoline and a fine lace shawl. 'The photo of Charlotte Vansittart Neale as a young girl is interesting I think because of her lovely dress.'[25]

The Italian upbringing of the Strettell children was unusual, and it produced unusual results in terms of the children's education. Both Alice and her

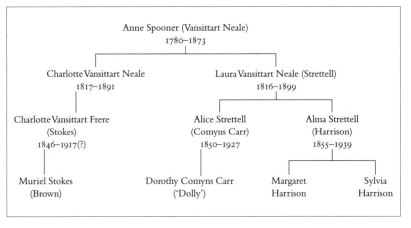

FAMILY TREE 7: The Strettell connection.

sister had linguistic accomplishments. Alice spoke Italian like a native. Many years later she remembered her husband's delight, when he was trying to purchase something from an Italian vendor, 'at the sudden drop of five francs in the demand of the astounded plunderer upon hearing his own vernacular from my indignant English lips'.[26] As Alice admitted later, however, she did not fully appreciate all the advantages of her upbringing at the time:

> There was much that must have been, unconsciously to myself, of rare educational advantage in the lovely scenery and picturesque surroundings of my childhood's life on the Riviera and in the Apennines; and my parents so loved both Nature and Art that they gave us contant change of opportunities in these directions. Yet I must confess that as I grew up, the chestnut groves of the Apennines and the shores of the blue Mediterranean became empty joys to me, … and I longed for freedom and the attractions of the world – more especially in London, which I only knew through visits to relatives during the holidays of a short period of my life at a Brighton School. [So I] cajoled my father, then English chaplain at Genoa, into letting me 'see London' under the care of my brother, resident there.[27]

At that time, Alice's brother, Arthur Edward Vansittart Strettell[28] was living in rooms facing the British Museum, though he would later leave England for the United States[29] Alice stayed in a boarding house near Arthur's lodgings, and soon after her arrival in London she met her future husband. This was in 1873 and 'I had but lately arrived from Italy'. Joseph William Comyns Carr was then aged 24, and of Irish extraction, though at that time he had never yet visited his homeland. Henry Irving, would later describe Joe as 'the wittiest man in England'.[30]

Joseph and Alice were married in December 1873, in Dresden, where Alice's father had taken a temporary chaplaincy. The civil ceremony took place in the hotel and, in Alice's words, they were then 'finished off' by her father in the local English Church. The young couple settled in Bloomsbury. They 'were at the center of what they termed the "Bohemian World" (vis-à-vis the "Social World") which had begun to gravitate to London's Bloomsbury District'.[31] Alice later remembered:

> the beautiful Adams room where Burne-Jones had once painted and that Whistler had not long left . [Here] a light rap fell on the door and a voice loved by us all called out: 'Anybody at home?' as the radiant face of Ellen Terry peeped merrily in upon us.[32]

Alice was to be very close to Ellen for the rest of her life. As Ellen later recalled, Alice designed her stage costumes for many years:

> As Katherine [of Aragon, in Shakespeare's Henry VIII] she wanted me to wear steely silver and bronzy gold, but all the brocades had such insignificant designs. … At last Mrs Carr found a black satin which on the right side was timorously and feebly patterned with a meandering rose and thistle. On the wrong side it was a sheet of silver – just the right steely silver because it was the wrong side! Mrs Carr then started on another quest for gold that should be as right as that silver. She found it at last in some gold-lace antimaccassars at Whiteley's! From these base materials she and Mrs Nettleship constructed a magnificent queenly dress. Its only fault was that it was heavy.[33]

Alice also designed the very famous costume, sewn all over with the irridescent wing cases of beetles, which Ellen wore in the role of Lady MacBeth: a dress which figures in the well-known portrait of Ellen by John Singer Sargent.[34]

John Singer Sargent was also a friend of Alice and Joe, and has left us both a pencil sketch and a painting of Alice, together with portraits of her sister and of one of her nieces. In fact Joseph and Alice had many friends among the artists then resident in London, and in the world of the London theatre. These included Sir Authur Sullivan, Oscar Wilde, and the artists Edward Burne-Jones, and Laurence Alma Tadema. The couple also had a number of American friends, with the result that several members of their family eventually visited the United States. In the 1870s they met the wealthy General William Jackson Palmer, founder of Colorado Springs, and his family. Subsequently Alice's brother, Arthur Strettell, her daughter, Dolly, and sister and brother-in-law, Alma and 'Peter' Harrison all stayed at Glen Eyrie as guests of the Palmers. The Comyns Carrs also frequently stayed at Ightham Mote, a medieval manor house with Ricardian connections, 'which our American friends, General and Mrs. Palmer had made their English home'.[35]

Alice's younger sister, Alma Gertrude Vansittart Strettell was born in Italy. She grew up with linguistic and literary interests and later published several books: *Spanish and Italian Folk Songs*, London 1887; *Legends from River and Mountain*, co-written with Carmen Sylva, London 1896, and *The Bard of Dimbovitsa*, translated by Alma, and Carmen Sylva, London 1914. 'Carmen Sylva' was the *nom de plume* of Alma's friend, Elisabeth von Wied, the then Queen of Romania.[36] Alma collected Balkan folk music, and had many artistic friends including the painter John Singer Sargent (who painted two portraits of Alma) and the composer Elgar. Her eventual husband, 'Peter' Harrison, was also a painter, though a minor one.

Alma was younger than Alice, who described her as being of a light and merry disposition. Having Alice as her older sister undoubtedly helped to bring Alma out. Alice and her husband went on a visit to Paris, where Alice recalled 'cheerful meals in the humblest of restaurants ... my sister, Mrs. Harrison – then Alma Strettell – was bidden as being of our party'.[37]

In the 1880s, while she was still unmarried, Alma paid her first visit to the United States, where she stayed at Glen Eyrie, the Colorado Springs 'castle' of General and Mrs Palmer. Alma married Laurence Alexander ('Peter') Harrison at King's Langley on 18 December 1890. The marriage was solemnised by Alma's father, the vicar of King's Langley. 'Peter' Harrison, a tall, slim man, was a portrait painter and landscape artist, though he described himself on the marriage certificate simply as 'gentleman'. In fact Peter rarely exhibited paintings, though he was a member of the 'Chelsea set' and joined the *New English Art Club* in 1904. Although Peter had mistresses, and the couple were sometimes apart (as in May 1903, when he visited General Palmer at Colorado Springs, where he painted several extant studies),[38] in general the marriage seems to have been a success.

Alma died at Chelsea in 1939, leaving to her three children not only money but also pearl and diamond necklaces and tiaras, and further treasures, including an impressive collection of paintings by Sargent and others. Her property included a diamond ring which she had inherited from her mother, Laura, and a silver sugar sifter which had been a present to her from John Singer Sargent. The water-colour sketch of herself by Sargent, she left to her younger daughter, Sylvia, and her Sargent portrait in oils, to her son, Nicholas. Nicholas also received a landscape painting of Colorado by his father. Alma is still well known in certain literary circles, and has a website devoted to her on the internet. She left one son and two daughters. Her younger daughter, Sylvia, died unmarried. Through her elder daughter, Margaret, Alma does have living descendants – but they do not carry her mtDNA.

Like her cousin, Dolly Comyns Carr, Margaret (also known to her family as Meg or Margot) had an interest in music, which she studied under Percy Grainger (1882–1961, Australian-born pianist and composer). In about 1913 Margaret Harrison became engaged to Percy. However, her parents reportedly broke off this engagement (possibly because they were aware of Grainger's taste for flagellation), and they sent Margaret to America to get her away. There, on 7 March 1916, Margaret married a fellow Christian Scientist, Ames Nowell (b. 30 December 1892 in Newton, Mass). They had one son: Lawrence Ames Nowell. Later Margaret had a second son, Leonard Nowell, but his real father was Percy Grainger. In 1933 Margaret and Ames Nowell divorced, and in 1934 Margaret married her second husband, in London. He was Francis W. ('John') Bacon-Armstrong , but they had no children. After the Second World War they emigrated to South Africa where John died in about 1952. Margaret then moved to Colorado to be near her son. She was married a third time, to Arthur Porter, in about 1956. She died in Carmel, CA in 1979. Margaret inherited her Christian Scientist religion from her mother, Alma.

Alice and Joe Comyns Carr had three children: Philip Alfred Vansittart Comyns Carr, Arthur Strettell Comyns Carr, and Dorothy Comyns Carr (known as 'Dolly'). Naturally, all of Alice's children inherited her mitochondrial DNA; the DNA of Richard III and his siblings; but only her daughter Dolly had the possibility of passing this on to future generations. Given the background in which she was brought up, 'it is not surprising that Dolly Carr had artistic ambitions'.[39]

> By the time she visited Glen Eyrie in 1902–03, she had exhibited in several galleries in London and had sold a few of her paintings. Dolly was urbane and well-educated. She had traveled on the Continent and spoke French. … she had a generous heart and was a charming companion and delightful guest during her extended stay at the stately Palmer residence' in Colorado Springs.[40]

Dolly's impressions of America in the first years of the twentieth century are fascinating. She noticed of course that everything, including the country itself, seemed very big. 'At the turn of the century, New York was already the second largest city in the world, with a largely immigrant population of over 3,000,000.' Dolly pronounced the Brooklyn Bridge 'enormous', and declared the Hudson 'the biggest thing in rivers I have seen'. After leaving New York she found herself travelling westwards across the prairie. Dolly very much enjoyed General Palmer's hospitality at Glen Eyrie. She continued to paint while she was there, joined later by her artist uncle, 'Peter' Harrison.

Sadly, Dolly's artistic ambitions were not ultimately to be crowned with success. After returning to England, Dolly Carr continued to pursue her vocation as a painter (oils and watercolors) of flowers and landscapes. Her work was exhibited occasionally in London, but, despite some modest success, she did not achieve prominence as a professional artist. She remained unmarried and without children. On 10 May 1918, only a few days before her 40th birthday, she committed suicide near her home in Bedford. The coroner's report reads: 'Drowned herself in a certain pond whilst temporarily insane.'[41] This must have been an enormous shock and a great tragedy for Dolly's family. Her father was already dead, but her mother was then still living. However, Alice makes no reference whatsoever to her daughter's suicide in her later published writings about her family. Alice herself died in 1927, a year before her old friend, Dame Ellen Terry.[42] Unfortunately, neither she not her sister Alma seemed destined to pass on Richard III's mtDNA into the twenty-first century. The family line which was destined to preserve that mtDNA into the second millennium was that of Laura Vansittart Neale (Strettell)'s elder sister, Charlotte, and the descendant who made that mtDNA available for research was Charlotte Vansittart Neale's great granddaughter, Joy Brown (Ibsen).

Joy Ibsen was born in London, England, on 25 May 1926, the third child (and only daughter) of Muriel Charlotte Folliott Stokes and her husband, Orlando Moray Brown. The couple had married just after the end of the Great War:

> By 1919, when my parents met, there were not many young men left in England and I suspect that my parents' marriage that year was a hasty grasping at happiness after the horrors of 1914-18. At any rate, it was not a success. He was thirty-nine, she was thirty-five, and anxious to have children. ... [My father] was to spend the next twenty years working as a mining engineer in Chile and Bolivia, living in fairly primitive places which seemed to suit him. His wife would join him briefly before returning to England for the birth of her children. After I was born she never returned. But he continued to live abroad for most of his life.[43]

Joy's two older brothers were Kenneth Patrick Brown (born 29 March 1920) and Patrick Hugh Brown (born 19 March 1924). Both of them shared with Joy and their mother the mitochondrial DNA of Anne of York and her family, but of course, being male, they could not pass it on.

Joy's birth was registered under the name Muriel Joyce Brown, but she preferred to reverse the order of her names, and to shorten 'Joyce' to 'Joy'. One of her godmothers was her grandmother's first cousin, Alma Strettell (Mrs Harrison). 'I have no memory of her but I recall my mother talking about "Aunt Alma". I think there is a slight resemblance between the two'.[44] Joy and her brothers were brought up by their mother in Sussex and Shropshire, where her eldest brother, Ken, attended Shrewsbury School. Ken also recalls staying with his godfather, Arthur Comyns Carr,[45] in London in 1936 or 1937.

Although her father was absent, Joy recalls that 'my grandfather, Allen Gardiner Folliott Stokes ... was very dear to me as a child.'[46] Stokes, who died in 1939,[47] was the author of a number of books,[48] and a great lover of Cornwall, which he knew intimately. 'He was a friend of the writer C. Ranger-Gull who dedicated his novel *Portalone* (1904) to him [saying]: "it was owing to him that I made knowledge of the wildest and most untrodden parts of Cornwall".'[49]

Joy's mother, Muriel, suffered from asthma and rheumatoid arthritis and in 1937 the family moved to Nassau, Bahamas, and in 1945 to Canada, where Joy attended McGill University in Montreal, graduating with a BA in English and history:

> My eldest brother embarked on a long career with the Canadian Broadcasting Corporation in Montreal, London (England) and Ottowa. My other brother, Patrick, has had a varied career and lives in retirement in British Columbia. I wanted a career in journalism but at that time women were not welcome in daily newspaper newsrooms. Having mastered typing and shorthand I got my foot in the door of a western Canadian newspaper as secretary to the editor, a crusty ex-alcoholic (and crackerjack newspaperman). That newsroom was a great place for a young, aspiring writer. Some very good journalists worked there (I was to marry one of them later) as well as some odd characters! The pressure of daily deadlines was exciting, especially when I graduated to writing features or reviews. I learned a lot here. After one and a half years I moved on to an eastern paper as a reporter in the Women's Department, leaving that job for a two-year stint as Women's Editor at a small daily.[50]

Joy and Norm Ibsen were married in May 1956. 'We ended up in London, Ontario, where we still live. Norm has had a thirty-eight-year career at the London Free Press and is now retired. After producing three children I became a freelance writer, contributing articles to magazines and newspapers, and reviewing books'.[51] As for Joy's mother, Muriel Charlotte Folliot Brown lived in a number of places including London, Ontario. She died in London, Ontario, on 25 May 1961 at the age of 77. Her husband died in 1965.

Joy had an interest in her family tree before I contacted her, and she knew a good deal of information from family tradition, by word-of mouth from relatives. 'Although I have spent most of my life away from England, I have often looked back at the rich genealogical history I have inherited, and have felt grateful to those who have preserved my "roots" over the centuries'.[52] However, Joy had tended to concentrate on male lines of ancestors, and readily admits that she had not made a great deal of progress with her female line ancestry. Her previous knowledge on that side of her family extended back a mere three generations, to her great grandmother, Charlotte Vansittart Neale. The family's descent from the house of York, and its relationship with Richard III, were lost in the mists of time. 'How puzzling that a family interested in their ancestors would not have known of this connection and passed the information down the generations! ... Possibly the widely-held traditional view of Richard III as an infamous murderer was a reason to play down the Plantagenet connection.'[53]

When I first contacted Joy with details of her descent from Anne of York, Cecily Neville and Catherine de Roët, the information came as a complete surprise to her. Fortunately, she was also fascinated to be presented with a family tree that went back to the Emperor Charlemagne and beyond. 'For my part, I am delighted to have been tracked down and identified ... as a living descendant of Anne of Exeter, eldest sister of Edward IV and Richard III'.[54] In July 2004, Joy told me:

> we are off shortly to Vancouver Island to dog-sit for our daughter at her sea-side house. Our sons are flying in from Toronto and England for a small family reunion and I plan to surprise them with all your startling revelations about my family tree, the DNA etc. They are aware of the Pitt and Frere ancestors but not of their mother's descent in the female line from Cecily Neville, Duchess of York. They'll have to start showing me due respect![55]

16

The Future of Richard III

It may seem perverse to conclude this book by seeking to discuss the future of a man and king who has been dead for more than 500 years. However, historical interest in Richard III continues, and the controversy surrounding his name still rages. In one way, of course, this is a pity, since it leads to a vast quantity of circular and rather predictable writing about Richard, based on *partie-prise* attitudes, and offering few, if any, fresh insights.

But Ricardian study is not obliged to restrict itself to well-worn and unproductive ruts. This present book constitutes a conscious attempt to avoid the deepest and best-known ruts of the Ricardian controversy, seeking new ways of understanding Richard and the events of his short reign. Its chosen time frame in terms of Richard's life has mercifully allowed us to largely eschew the hoary and currently unproductive chestnut of 'who murdered the princes in the Tower'. Nor has it sought to pass any kind of inappropriate retrospective judgement on Richard, whether favourable or unfavourable. Instead, it has tried to give an account of what actually happened during the last months of his life and afterwards. The justification for this approach hopefully lies in the fact that what has emerged as a result is a fresher, rather different picture of Richard III in 1485.

Perhaps the way to a better understanding of Richard III is by means of a deliberate endeavour to avoid the pantomime, black *versus* white, good *versus* bad arguments which have so bedevilled the study of his life and reign, for these merely tend to produce a somewhat *1066 and All That* impression.[1] By concentrating instead on the *minutiae* of Richard's day-to-day life, and by seeking entirely new kinds of evidence, as this present study has sought to do, it may be possible to arrive at a clearer and better picture of the real man and king: a picture which is hopefully not black and white, but full of rich colours and shadings.

The revelation of Richard III's mtDNA sequence is one piece of new evidence. In connection with my Belgian research concerning possible Margaret of York remains, Joy Ibsen kindly provided a DNA sample which was analysed initially by *Oxford Ancestors*, a commercial company engaged in DNA testing for genealogical purposes. The resulting mtDNA sequence was communicated to Professor Jean-Jacques Cassiman of the Centre for Human Genetics, Catholic University of Leuven, who had been requested by the authorities in Mechelen to attempt to extract and sequence DNA from the various sets of potential 'Margaret of York' remains. Professor Cassiman repeated DNA tests on further samples provided by Joy Ibsen, and also succeeded in sequencing DNA from the Mechelen remains. As a result, it emerged that Richard III and his siblings belonged to mtDNA haplogroup J, and that their 'clan mother' was 'Jasmine'. It also appeared that none of the three sets of female remains which had at that time been recovered from the Franciscan church in Mechelen could be those of Margaret of York. A summary of the results of the DNA tests on the three sets of Mechelen bones is given in appendix 5.

The first edition of this book highlighted one huge gap in the evidence that was then available, relating to England's last Plantagenet king – namely the fact that the precise location of his physical remains was at that time still unknown. In fact, my original text ended with the words 'Perhaps one day the search for Richard III will begin!'. Screenwriter Philippa Langley, who is also the Secretary of the Scottish Branch of the Richard III Society, had been working on the project to go in search of Richard's grave for quite some time at that point and was awaiting the first edition of this book, and the research it included, before taking the project proper to Leicester City Council. In particular, Philippa was impressed by:

- the potential evidence for identification which was implicit in my publication of Richard III's mtDNA sequence
- my demonstration that Speede's story of Richard's exhumation in the sixteenth century was nonsense
- my indication – based upon my knowledge of medieval Catholic practice, and of the layout of medieval friaries – that existing reconstructions of the layout of the Leicester Greyfriars, which postulated a church located on the southern side of the site, were incorrect, and that Richard's remains should, therefore, be sought on the exposed northern side of the central Greyfriars car park.

As a result of the publication of this book, Philippa decided to ensure that investigation of the three car parks in Leicester which now occupy the Greyfriars site would take place. She had to overcome major hurdles to achieve this, but finally, in August 2012, thanks to her tremendous work, the archaeological investigation commenced, and on the very first day of the dig the bones which ultimately proved to be the remains of Richard III were found, in precisely the area which I had indicated as the most likely location for the choir of the vanished priory church.

Subsequently, with the help of DNA samples from Joy Ibsen's elder son Michael, those remains were proved to have an mtDNA sequence consistent with the proposition that they were the bones of Richard III. The bones showed evidence of scoliosis which would have made the left shoulder lower than the right in life (just as Richard's contemporary, John Rous, had described). The body was male and of the right age and social class, it showed evidence of a violent death and of significant post mortem injuries. carbon-14 dating indicated that the individual had died in about 1490.

When the remains had been carefully removed, one by one, from their grave by gloved and masked osteologist, Dt Jo Appleby, they were packed individually in labelled polythene bags and then carefully stacked in a long cardboard box. *I* was then asked by Philippa to carry that box to the white van that was waiting to remove the remains to Leicester University, where they would be kept safe and subjected to detailed examination. As I carried that box my mind was full of very strange thoughts and reflections. At that moment, I felt that I was as close as I would ever be to the real Richard III.

I believe that my search for Richard's mtDNA showed what could be achieved by taking a new approach, but this is not the end of the story. At the time of my initial DNA research I was aware that, ideally, the mtDNA sequence obtained from samples supplied by Joy Ibsen – direct female-line descendant of Anne of York, Duchess of Exeter – should be confirmed from other sources. I made one attempt to obtain such confirmation, using a sample of the hair of King Edward IV, cut from his body when his tomb was opened in the eighteenth century, and kindly supplied to the present author by the Ashmolean Museum, Oxford. Unfortunately, that attempt was unsuccessful. The DNA of the Edward IV hair sample was too degraded to produce a sequence. Now, however, Dr Turi King and her colleagues from the University of Leicester have succeeded in finding independent confirmation of the mtDNA sequence of Michael and Joy Ibsen, and matching the mtDNA with the sequence obtained from the Leicester bones.

Sadly, in November 2008, Joy Ibsen died of cancer. One of my lasting regrets is that she was not alive in the first months of 2013, to hear the news that the body of her uncle sixteen generations removed had been found and identified thanks to her assistance. Although for the moment the living members of her family still preserve the line of her mtDNA, this almost unique heritage is now coming to an end. It is extremely fortunate, therefore, that,

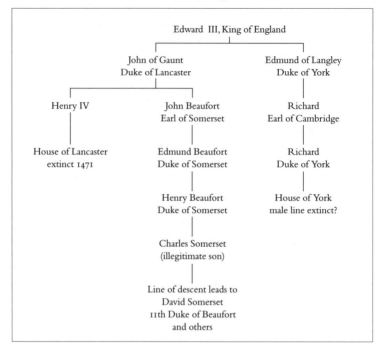

FAMILY TREE 8: The Plantagenet Y-chromosome

with the active co-operation and support of Joy and subsequently of her children – in particular of her elder son, Michael – details of this fascinating mtDNA sequence are now on permanent record.

It would also be desirable to seek to analyse and hold on file similar independent information in respect of Richard III's Y-chromosome – the only component of the nuclear DNA whose origin can currently be traced for certain. Dr Turi King and her team at Leicester University have already made some progress in that direction. Richard III's Y-chromosome was that of the entire Plantagenet dynasty, back to its earliest known male line progenitor, Geoffrey, Count of Gâtinais, who lived in the first half of the eleventh century. Of course, there are no individuals bearing the surname Plantagenet living today. The 'Tudor' kings took good care to see that this surname and all the males who carried it were exterminated. However, the members of the Somerset family are surviving descendants of the Plantagenets in an unbroken (though illegitimate) male line. As shown in Family Tree 8 (above) they can claim direct patrilineal descent from King Edward III via his illegitimate grandson, John Beaufort. From John the fifteenth century earls and dukes of Somerset were descended. And although John's legitimate male heirs died out in 1471, one of his grandsons, Henry third Duke of Somerset (died 1464), left an illegitimate son, Charles Somerset, whose line of descent leads directly to the present Duke of Beaufort. Thus in this family the Plantagenet Y-chromosome – Richard III's Y-chromosome – theoretically still flourishes at the present day.[2] A suitable DNA sample could be provided by any male member of the Somerset family, and volunteers to provide such samples have now come forward.

Comparing the Somerset male line DNA to that of the remains which we now know to be Richard III will potentially be very interesting, and it is one of the many things that we still have to look forward to in the coming years. Unfortunately, unlike female line genealogy, male line genealogy as recorded on paper is not always consistent with the biological facts. The person who is recorded as having been someone's father may not have been their true *biological* father. Therefore, the comparison of the living Somerset Y-chromosome with that of Richard III is open to various possible outsomes and interpretations. Whatever future research in this area reveals is, however, certain to be of interest in one way or another.

Holding on record such DNA sequences relating to ancient royalty, might in the future help to resolve further historical mysteries. One particular way in which DNA analysis could yet serve to clarify an important aspect of Richard III's story relates to the fate of Richard III's nephews, the so-called 'princes in the Tower',[3] a story which has long bedevilled Ricardian research. Although there is absolutely no proof that either 'prince' was ever murdered by anyone, a perennial theme of popular histories is 'who murdered the "princes in the Tower"?'. Or, even better, 'did Richard III murder the "princes in the Tower"?'. Given that some historians consider that Henry VII's aim was to exterminate the entire posterity of the house of York, and view this policy as an example of 'strong kingship', the whole debate about the fate of the 'princes' seems curiously unfair. However, it would be good to be able to shed light on this issue if possible – if only in the hope of finally closing the debate.

Although the fate of the 'princes' is unknown, there is a marble urn in the Henry VII chapel at Westminster which bears their names and purports to contain their bones. The urn was created by Sir Christopher Wren at the behest of Charles II, to house some fragmentary remains which were discovered during some demolition work at the Tower of London in the 1670s. We have no idea from what period these bones date, nor is it known whether they represent boys or girls. The remains have never been subjected to any rigorous scientific examination. Nevertheless, the requisite information which would make it possible to show whether or not these could indeed be the bones of

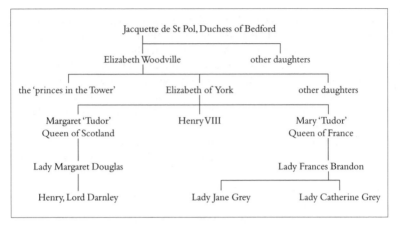

FAMILY TREE 9: The mtDNA family tree of the 'princes in the Tower' (simplified).

the 'princes' may in due course become available, and I have been struggling with this for some years now.

In 1787, the tomb of Mary 'Tudor', Queen of France and Duchess of Suffolk was opened in St Mary's Church, Bury St Edmunds, Suffolk. The queen's body was found to be well preserved, and locks of her long red hair were cut off as souvenirs. One such lock of hair remains in Bury St Edmunds, where it is displayed at Moyses Hall Museum. Mary 'Tudor', younger sister of King Henry VIII, was a daughter of Elizabeth of York, and thus the female line niece of the 'princes'. In 2007, I was given permission by the Bury St Edmunds museum authorities to attempt DNA testing of a few strands of this hair. Sadly, however, in the event it proved impossible to open the Bury St Edmunds locket without risking damage both to the locket itself and to the hair. Finally, the attempt had to be abandoned.

But the hair in the Moyses Hall Museum locket is not the only lock of Mary 'Tudor''s hair in existence above ground. After a prolonged search I located a second locket, and a sample of hair from this locket was tested in the hope of thereby obtaining the mtDNA sequence of the 'princes in the Tower'. The initial tests did not succeed in producing a complete and uncontaminated mtDNA sequence, but a few strands of the hair remain in a sealed container in my keeping, and since DNA testing has progressed in the last few years in may, at some stage, be possible to repeat the attempt.

The obvious alternative line of investigation, which would seek to replicate the research which led to Joy Ibsen in Canada, by identifying a living female-line descendant of Elizabeth Woodville or one of her sisters, is sadly impossible in the case of the 'princes', because research by myself and others has shown that there are now no known living all-female-line relatives of Elizabeth Woodville. Although my work on the DNA of the 'princes' has yet to yield positive results, it goes to show that there are still new avenues of research to be explored, and that in due course more may be known about Richard III. If we keep searching for new sources, new evidence, new approaches, some of the other aspects of Richard's story which have been contentious for the last five centuries may finally be resolved. Philippa Langley's determination to seek the real Richard III beneath a Leicester car park shows very clearly what can be achieved.

Meanwhile, hopefully at some suitable moment in the not too distant future, Richard III's remains will be given an honourable reburial. Provisional plans for a suitable tomb in Leicester Cathedral – just across the road from the Greyfriars site where his body lay for more than 500 years – have already been made. Of course today this cathedral is an Anglican church. Since I myself share Richard III's Catholic faith, I explored with the Dean of Leicester the possibility of the inclusion of elements of Catholic liturgy in plans for the reburial service, together with the invitation of members of the Catholic hierarchy. I was very happy to be reassured upon these points, because one of the things which we do know for certain about Richard III is that his religious beliefs were important to him during his lifetime.

As for the present position, we already know rather more about Richard III than we did before. We have a clear impression of his build and appearance. We know how he died. We know that, like the bodies of many defeated leaders, Richard's corpse was almost certainly mal-treated in the immediate aftermath of his defeat and death. We are now certain of his mitochondrial DNA sequence and have the possibility of learning more about his genetic make-up in the future.

Richard III's historiography has been the victim of more than 500 years of mythology and legends. One of the best-known of these was the story that his body was dug up at the Reformation and thrown into the River Soar. In the first edition of this book, I produced strong evidence against that story, and we can now be absolutely certain that it was nothing but a myth with no basis in fact. How many of the other stories about Richard III, which have been widely believed for centuries, belong in the same category? We cannot be sure. But the final debunking of the 'body in the river' legend and the positive identification of Richard's undisturbed burial at Leicester Greyfriars will hopefully warn the historians of the future to tread very carefully when handling the many other tales that have been passed down to us about Richard III.

Appendix 1

Richard III's Itinerary for 1485 [1]

MARCH
1 Tuesday –28 Monday	Westminster
[16 Wednesday	death of Queen Anne, Palace of Westminster]
[25 Friday	burial of Queen Anne, Westminster Abbey]
28–30	London (city)
30	Clerkenwell (Priory St John)
31	London

APRIL
1 Friday – 17 Sunday	London
18 Monday –20 Wednseday	Windsor
22–26	London
26–30	Westminster

MAY
1 Sunday –11 Wednesday	Westminster
12–16	Windsor
17	Berkhamsted

18–21	?
22–31	Kenilworth

JUNE

1 Wednesday	Coventry
2–5	?
6	Kenilworth
7–8	?
9–30	Nottingham

JULY

1–31 (? There are gaps)	Nottingham

AUGUST

1–9	Nottingham
10	?
11–17 (? There are gaps)	Bestwood
18	?
19?–20	Leicester
21	camp
[22	*battlefield, then Leicester – ?embalmers]*
[23–24	*Leicester – ?Newark]*
[25 onwards	*Leicester – Greyfriars choir]*

Appendix 2

Calendar for 1485 (March to August)

MARCH 1484/85 (OLD STYLE)

S	M	T	W	Th	F	S
		1	2	3	4	5
6	7	8	9	10	11	12
13	14	15	16[1]	17	18	19
20	21	22	23	24	25[2]	26
27[3]	28	29	30	31[4]		

APRIL

S	M	T	W	Th	F	S
					1[5]	2
3[6]	4	5	6	7	8	9
10	11	12	13	14	15	16
17	18	19	20	21	22	23
24	25	26	27	28	29	30

MAY

S	M	T	W	Th	F	S
1	2	3	4	5	6	7
8	9	10	11	12[7]	13	14
15	16	17	18	19	20	21[8]
22[9]	23	24	25	26	27	28
29[10]	30	31				

JUNE

S	M	T	W	Th	F	S
			1	2[11]	3	4
5	6	7	8	9	10	11
12	13	14	15	16	17	18
19	20	21	22	23	24	25
26[12]	27	28	29	30		

JULY

S	M	T	W	Th	F	S
					1	2
3	4	5	6	7	8	9
10	11	12	13	14	15	16
17	18	19	20	21	22	23
24	25	26	27	28	29	30
31						

AUGUST

S	M	T	W	Th	F	S
	1	2	3	4	5	6
7	8	9	10	11	12	13
14	15	16	17	18	19	20
21	22[13]	23	24	25[14]	26	27
28	29	30	31			

Appendix 3

Approximate Timetable for Monday 22 August 1485

All times are BST.

06.00	Prime.
06.10	Sunrise. Richard III gets up.
06.40	Mass begins in the royal tent.
07.10	Richard III starts his breakfast; meanwhile his esquires arm him.
07.30	Richard III leaves his tent to address his army.
08.00	The battle commences.
09.00	Terce. Richard III starts his charge towards Henry 'Tudor'.
09.15	Death of Richard III.
10.00	The battle ends.
11.00	Richard III's body, together with his crown, are brought to Henry 'Tudor', who is proclaimed king, has lunch, and conducts various urgent business.
12.00	Sext.
13.00	Henry VII orders his men to make ready to march to Leicester.
14.00	Henry VII's army leaves the battlefield.
15.00	None.
18.00	Vespers. The tail end of Henry VII's baggage train, including Richard III's dead body, arrives in Leicester. Richard's body is washed and embalmed(?), ready to be placed on display the following morning.
19.55	Sunset.

Appendix 4

John Speede's Account of the Burial of Richard III [1]

The slaine body of the usurping Tyrant, all tugged and torne, naked, and not so much as a clout left to cover his shame, was trussed behind *Blanch Seint-Leger* [*sic*] (or *White Bore*, a Pursevant at Armes,) like a hogge or Calfe, his head and Armes hanging on the one side of the horse, and his legges on the other, and all besprinckled with mire and bloud, was so brought into *Leicester*, and there for a miserable spectacle the space of two days lay naked and unburied, his remembrance being as odious to all, as his person deformed and loathsome to be looked upon: for whose further despite, the white Bore his cognizance was torne downe from every Signe, that his monument might perish, as did the monies of *Caligula*, which were all melted by the decree of the Senate: [2] Lastly his body without all funeral solemnity was buried in the Gray-Friers Church of that city. But King Henry his Successor, of a princely disposition, caused afterward his Tombe to bee made with a picture of Alablaster [*sic*], representing his person, and to be set up in the same church, which at the suppression of that Monastery [*sic*] was pulled downe, and utterly defaced; since when his grave overgrown with nettles and weedes, is very obscure and not to be found. Only the stone chest wherin his corpse lay is now made a drinking trough for horses at a common Inne, and retaineth the onely memory of this Monarches greatnesse. His body also (as tradition hath delivered) was borne out of the City and contemptuously bestowed under the end of *Bow-Bridge*. [3]

Appendix 5

DNA evidence relating to the putative remains of Margaret of York preserved in Mechelen, Belgium

The Mechelen Bones

During the twentieth century three sets of female remains were found in the former Franciscan church of Mechelen in locations which could potentially be interpreted as being consistent with the approximate site of the lost tomb of Richard III's sister, Margaret of York.[1]

1. remains found in 1936 (excavations led by Vaast Steurs)[2]
2. remains found in 1937 (excavations associated with the name of Maximilien Winders)[3]
3. remains found in 1955 (accidental discovery, subsequently examined by Professor François Twiesselmann).[4]

The bones from the 1955 discovery were photographed at the time, and these bones were subsequently coated with varnish. As a result, they can still be relatively easily identified. It is not now possible to distinguish for certain which of the other female remains from Mechelen's Franciscan priory site were discovered in 1936, and which in 1937.[5]

The Samples

On 27 April 2005, in the presence of M. Henri Installé (then archivist of the town of Mechelen), Professor Cassiman of the Catholic University of Leuven took samples of the female remains from the former Franciscan church of Mechelen as follows:

V812/1   right radius, left ulna and right humerus
V812/2   left humerus, right ulna, fibula and left femur
V812/3   a piece of left side lower jaw, right humerus, left femur and a metatarsus

The numbering of the samples corresponds to the numbering of the boxes in which the bones were then stored at the Mechelen Town Archives. V812/2 comprises varnished bones from the 1955 (Twiesselmann) discovery.[6] V812/1 and V812/3 are the remains excavated in the 1930s (Steurs; Winders). As has already been noted, it is not currently possible to state categorically which set of remains are the Steurs bones and which set the Winders bones.

Mitochondrial DNA Analysis of the Mechelen Bones

Professor Cassiman subsequently reported to the town of Mechelen that mtDNA analyses had been successfully carried out, yielding sequences, or partial sequences[7] for some, at least, of the samples taken from each of the three sets of remains (for details, see Appendix 1).

V812/1 and V812/3 (comprising the two sets of bones discovered in the 1930s) both yielded uncontaminated results. In the case of each of these skeletons, two distinct specimens had produced consistent and mutually confirmatory results which reveal that the mtDNA of V812/1 belongs to haplogroup V, while the mtDNA sequence of V812/3 belongs to haplogroup J.

Sample V812/2.7[8] also yielded 'pure' results, but the remaining samples from V812/2 were contaminated.[9] Supporting evidence in favour of the 'pure' sequence found in V812/2.7 was found in each of the other samples from V812/2. However, it remains uncertain whether this sequence is really that of V812/2 or whether it derives from the source of the contamination (possibly the varnish with which the bones had been treated – see above). If the mtDNA sequence yielded by sample V812/2.7 is indeed the mtDNA sequence of the person in question, then that individual belonged to haplogroup H, the most widespread group in Europe.

Comparison with the mtDNA sequence for Margaret of York

The DNA results from the Mechelen remains were compared with the mtDNA sequence of Mrs Joy Ibsen, descendant in an all-female line of Margaret of York's elder sister, Anne of York, Duchess of Exeter. The mtDNA sequence of Joy Ibsen was checked by Professor Cassiman, using cheek swabs (G3993-1.1 and G3993-1.2). Joy's mtDNA sequence belonged to haplogroup J.[10] This indicated that she was, in fact, related in the female line of descent to V812/3 (the individual whose bones were discovered at Mechelen in the 1930s by either Steurs or Winders). This is not particularly surprising, since it is known that Cecily Neville's mtDNA derives from her unknown maternal great grandmother, who quite probably came from the region of modern Belgium. However, Professor Cassiman's detailed examination of mutations in the nucleotide bases outside of the control region normally tested in mtDNA analyses revealed that Joy Ibsen's mutations were not identical to those of V812/3. There were four points of difference between the sequence of Joy Ibsen and that of V812/3,[11] suggesting that their relationship could be quite remote.[12] Moreover, since V812/3 exhibited mutations which Joy did not possess, V812/3 can neither be in, nor close to, Joy Ibsen's direct female ancestral line.

Conclusions

On the basis of this mtDNA analysis, neither skeleton V812/1 nor skeleton V812/3 can be the remains of Margaret of York. This outcome appears consistent with the results of carbon-14 dating tests, carried out on the Steurs and Winders bones in 1969–70, which indicated that these bones were too early in date to be those of the duchess.[13]

In the case of skeleton V812/2 the DNA result is necessarily less definitive, due to contamination. The mtDNA sequence apparently revealed for this skeleton certainly does not correspond with Joy Ibsen's sequence. However, it remains uncertain whether the mtDNA sequence yielded equivocally by the V812/2 samples is really that of the skeleton itself. The apparent sequence may merely be the result of contamination. At the present time it is, therefore, impossible to state with absolute certainty that skeleton V812/2 cannot belong to Margaret of York.

In some ways, this is unfortunate. V812/2 is the set of Mechelen remains which some previously considered the most likely (of the three sets of bones found to date) to actually be the remains of Margaret of York.[14] The bones and hair of V812/2 seem to come from the reburial of a corpse which had been disturbed and parts of which had been lost. This hypothesis is not inconsistent with the presumed circumstances surrounding the destruction of Margaret of York's original tomb during the religious disturbances of the sixteenth century. It still remains desirable, therefore, to seek to clarify the position in respect of V812/2.

Summary of the Results of the DNA tests

N.B. only points of difference from the Cambridge Reference Sequence are noted here.

V812/1.1 (humerus) and **V812/1.2** (radius) both yielded: **16298 C; 72 C**

V812/2. 7 (tibia) yielded **16354 T**; **263 G**; **315.1 C**
This was the only clear set of results for V812/2. The other samples all yielded contra-dictory double readings in one or more positions.

V812/3.1 (tooth 1) and **V812/3.2** (tooth 2), both yielded:
16069 T; **16126 C**; **16311 C**; **73 G**; **152 C**; **185 A**; **188 G**; **228 A**; **263 G**; **295 T**; **315.1 C**

G3993-1.1 and **G3993-1.2** both yielded:
16069 T; **16126 C**; **73 G**; **146 C**; **185 A**; **188 G**; **263 G**; **295 T**; **315.1 C**

b. The following two tables set out Professor Cassiman's detailed results

mtDNA sequence		16069	16126	73	146	185	188	263	295	315.1
ference		C	T	A	T	G	A	A	C	/
993-1.1	16020–16390; 58–367	T	C	G	C	A	G	G	T	C
993-1.2	16020–16390; 58–367	T	C	G	C	A	G	G	T	C

TABLE 1: The mtDNA sequence of Richard III and his siblings.

mtDNA sequence		16069	16126	16162	16209	16291	16294
Reference		C	T	A	T	C	C
V812/1.1 humerus	16009-16365; 49-154	★	★	★	★	★	★
V812/1.2 radius	16009-16365; 49-154	★	★	★	★	★	★
V812/2.1 humerus (1)	16100-16365; 49-154; 175-347	?	C/T	★	★	★★	C/
V812/2.2 humerus (2)	16100-16365; 49-154; 175-347	?	★	★	★	★	★
V812/2.3 humerus (3)	16100-16365; 49-154; 175-347	?	★	★	★	★	★
V812/2.4 humerus	16100-16365; 49-154; 175-347	?	★	A/G	C/T	C/T	★
V812/2.5 humerus	16100-16365; 49-154; 175-347	?	★	A/G	C/T	C/T	★
V812/2.6 tibia	16100-16365; 49-154; 175-347	?	★	★	★	★	★
V812/2.7 tibia	16100-16365; 49-154; 175-347	?	★	★	★	★	★
V812/2.8 ulna	16100-16365; 49-154	?	★	★	★	★	★
V812/3.1 tooth1	16009-16365; 49-154; 175-347	T	C	★	★	★	★
V812/2.2 tooth2	16009-16365; 49-154; 175-347	T	C	★	★	★	★

The table shows the various positions in the sequence where a difference from an international reference sequence ('Anderson' or 'Cambridge Reference Sequence') of human mtDNA was observed.

/ = nucleotide not present in the reference sequence
? = sequence could not be determined
★ = identical to the reference sequence
★★ = not possible to obtain confirmation even by the analysis of several DNA fragments
G/A (&c) = the presence of two nucleotides

16298	16304	16311	16354	72	73	152	185	188	228	263	295	315.1
	T	T	C	T	A	T	G	A	G	A	C	/
	★	★	★	C	★	★	?	?	?	?	?	?
	★	★	★	C	★	★	?	?	?	?	?	?
	★★	★	T	★	A/G	C/T	★	★	★	G	★	C
	★	★	C/T	★	★	★	★	★	★	G	★	C
	★	★	C/T	★	★	C/T	★	★	★	G	★	C
	★	★	C/T	★	A/G	★	★	★	★	G	★	C
	★	★	C/T	★	A/G	★	★	★	★	G	★	C
	★	★	T	★	★	C/T	★	★	★	G	★	C
	★	★	T	★	★	★	★	★	★	G	★	C
	C/T	★	C/T	★	★	★	?	?	?	?	?	?
	★	C	★	★	G	C	A	G	A	G	T	C
	★	C	★	★	G	C	A	G	A	G	T	C

Appendix 6

Richard III's Epitaph

George Buck's Latin Text

George Buck's *History of the Life and Reigne of Richard the Third* is extant in two versions: a posthumous edition published in London in 1647, and reprinted in facsimile with an introduction by A.R. Myers at Wakefield in 1973[1] (hereinafter 'Buck 1647'), and an earlier and more accurate text which dates from 1619, but which was not published until the twentieth century, in the edition by Kincaid[2] (hereinafter 'Buck 1619'). The following (with one modification – where the text of Buck 1647 appears to give a grammatically more accurate reading)[3] is the epitaph as published in Buck 1619. The punctuation is modern.[4] Variant readings from Buck 1647, and from Sandford are supplied in the footnotes. The greater part of the Latin text of the epitaph is agreed by all the published sources, but there are a number of minor variations, making it somewhat difficult to establish a completely authoritative version.[5]

Epitaphium Regis Ricardi[6] tertii, Sepulti apud[7] Leicestriam, iussu et sumptibus Sancti[8] Regis Henrici Septimi[9]

Hic ego quem vario tellus sub marmore claudit
Tertius a iusta[10] voce Ricardus[11] eram.
Tutor eram patriae,[12] patruus[13] pro iure nepotis
Dirupta, tenui regna Britanna fide.
Sexaginta dies binis dumtaxat[14] ademptis
Aestatesque[15] tuli tunc[16] mea sceptra duas.[17]
Fortiter in bello certans[18] desertus ab Anglis

Rex Henrice tibi septime succubui.
At sumptu pius ipse tuo sic ossa decoras[19]
Regem olimque facis regis honore coli
Quattuor[20] exceptis iam tantum quinque[21] bis annis
Acta trecenta[22] quidem lustra salutis erant.[23]
Anteque[24] Septembris undena luce Kalendas[25]
Reddideram[26] rubrae[27] iura petita[28] rosae.[29]
At mea, quisquis eris, propter commissa precare,[30]
Sit minor ut precibus poena levata[31] tuis.

Buck's published 'translation' of Richard III's epitaph

In the early nineteenth century the epitaph was reprinted in John Nichols' *History and Antiquities of the County of Leicester*. His text, complete with notes, appeared also in the additions Nichols made to Hutton's *The Battle of Bosworth Field*, second edition.[32] There, Nichols also supplied the following versified English translation, which he ascribed to Buck.[33] Although the translation is rather free (and indeed, sometimes inaccurate), hitherto this appears to have been the only published English version of the epitaph.

I who am laid beneath this marble stone,
Richard the Third, possessed the British throne.
My Country's guardian in my nephew's claim,
By trust betray'd[34] I to the kingdom came.
Two years and sixty days, save two, I reign'd;
And bravely strove in fight; but, unsustain'd
My English left me in the luckless field,
Where I to Henry's arms was forc'd to yield.
Yet at his cost my corse this tomb obtains,
Who piously interr'd me, and ordains
That regal honours wait a king's remains.
Th'year thirteen hundred 'twas and eighty four[35]
The twenty-first of August, when its power
And all its rights I did to the Red Rose restore.
Reader, whoe'er thou art, thy prayers bestow,
T'atone my crimes and ease my pains below.[36]

The Epitaph of Catherine of France (widow of Henry V)[37]

This epitaph is comparable in date, metre and length to that of Richard III. Note the use of direct address in line 2, and the use of the word *Britanna* in lines 7 and 16.

Hic Katherina iacet Francorum filia regis,
Heres & regni, Carole sexte, tui.
Henrici quinti thalamo bis leta iugali
Nam sic vir duplici clarus honore fuit:
Iure suo Anglorum, Katherine iure triumphans
Francorum obtinuit ius, decus imperij.
Grata venit letis felix regina Britannis
Perque dies celebrant quatuor ore Deum.
Edidit Henricum genebunda puerpera regem.
Cuius in imperio Francus & Anglus erat.
Non sibi sed regno felici sidere natum;
Sed patri & matri religione parem.
Post ex Owino Tiddero tertia proles,
Nobilis Edmundus te Katherina beat:
Septimus Henricus quo non prestantior alter
Filius Edmundi, gemma Britanna fuit.
Felix ergo uxor, mater, ter filia felix,
Ast avia hec felix terque quaterque fuit.

One of the epitaphs from the tomb of Henry VII and Elizabeth of York:[38]

Septimus hic situs est Henricus, gloria regum
Cunctorum, ipsius qui tempestate fuerunt,
Ingenio atque opibus gestarum & nomine rerum,
Accessere quibus nature dona benigne:[39]
Frontis honos, facies augusta, heroica forma,
Iunctaque ei suavis coniunx perpulchra, pudica,
Et secunda fuit: felices prole parentes,
Henricum quibus octavum terra Anglia debes.

Notes

Introduction

1. For Henry VII's surname see below, and also J. Ashdown-Hill, *Royal Marriage Secrets*, Stroud 2013 (forthcoming), chapter 5.

1. 'Your Beloved Consort'

1. Letter of condolence to Richard III from the Doge and Senate of Venice: *Calendar of State Papers – Venetian, vol 1, 1202–1509*, p. 154.
2. The precise nature of Queen Anne Neville's fatal illness is nowhere recorded, but it was probably tuberculosis (consumption): *Road*, p. 196. Myers/Buck, p. 44, describes her as 'languishing in weaknesse and extremity of sorrow' following the death of her son. My description of her likely symptoms is based on the account of tuberculosis in R. Porter, *The Greatest Benefit to Mankind*, London 1997, pp. 309–10.
3. 'Suger candy', 'wyne' and 'water of honysoclys' were listed together with additional unspecified 'medesyns' supplied to the sick Lady Howard in 1465, though details of her symptoms are not recorded: BL, Add. MS 46349, f. 87r; *HHB*, part 1, p. 304.
4. *vanisque mutatoriis vestium Annae, reginae, atque Dominae Elizabeth, primogentiae defuncti regis eisdem colore et forma distributis*: *Crowland*, p. 174. However, I take issue with the translation of this passage given by Pronay and Cox, and a different translation is offered here. See also L. Visser-Fuchs, 'A Commentary on the Continuation', *Ric.* 7 (1985–87), p. 521, and also www.r3.org/bookcase/croyland/index.html (consulted June 2009).

5. In terms of the medieval English calendar, Anne Neville and her son died in the *same* year (1484). This is because in England the medieval calendar year began not on 1 January, but on Lady Day (25 March). Edward of Middleham died in April 1484, and Anne Neville eleven months later, on 16 March, eight days before the end of 1484 according to the medieval reckoning.

6. *Crowland*, p. 175 – see *R3MK*, pp. 250 and 309, n. 2.

7. For the date, the solar eclipse and anne's death see *Crowland*, p. 175.

8. Collop Monday (which fell on 14 February in 1484/5) was the day for using up the last scraps of meat before Lent. Ash Wednesday (16 February 1484/5) is the first day of Lent and a fast day. It is so called because a cross of ashes is traced on the foreheads of the faithful at mass that day.

9. See above, note 5.

10. The time was recorded at Augsburg, where the eclipse was total: http://ls.kuleuven.ac.be/cgi-bin/wa?A2=ind0103&L=vvs&P=1445, citing Achilli Pirmini Gassari: *Annales Augustburgenses*.

11. The central duration of the eclipse was 4 minutes 53 seconds: http://sunearth.gsfc.nasa.gov/eclipse/SEsaros/SEsaros121.html.

12. *Crowland*, p. 175.

13. C.A. Halsted, *Richard III*, London, 1844, vol. 2, p. 399, citing BL, Cotton MS Faustina, c. Iii. 405 and Cooper's *Annals of Cambridge*, p. 229.

14. There were, of course, fifteenth-century reports suggesting that Cecily Neville was unfaithful to her husband on at least one occasion, leading to the supposed bastardy of Edward IV. However, these rumours were very firmly countered by Cecily herself in her last months of life, as the words of her will clearly demonstrate. In that document she insisted on the fact that Edward IV was the son of her husband: J. Nicholls and J. Bruce, eds, *Wills from Doctors' Commons. A selection of Wills of eminent persons proved in the PCC 1495–1695*, Camden old series, vol. 83, London, 1863, p. 1.

15. Based upon no real evidence, two other bastard sons have been imputed to Richard by some writers. However, the dates of birth of these children are also unknown.

16. Both Anne and her sister, Isabel, Duchess of Clarence, died comparatively young, and Isabel was survived by only two children. Moreover, Eleanor and Elizabeth Talbot, who were first cousins of Anne and Isabel Neville, also seem to have had difficulty in producing children. See Ashdown-Hill, 'Norfolk Requiem', *Ric.* 12, pp. 198–217 (pp. 198–203).

17. See, for example, A.F. Sutton and L. Visser-Fuchs, *The Hours of Richard III*, Stroud, 1990; and J. Hughes, *The Religious Life of Richard III*, Stroud, 1997.

18. See Introduction.

19. For details of the funeral arrangements for Edward IV, see *Beloved Cousyn*, pp. 83–84.

20. 'Quene Anne deseyd thys same yere at Westmynster that Thomas Hylle was mayor the xvj day of Marche and bered the ix day after ate Westmynster. God have merci on her soulle.' BL, Harl. MS 541, f. 217v, as quoted in J. Gairdner, *History of the Life and Reign of Richard the Third*, Cambridge, 1898, p. 205, n. 1.

21. *Sepulta est … non cum minore honore quam sicut reginam decuit sepeliri*, *Crowland*, pp. 174–75. Such a specific statement from a rather variable source, often hostile to Richard III, makes it quite certain that Queen Anne Neville was buried with the full panoply of late medieval royal honours.

22. English kings at this period did not openly attend funerals of members of the royal family, though they were sometimes present semi-secretly, in a screened 'closet': A.F. Sutton, and L. Visser-Fuchs with R. A. Griffiths, *The Royal Funerals of the House of York at Windsor*, London, 2005, p. 50.

23. The Stuart sovereigns seem to have especially favoured Holy Week and Michaelmas for this ceremony (though it could be performed at any time). French sovereigns also regularly favoured Easter for 'touching'.

24. M. Bloch (trans. J.E. Anderson), *The Royal Touch, Sacred Monarch and Scrofula in England and France*, London, 1973, p. 224. To take Holy Communion at or around Easter was and is the minimum requirement for a practising Catholic.

25. Bloch, *Royal Touch*, p. 22.

26. Edward III is reported to have challenged his rival, Philippe VI, to compete with him in a 'touching' ceremony to establish which of them was rightful King of France: Bloch, *Royal Touch*, pp. 1–2. See also *ibid.*, pp. 65, 220. Subsequently, the ritual was particularly promoted by the incoming 'Tudor' dynasty – the legitimacy of whose claim was more than a little suspect. Later still, the exiled legitimist Stuart claimants to the throne would continue to 'touch' in exile until the death of the dynasty's last direct descendant in 1807. The Hanoverian kings, however, never attempted to perform this rite, despite receiving requests to do so.

27. Bloch, *Royal Touch*, p. 54.

28. *Ibid.*, p. 249.

29. *Ibid.*, p. 65. Fortescue was later reconciled to the Yorkist regime, and retracted his comments. See also N. Woolf, *The Sovereign Remedy, Touch Pieces and the King's Evil*, British Association of Numismatic Societies, 1990, pp. 6–7.

30. Bloch, *Royal Touch*, pp. 181–82.

31. By the 'Tudor' period, the 'touch pieces' presented to the sick who had received the royal touch were undoubtedly gold 'angels'. Prior to the Yorkist period each person touched by the king had subsequently been given a silver penny by the royal almoner, but the gold angel was introduced by Edward IV, and Bloch has suggested that this may have been with the

deliberate intention of encouraging the sick to come to him for healing (thereby gaining 80 pence rather than a single silver penny): Bloch, *Royal Touch*, pp. 66, 182; Woolf, *The Sovereign Remedy*, p. 6.

32. The gatehouse, and parts of the church, of the Priory of the Knights Hospitaller at Clerkenwell survive, and are now in the hands of the so-called 'Venerable Order of St John of Jerusalem', a Victorian Protestant English 'recreation' of the Order of Knights Hospitaller. The original Sovereign Order of St John of Jerusalem still survives as an order of the Catholic Church, based nowadays in Rome.

33. The first antiphon begins: *Mandatum novum do vobis* ('a new commandment I give unto you'). The word 'Maundy' is a corruption of the Latin *mandatum*.

34. E.E. Ratcliffe and P.A. Wright, *The Royal Maundy, a brief outline of its history and ceremonial* (The Royal Almonry, Buckingham Palace, seventh edition, 1960), pp. 6–9, citing a manuscript account in the College of Arms describing the practice in the early 'Tudor' period. The sovereign continued to perform the annual foot-washing ceremony in person until the deposition of James II.

35. Bloch, *Royal Touch*, p. 92.

36. *Ibid.*, p. 93.

37. *Ibid.*, p. 251.

38. *Ibid.*, p. 100. No Good Friday fell within the very short reign of Edward V, who therefore never made this offering as king.

39. *Tenebrae* ['Darkness'] was the traditional name given to the office of Matins during Holy Week.

2. 'It Suits the King of England to Marry Straight Away'

1. See below, note 15.

2. J. Ashdown-Hill, '"Yesterday my Lord of Gloucester came to Colchester …"', *Essex Archaeology & History* 36, 2005, pp. 212–17. There is some evidence that Howard condoned the sexual experimentation of young men. He financed a trip by his young cousin John Mowbray, 4th Duke of Norfolk to a brothel, and Howard's own eldest son seems to have had an illegitimate son. Θ, subsection 5.8.10 and *Beloved Cousyn*, chapter 4. For the name 'John de Pountfreit' (John of Pontefract), see Harl. 433, vol. 1, p. 271.

3. *Beloved Cousyn*, chapter 4, n.19. The surname 'de Pountfreit' appears to imply that John may have been either born or brought up at Pontefract.

4. *Road*, p. 202.

5. On the legitimist stance of the Yorkists in general, and Richard III personally, see *Eleanor*, pp. 10–12.

6. See below: Elizabeth of York's letter to the Duke of Norfolk.

7. From Edward I to Henry VI all the kings of England had married foreign ladies as their queens consort (though Henry IV's first wife, married before his accession, was from the English aristocracy). Edward IV had broken this traditional marriage pattern, arguably with disastrous results.

8. Or possibly '… greatly serving God and honouring Him …' The Portuguese possessive adjective *sua* could refer to either sex. Its intended application in this sentence is therefore ambiguous. It might refer either to the princess or to the Deity. I am grateful to Carolina Barbara for drawing my attention to this point.

9. *pela concordia que no mesmo Reyno de Ingraterra com seu casamento e ajuntamento com a parte del Rey se segue, de tanto seruiço de Deos e honra sua por se unir em hum a parte de Alencastro e Jorca que são as duas partes daquelle Reyno, de que nascem as divisiões e males sobre a socessão*: A.J. Salgado, *Álvaro Lopes de Chaves, Livro de Apontamentos (1438–1489), Códice 443 da Colecção Pombalina da B.N.L.*, Lisboa, 1983, p. 256; also quoted in D.M. Gomes dos Santos, *O Mosteiro de Jesus de Aveiro*, 3 vols, Lisboa, 1963, vol. 1, p. 93. The council meeting was held in Alcobaça in 1485, but the precise date is not recorded; *Conselho que se teue em Alcobaça na era de 1485 sobre o casamento da Ifante Dona Joana com el Rej de Ingrayerra Richarte que foj Duque de Gronsetra e jrmão del Rej Duarte do ditto Rejno*: Salgado, *Álvaro Lopes de Chaves*, p. 254.

10. She is frequently referred to in English as *Isabella*, but there is no good reason for this. Her name in Spanish was *Isabel* and that form of the name also exists in English.

11. J. Ashdown-Hill, 'The Lancastrian Claim to the Throne', *Ric.* 13 (2003), pp. 27–38.

12. TNA, Warrants for Issues E404/78/3/47, 22 March 1485, cited in B. Williams, 'Rui de Sousa's embassy and the fate of Richard, Duke of York', *Ric.* 5, pp. 341–45, n. 20.

13. My italics. *Poderá casar com a Ifante Dona Isabel de Castella e fazer su ligua com os Reys della e ficaros por imigo e contrajro*: Salgado, *Álvaro Lopes de Chaves*, p. 255; also quoted in Gomes dos Santos, *O Mosteiro de Jesus de Aveiro*, vol. 1, p. 92.

14. *poderlheam os Reis de Castella dar soa filha major por molher*: Salgado, *Álvaro Lopes de Chaves*, p. 255; Gomes dos Santos, *O Mosteiro de Jesus de Aveiro*, vol. 1, p. 92. Although the Portuguese account refers to Isabel as 'of Castile' (which she was, on her mother's side), it would be more usual to refer to her as 'of Aragon', acknowledging her father's title. It is possible that records of Richard's enquiries regarding a possible marriage with the Infanta Isabel survive in Spanish archives, but if so they have not yet surfaced.

15. *a El Rej de Ingraterra convem de casar loguo*: Salgado, *Álvaro Lopes de Chaves*, p. 255; Gomes dos Santos, *O Mosteiro de Jesus de Aveiro*, vol. 1, p. 92.

16. *casamento da filha del Rej Duarte de Inglaterra … com o duque de Beja Dom Manuel … o qual casamento antes fora a el Rej apontado por Duarte Brandão sendo uindo por embaixador del Rej Richarte jrmão do ditto Rej Duarte a jurar as ligas e commeter*

casamento com a Iffante Dona Joana: A. Mestrinho Salgado and Salgado, *Álvaro Lopes de Chaves*, as cited in A.S. Marques 'Álvaro Lopes de Cheves [*sic*]: A Portuguese Source', *Ricardian Bulletin*, Autumn 2008, pp. 25–27. For a discussion of this second aspect of the Portuguese marriage proposal, see below.

17. Lopes de Chaves, cited in Gomes dos Santos, *O Mosteiro*, p. 95.

18. B. Williams, 'The Portuguese Connection and the Significance of "the Holy Princess"', *Ric.* 6 (1983), pp. 138–45 (pp. 141–42).

19. I am grateful to Lynda Pidgeon for her comments on the inheritance of the Scales title. This ultimately fell into abeyance between the heirs of the two daughters of Robert, 3rd Lord Scales: *Complete Peerage*, vol. 11, London, 1949, p. 507.

20. King John II of Portugal, 'in his letter sent from Santarém (transcribed by Lopes) makes it clear that even at the time of Edward Woodville's first stop in Lisbon, Henry was already married to Elizabeth and reigning over England': personal communication from Antonio Marques, January 2009.

21. See below: chapter 8.

22. Isabel of Aragón was born on 2 October 1470. She was heiress presumptive to the thrones of Castile and Aragon until the birth of her only brother Juan, in 1478, and again, briefly, from Juan's death in 1497 until her own demise the following year. She ultimately married first Alfonso of Portugal, son and heir of John II, and later John's cousin, Manuel I (formerly Duke of Beja).

23. Lopes de Chaves, cited in Gomes dos Santos, *O Mosteiro*, p. 95. By comparison, Edward IV's negotiations for his daughters' marriages with France and Scotland were very specific. Edward named Cecily as the bride for James III's son and specified arrangements for a replacement should Cecily die. The Treaty of Picquigny stipulated that Elizabeth was to marry the Dauphin, and if she should die Mary was to take her place.

24. In the Iberian peninsular the title 'the Infanta' *tout court* was generally applied to the *eldest* daughter of a sovereign, and it meant roughly 'the [royal] daughter'. Younger daughters of a monarch, on the other hand, were designated as 'the Infanta [+ first name]'.

25. Their second daughter, Mary, had died in 1482, aged fifteen; their third son, George, died in 1479 at the age of two, and it is possible that their eldest son, 'Edward V', had by this time also succumbed to death by natural causes.

26. 'To the archbishop of Canterbury, mandate. The tenor of the petition presented to the pope of Manuel, Duke of Beja and Viseu [*Begie et Visen' Ducis*], and Anne Plantagenet, daughter of the late Edward, king of England, was that for certain reasonable causes they desire to be joined together in marriage, but that since they are related in the fourth and fourth degrees of consanguinity, they cannot do so without apostolic dispensation. Manuel is also, as is alleged, administrator, deputed by the apostolic see, of the military order of Jesus Christ. At their supplication, and since, as is also alleged, Anne has no fixed dwelling place but

follows the court of Henry, king of England, the pope hereby commissions and orders the above archbishop to dispense them – if the foregoing is true and if Anne shall not have been ravished on this account – freely to contract marriage together and to remain therein after it has been contracted, notwithstanding the said impediments, declaring the offspring of this marriage legitimate': *Calendar of Entries in the Papal Registers relating to Great Britain and Ireland*, Vol XV 1484–92, no 631, cited by M. Barnfield, 'Diriment Impediments, Dispensations and Divorce: Richard III and Matrimony', *Ric.* 17, pp. 84–98 (p. 98, n. 45).

27. It may even be that, initially, Henry tried to adopt Richard III's entire marriage package, with himself as Infanta Joana's substitute bridegroom. On this basis Elizabeth of York would still have married Dom Manuel. It is noteworthy that Henry did not, in fact, immediately contract a marriage with Elizabeth of York. However, Joana's matrimonial record, together with the story of her prophetic dream (see below, chapter 8) suggest she would have been unlikely to accept Richard's supplanter as an alternative spouse. Subsequently (perhaps because of Joana's reluctance), Henry therefore revised his plans, marrying Elizabeth of York himself. Nevertheless, the projected marriage with the Duke of Beja was not abandoned, and ultimately Anne of York took her elder sister's place as the proposed bride. This revised marriage project was also later abandoned, when Dom Manuel became heir presumptive to the Portuguese throne on the death of his first cousin once removed, the Infante Dom Alfonso. At that point Manuel married Alfonso's widow, Isabel of Aragón (who, intriguingly, had been the second string to Richard III's matrimonial bow in the spring of 1485).

28. Harl. 433, f. 308v; vol. 3, p. 190.

29. This marriage was annulled by Henry VII soon after his accession, and although he subsequently married Cecily to Lord Welles, Cecily was actually available in 1486, at the time when her uncle, the self-styled 'Count Scales', was talking to the King of Portugal. For references to Cecily's Scrope marriage, see: Ellis/Vergil, p. 215; P. Sheppard Routh, '"Lady Scroop Daughter of K. Edward": an Enquiry', *Ric.* 9 (1991–93), pp. 410–16 (pp. 412, 416, n. 12); and J. Laynesmith, *The Last Medieval Queens*, Oxford, 2004, p. 199.

30. *R3MK*, p. 257, quoting Kincaid's edition of Buck's reported text of Elizabeth of York's letter. Also Myers/Buck, p. 128. This letter apparently remained amongst the Howard family papers until at least the early seventeenth century, but is now lost.

31. Myers/Buck, p. 128.

32. *Crowland*, pp. 174–75.

33. *Ibid.*, pp. 176–77.

34. *R3MK*, pp. 262, 264.

35. See, for example, Myers/Buck, p. 44.

36. It is possible that later in the year, and on the eve of battle, Richard may have made some statement about the succession (see below, chapter 7).

37. R. Horrox, 'John de la Pole, Earl of Lincoln', *ODNB*.

38. *Ibid.*

39. R. Horrox, *British Library Harleian Manuscript 433*, vol. 4, London, 1983, p. 66.

40. Horrox, 'John de la Pole, Earl of Lincoln', *ODNB*.

41. C. Carpenter, 'Edward, called Earl of Warwick', *ODNB*. Carpenter also refers to Warwick as potentially Richard III's 'heir apparent'. This is also an error. Warwick could only possibly have been regarded as an heir *presumptive*.

42. Confirmed by the York city register, 13 May 1485, '*when it was determyned that a letter should be consaved to be direct to the lordes of Warwik and Lincoln and othre of the counsail at Sheriff Hoton ffrome the maire and his bretherne*': L.C. Attreed, ed., *York House Books 1461–1490*, vol. 1, Stroud, 1991, p. 361.

3. 'Tapettes of Verdoures with Crownes and Rooses'

1. Nicolas, p. 144.

2. E. Power, ed., *The Goodman of Paris (Le Ménagier de Paris) a Treatise on Moral and Domestic Economy by a Citizen of Paris c. 1393*, London, 1928 (1992), pp. 35–37.

3. J. Ashdown-Hill, 'Queen Elizabeth Woodville and the *Angelus*', *Ric.* 10 (1994–96), pp. 326–27.

4. Power, ed., *The Goodman of Paris*, pp. 39–41. The *Gloria* is not said or sung at ordinary weekday masses. Its inclusion in the list indicates that a Sunday or feast day mass is being described. However, at this period, more feast days would have been celebrated than is the norm in the modern ecclesiastical calendar. In the modern mass rite only very major feasts still have a 'sequence' said or sung before the *Alleluia*.

5. Power, ed., *The Goodman of Paris*, p. 41, present writer's emphasis.

6. See Sutton & Visser-Fuchs, 'The Hours of Richard III'.

7. *Beloved Cousyn*, chapter 7.

8. http://www.godecookery.com/how2cook/howto05.htm (consulted December 2008).

9. http://www.godecookery.com/how2cook/howto05.htm (consulted December 2008).

10. P. W. Hammond, *Food & Feast in Medieval England*, Stroud, 1993, p. 105.

11. A reduced pre-Communion fast of one hour is stipulated for Catholics, even today.

12. www.probertencyclopaedia.com/cgi-bin/res.pl?keyword=Fifteenth& offset=0 (consulted December 2008).

13. http://www.godecookery.com/how2cook/howto05.htm (consulted December 2008).

14. T. Scully, *The Art of Cookery in the Middle Ages*, Woodbridge, 1995, pp. 119–120.

15. Soc. Ant., MS 77, f. 26r; *HHB*, part 2, p. 327.

16. Power, ed., *The Goodman of Paris*, pp. 148–55.

17. The final course of the 'Goodman's' dinner menu 1 comprises pears, comfits, medlars, nuts, hippocras and wafers, and his second dinner menu also ends with a sweet course. However, menu 23 (a fish dinner) *begins* with fruit (cooked apples and ripe figs) and ends with porpoise, mackerel, oysters and cuttle fish. His twenty-two other sample menus have courses which, to modern eyes, do not noticeably differ from one another. In general terms there was no medieval concept of a fish course, a meat course or a sweet course.

18. Quoted in D. Hartley and M.M. Elliot, *Life and Work of the People of England – the Fifteenth Century*, London, 1925, p. 17.

19. L. and J. Laing, *Medieval Britain, the Age of Chivalry*, London, 1996, p. 180.

20. See, for example, M. Black, *The Medieval Cookbook*, London, 1992.

21. *Eleanor*, p. 15.

22. Laing, *Medieval Britain*, p. 181.

23. *Ibid.*

24. *Ibid.*, pp. 182–83.

25. The eldest, Anne, Duchess of Exeter, had died in 1476.

26. Certainly during Richard's reign, envoys to the Habsburg court regularly passed through England (see below).

27. Richard III had been eight years old when his father was killed.

28. *Beloved Cousyn*, pp. 25–26 and figure 11.

29. *Itinerary*.

30. Nicolas, p. 123: 'Reparacion off the Kinges Carre'.

31. For example, one possibility might be that the king used a carriage in order to attend funerals at which he was not officially present.

32. A.F. Sutton & P.W. Hammond, eds, *The Coronation of Richard III, the extant documents*, Gloucester, 1983, p. 47.

33. Sutton & Hammond, *Coronation*, p. 68.

34. A. Prockter and R. Taylor, *The A to Z of Elizabethan London*, London, 1979, p. 21 (map reference K5).

35. www.maney.co.uk/files/misc/HenryChapter3.pdf (consulted January 2009). In September 1485 Curteys was reappointed by Henry VII.

36. Nicolas, p. 132. For evidence of the use of tapestry by John Howard (Duke of Norfolk), see Θ.

37. Nicolas, p. 140. 'Paled' means arranged '*per pale*' (see below note 38).

38. This is a heraldic term, meaning in two broad stripes, set side by side.

39. Nicolas, pp. 132–33, repeated pp. 143–44.

40. The former London home of Richard Neville, Earl of Warwick, and subsequently of his son-in-law, the Duke of Clarence, on the site of the present Canon Street Station.

41. Nicolas, pp. 140–42.

42. *Ibid.*, p. 144.

43. Bishop Thomas Langton, an admirer and supporter of Richard III, is said to have remarked that 'sensual pleasure' held sway at Richard's court, and Ross has therefore argued that 'Richard's court was perhaps as gay and hedonistic as Edward's had been': Ross, *Richard III*, p. 142, and citing Alison Hanham's reconstruction of Langton's Latin sentence.

44. At this period shirts were underclothes.

45. Originally, at least, 'cordwain' described sheep or goat leather imported from Córdoba in Spain.

46. Nicolas, pp. 146–52.

47. A.F. Sutton & L. Visser-Fuchs, 'Richard III's Books', *Ric.* 7–10 (1985–96).

48. Θ.

49. See also chapter 7 below.

50. A.F. Sutton and L. Visser-Fuchs with R.A. Griffiths, *The Royal Funerals of the House of York at Windsor*, London, 2005, p. 116.

51. In 2008 a small copy in oils of this portrait of Richard III was produced in less than a week. In the fifteenth century, the small panel portrait by Petrus Christus of one of the nieces of the Duchess of Norfolk seems to have been easily completed during the weeks when the Duchess and her family were in Flanders for Margaret of York's wedding in 1468: *Eleanor*, p. 68.

52. For the history of wedding rings, see Ashdown-Hill, *Royal Marriage Secrets*.

53. This portrait of Richard III – together with a matching panel portrait of Edward IV – was later owned by members of the Paston family. However, its original owner is unknown.

54. Harl. 433, f. 211v: vol. 2, p. 211. There has been much debate as to the identity of 'the lord Bastard'. Does this refer to one of the sons of Edward IV? (Richard's own son, John of Gloucester, is not referred to elsewhere as a 'lord'.)

55. *Ibid.*

56. Harl. 433, f. 217r: vol. 2, p. 223.

57. Harl. 433, f. 212v: vol. 2, pp. 213–14. From 1 June 1485 the King of Hungary claimed the title 'Duke of Austria', but in April 1485 the reference is almost certainly to a member of the Habsburg family, probably Sigismund, Archduke of Upper Austria (since his cousin, Frederick, Archduke of Inner Austria, was also Holy Roman Emperor, and would more probably have been referred to by that title). There were similar authorisations on other dates to other named servants of Salasar, to a servant of the Duke of Burgundy, and to the Pope's sergeant-at-arms.

58. Harl. 433, f. 213r: vol. 2, p. 214.

59. Harl. 433, f. 213v: vol. 2, p. 216.

60. *Ibid.*, p. 215.

61. Harl. 433, f. 217v: vol. 2, p. 223.

62. Harl. 433, f. 214v: vol. 2, p. 219.

63. Harl. 433, f. 218v: vol. 2, p. 227.

64. *Ibid.*

65. www.1911encyclopedia.org/Pheasant (consulted January 2009).

4. Tombs of Saints and Queens

1. *Crowland*, p. 177, dates these rumours after Holy Week and prior to Whitsun (April–May 1485). The octave of a major religious feast comprises the feast day itself and the seven days following.

2. This comparatively close blood relationship between Richard III and Henry 'Tudor' (Henry VII) stemmed from their common Beaufort descent, by virtue of which Richard III was the second cousin of Henry VII's mother, Margaret Beaufort, Countess of Richmond.

3. The fact that Henry's father, Edmund 'Tudor' and his uncle, Jasper 'Tudor', used versions of the royal arms based apparently upon those of Edmund Beaufort indicates that their patrilineal ancestry was, in reality, not Tudor but royal, probably via the Beaufort line. See Ashdown-Hill *Royal Marriage Secrets*.

4. *fils du feu roy Henry d'Angleterre*: M. Jones, *Bosworth 1485: Psychology of a Battle*, Stroud, 2002, pp. 124–25.

5. *Crowland*, p. 173.

6. Kendall *R3*, p. 300, citing *CPR 1476–1485*, pp. 544–45. The fleet remained on guard in the Channel until at least the end of May.

7. C. Ross, *Richard III*, London, 1981, pp. 204–5.

8. *Beloved Cousyn*, chapter 6.

9. G.F. Beltz, *Memorials of the most Noble Order of the Garter from its foundation to the present time*, London, 1841, p. 75, citing BL, Harl. MS 36B.18, p. 213; also Harl. 433, vol. 2, pp. 215–16.

10. R.A. Griffiths, 'Henry VI', *ODNB*.

11. Cited in W.J. White, 'The Death and Burial of Henry VI', part 1, *Ric. 6* (1982–84), pp. 70–80 (p. 70). Warkworth's account was penned after July 1482. The 21 May 1471 was indeed a Tuesday.

12. B. Wolffe, *Henry VI*, London, 1981, p. 347.

13. Ellis/Vergil, pp. 155–56.

14. White, 'The Death and Burial of Henry VI', part 1, pp. 70–71.

15. Cited in White, 'The Death and Burial of Henry VI', part 1, p. 71. White argues that this is the most nearly contemporaneous account.

16. A. Breeze, 'A Welsh Poem of 1485 on Richard III', *Ric. 18* (2008), pp. 46–53 (p. 47). If Henry VI's death was *not* natural, Edward would probably have preferred to distance himself physically from this event, and may, therefore,

have arranged for the dispatch to take place after he himself had left the capital. On this basis Henry seems unlikely to have been killed on 21 or 22 May. Subsequent belief in the culpability of Edward's administration perhaps caused later Lancastrian accounts to deliberately adjust the date of his death to one of the two days when Edward and Gloucester were known to have been in London.

17. A. Hanham, 'Henry VI and his Miracles', *Ric.* 12 (2000–02), pp. 2–16 [erroneously numbered pp. 638–52 in the publication] (p. 2).

18. *Chenopodium bonus-henricus* is an easily cultivated and edible hardy perennial plant native to the Mediterranean, but introduced to England many centuries ago. It is widely known in Europe by variants of the name 'Good Henry', but the addition of the title of 'King' seems unique to England (where it had certainly been added by the beginning of the sixteenth century). Some writers have assumed that this addition was to honour Henry VIII, but Henry VI seems a more likely contender.

19. Given that the date of Henry's death can be debated, the supposed presence of Richard, as Duke of Gloucester, in the Tower of London during the night of 21–22 May is not necessarily significant, particularly since 'many other' people are also reported to have been there.

20. R.A. Griffiths, 'Henry VI', *ODNB*.

21. White, 'The Death and Burial of Henry VI', part 2, *Ric.* 6, pp. 106–17 (p. 112); Wolffe, *Henry VI*, p. 352. This first bay has subsequently become the site of the tomb of King Edward VII and Queen Alexandra. An alternative possibility is that Richard III intended to be buried at York Minster, where he proposed – and actually began constructing – a very splendid chantry chapel.

22. W.H. St John Hope, 'The Discovery of the Remains of King Henry VI in St George's Chapel, Windsor Castle', *Archaeologia*, vol. 62, part 2, pp. 533–42 (p. 533).

23. St John Hope, 'Remains of King Henry VI', p. 534.

24. A. Coldwells, *St George's Chapel, Windsor Castle* guidebook, 1993. Tresilian also made the iron work for the fine gate enclosing the tomb of Edward IV.

25. The accounts for the funeral expenses in 1471 mention spices and cere cloth, but there is no hint of a lead coffin. Warkworth's Chronicle suggests that a wooden coffin was used at the original interment: St John Hope, 'Remains of King Henry VI', p. 538.

26. St John Hope, 'Remains of King Henry VI', pp. 534–36.

27. It clearly achieved its objective, since John Rous wrote as though he had seen Henry VI's intact body in 1484 – though the archaeological evidence uncovered in the last century clearly shows this claim to be impossible.

28. St John Hope, 'Remains of King Henry VI', pp. 539, 541.

29. *Itinerary*.

30. Kendall *R3*, p. 332 (but Kendall gives no source for this information).

31. 'shortly before Whitsun' – *Crowland*, p. 177. Whit Sunday in 1485 fell on 22 May.

32. The *Calendar of State Papers – Venetian* attributes this letter to Agostino Barbarigo, but he was only elected Doge in 1486. The sender must rather have been Marco Barbarigo.

33. *Calendar of State Papers – Venetian, vol 1, 1202–1509*, p. 154.

34. A.G. Twining, *Our Kings and Westminster Abbey*, London, 1911, p. 139.

5. 'Þe Castel of Care'

1. 'Þat is þe castel of care who so cometh þerinne / May banne þat he borne was to body or to soule': W.W. Skeat, ed., W. Langland, *The Vision of William concerning Piers the Plowman*, Oxford, 1869, p. 10, lines 61–62. Richard III is supposed to have called Nottingham his 'Castle of Care', but actually there is no contemporary evidence that he did so, and the story seems to be a later invention. See A.F. Sutton, 'Richard III's "Castle of Care"', *Ric.* 3 (no. 49, June 1975), pp. 10–12.

2. 'The Body of Christ'.

3. A monstrance is a large vessel of precious metal, often bejewelled, with a glass or crystal compartment in which the Host is placed and through which it can be seen. Typically, medieval monstrances closely resembled contemporary reliquaries.

4. http://en.wikipedia.org/wiki/Coventry_Mystery_Plays (consulted January 2009).

5. E. Poston, ed., *The Penguin Book of Christmas Carols*, Harmondsworth, 1965, p. 64, dates the carol to the fifteenth century.

6. *Itinerary*, p. 20.

7. It is clear, at all events, that the king was not suffering from any kind of 'siege mentality', since he did not seek to defend himself behind the castle walls, but marched out of Nottingham to meet Henry 'Tudor' when he thought the time was ripe.

8. H. Gill, *A Short History of Nottingham Castle*, Nottingham, 1904, www.nottshistory.org.uk/gill1904/charlesi.htm (consulted January 2009).

9. Gill, *Nottingham Castle*, www.nottshistory.org.uk/gill1904/charlesi.htm.

10. P.W. Hammond and A.F. Sutton, *Richard III: the Road to Bosworth Field*, London, 1985, p. 209.

11. Henry 'Tudor' also knew this, as he clearly demonstrated after his accession to the throne, when he imprisoned the marquess.

12. Harl. 433, f. 220r: vol. 2, p. 228.

13. See Introduction.

14. Kendall *R3*, p. 334.

15. *Ibid.*, p. 337.

16. Ross, *Richard III*, p. 141.

17. *Ibid.*

18. Soc. Ant., MS 76, ff. 60r, 91v, 144v; *HHB*, part 2, pp. 70, 116, 207.

19. Soc. Ant., MS 77, f. 31v; *HHB*, part 2, p. 336.

20. The Romans had used the word *lusores* ('players') to refer to both singers and actors. This broad Latin term continued in use into the Middle Ages, and the usage passed into the various vernaculars.

21. C. Ricks, ed., *The Penguin History of Literature vol. 3: English Drama to 1710*, Harmondsworth: Penguin, 1971, pp. 3–4.

22. There is secondary evidence throughout the Middle Ages for the development of dramatic 'interludes' as aristocratic entertainment. Mummers from London entertained Richard II and his court in 1377. Early fifteenth-century texts survive of 'Prefaces' written by John Lydgate, a Dominican friar, which 'call not only for disguise of the persons involved, but for the use of substantial scenic properties' (Ricks, *English Drama*, p. 26). It is possible that Chaucer's *Franklin's Tale* contains a reference to similar entertainments: L.D. Benson, ed., *The Riverside Chaucer*, Oxford, 1987, p. 183, lines 1142–49.

23. Ross, *Richard III*, p. 135. All the benefactions to Queens' College of Richard III and his consort were later annulled by Henry VII.

24. *Crowland*, pp. 176–77; Ellis/Vergil, pp. 218–19; M.K. Jones, *Bosworth 1485, Psychology of a Battle*, Stroud, 2002, p. 157.

25. *Itinerary*.

26. Bestwood is the modern name; the medieval form was Beskwood.

6. Bucks at Bestwood

1. Kendall *R3*, p. 327, suggests that previously Richard took 'no marked interest' in hunting but this seems inaccurate. There is implicit evidence that Richard had hunted in his youth.

2. Harl. 433, vol. 2 (Upminster, 1990), p. 216 (f. 214), punctuation modernised.

3. *Ibid.*

4. *Ibid.* See also Kendall *R3*, p. 327, though Kendall misquotes the date of the third commission.

5. In December 1467, while staying in London (or more probably, at his house in Stepney), Sir John Howard purchased various paraphernalia for hawking, comprising a hawk's bag, two hawk's bells, and 'a tabere [*sic*, tabard? = hood?] for the hawk'. On 19 December 1482, 20*d*. was paid 'to Tymperleys man for

brynging of a hawke'. On 16 February 1483 there was a payment of 12*d*. 'to Seyncleres man for hawkynge': BL, Add. MS 46349, f. 153r; *HHB*, part 1, p. 431; Soc. Ant., MS 77, f. 26v; *HHB*, part 2, p. 328; Soc. Ant., MS 77, f. 43r; *HHB*, part 2, p. 360.

6. According to the *Boke of St Albans* the choice of falcon was entirely hierarchical. Only the emperor should use an eagle. Kings employed gyrfalcons, princes and dukes had peregrines, and so on: Reeves, *Pleasures and Pastimes*, pp. 113–14.

7. In 1368 Nicholas de Litlington, Abbot of Westminster, offered up prayers for the recovery of his sick hawk, accompanied by the presentation of a wax falcon as a votive offering: Reeves, *Pleasures and Pastimes*, p. 112.

8. J. Ashdown-Hill, 'Yesterday my Lord of Gloucester came to Colchester', *Essex Archaeology and History*, vol. 36 (2005), pp. 212–17.

9. Pollard, *North-Eastern England during the Wars of the Roses: Lay Society, War and Politics 1450–1500*, p. 198; L. Woolley, *Medieval Life and Leisure in the Devonshire Hunting Tapestries*, London: V&A, 2002, p. 25.

10. www.bbc.co.uk/nottingham/content/articles/2008/09/18/robin_hood_and_bestwood_feature.shtml (consulted December 2008).

11. www.bw-bestwoodlodge.co.uk/HistoryoftheLodge.asp (consulted December 2008).

12. In England, these comprised the native red deer, the smaller fallow deer (introduced by the Normans), and the roe deer – which had the advantage that roebuck could be hunted all year round.

13. Edward, Duke of York, considered hare the finest game: a swift and clever quarry which could be hunted all year round: C. Reeves, *Pleasures and Pastimes in Medieval England*, Stroud, 1995, p. 106.

14. They were not eaten, though their fur was used to adorn clothing.

15. Edward, Duke of York (d. 1415) translated into English, with additions of his own, the *Livre de Chasse* of Gaston III, Comte de Foix.

16. The Duke of York had, however, commented on the fact that foxes could provide cunning quarry for hounds, and produced an attractive pelt.

17. http://www.nottshistory.org.uk/Brown1896/arnold.htm (consulted December 2008).

18. The modern deer-stalking dates for Scotland are as follows:
Red Deer (Hart): July–Oct; Red Deer (Hind): Oct–Feb; Fallow Deer (Buck): Aug–Apr; Fallow Deer (Doe): Nov–Apr: www.woodmillshootings.com/holiday_packages.htm (consulted November 2008).

19. C.M. Woolgar, D. Sejeantson & T. Waldron, *Food in Medieval England – Diet & Nutrition*, Oxford, 2006, p. 178.

20. Edward, Duke of York, called scent-hounds 'harriers', 'crachets' or 'raches', and he preferred them to be tan in colour.

21. Even the alaunt tended to be given the protection of leather armour for this task. Alaunts were notoriously uncertain in temperament, and often vicious. They were favoured for bear and bull baiting.

22. So called because they originated in Spain.

23. Ashdown-Hill, 'Yesterday my Lord of Gloucester came to Colchester'.

24. Harl. 433, 1, 155.

25. Harl. 433, 2, 111.

26. BL, Add. MS 46349, f. 146r; Arundel Castle, MS, f. 96 (actually numbered 92 in MS); Soc. Ant., MS 76, ff. 87r, 91v, 149r; MS 77, f. 4v; *HHB*, part 1, pp. 419, 558; part 2, pp. 109, 115, 216, 287.

27. There appears to be no written source which recounts the exact details of the medieval Sudbury processions. This account is, therefore, based on local tradition.

28. *Beloved Cousyn*, pp. 105–6, 123.

29. Nicolas, p. 3.

30. N. Davis, ed., *Paston Letters and Papers of the Fifteenth Century*, 2 vols, Oxford: Clarendon, 1971 and 1976, vol. 2, p. 444.

31. It is true that the 'sweating sickness' or 'English Sweate' did first appear in England at about this time, and is mentioned in the Crowland Chronicle (pp. 168–69). The first known cases occurred early in August 1485, several weeks before the Battle of Bosworth. 'The symptoms and signs as described by Caius and others were as follows: The disease began very suddenly with a sense of apprehension, followed by cold shivers (sometimes very violent), giddiness, headache and severe pains in the neck, shoulders and limbs, with great exhaustion. After the cold stage, which might last from half an hour to three hours, the hot and sweating stage followed. The characteristic sweat broke out suddenly without any obvious cause. Accompanying the sweat, or after that was poured out, was a sense of heat, headache, delirium, rapid pulse, and intense thirst. Palpitation and pain in the heart were frequent symptoms. No skin eruptions were noted by observers including Caius. In the final stages, there was either general exhaustion and collapse, or an irresistible urge to sleep, which was thought to be fatal if the patient was permitted to give way to it. One attack did not offer immunity.' See http://en.wikipedia.org/wiki/Sweating_sickness (consulted March 2009).

32. *Crowland*, pp. 178–79. This story could be part of the Stanleys' subsequent rewriting of their role in the events of 1485. The chronicler at Crowland Abbey could well have derived his account from Lord Stanley's wife (see below: chapter 7, n. 21).

33. See *Beloved Cousyn*, appendix 4.

34. *Crowland*, pp. 178–79.

35. Ellis/Vergil, p. 223.

36. Contemporary sources suggest that this was a real crown, made of gold and set with jewels, and not a piece of gilt base-metal 'costume jewellery': Jones, *Bosworth 1485*, p. 187. Jones suggests that it may have been the crown of St Edward (the coronation crown), but this seems inherently improbable. The *precious* crown of an English sovereign was usually his personal, state crown. Even today the modern 'Imperial State Crown' is a far more valuable object than 'St Edward's Crown'. Moreover, it is the former, and not the latter, which is worn on state occasions.

7. Crossing the River

1. Most horses which appear to be white only have a white hair coat. Their underlying skin is dark in colour, as are their eyes. Such horses are, therefore, more accurately described as 'grey'. Rarely, true white horses do occur, which have pink skin under their coats and usually blue eyes. It is impossible at this late date to establish whether 'White Surrey' or 'White Syrie' – if indeed he existed – was in reality white or grey.

2. On 'White Syrie', see J. Jowett, ed., *The Tragedy of King Richard III*, Oxford, 2000, p. 336 and n. 43; also N. de Somogyi, ed., *The Shakespeare Folios: Richard III*, London, 2002, p. 267, n. 90. For the list of Richard III's horses, see Harl. 433, vol. 1, pp. 4–5.

3. See Θ, on John Howard's stable, and Harl. 433, vol. 1, pp. 4–5. The list of Richard III's horses includes twenty named mounts, which were either grey (*liard*, *lyard* or *gray*) or white (*whit*). Amongst these was 'the gret gray … being at Harmet at Nottingham'. There is no horse specifically named 'White Syrie', but not all the horses are named, nor are all described in terms of their colour.

4. See Θ.

5. Speede's account is cited in J. Throsby, *The Memoirs of the Town and County of Leicester*, Leicester, 1777, p. 61, n. b.

6. F. Roe, *Old Oak Furniture*, London, 1908, p. 286.

7. S.E. Green, *Selected Legends of Leicestershire*, Leicester, 1971, 1982, p. 21. Green cites no source for this quotation.

8. As we have seen (above), there is no actual evidence for any such change of name.

9. Green, *Legends*, p. 21. Thomas Clarke was Mayor of Leicester in 1583 and again in 1598: H. Hartopp, *The Roll of the Mayors of the Borough and Lord Mayors of the City of Leicester 1209–1935*, Leicester, 1935, pp. 75–76, 80. The story of Clark(e)'s treasure was first written down in Sir Roger Twysden's 'Commonplace Book' in about 1650, and published in Nichols' *History and Antiquities of the County of Leicester* (1815).

10. Throsby, *Leicester*, pp. 14, 62, n. b. The feet, which were cut off in the mid-eighteenth century, measured 6 inches square and were 2 feet 6 inches in height.

11. There are recent rumours of a 'Richard III bed' at a farmhouse in Sheepy Magna (J.D. Austin, *Merevale and Atherstone 1485: Recent Bosworth Discoveries*, Friends of Atherstone Heritage, 2004, section 21). But an indication of the ease with which 'Richard III beds' may be invented, is provided by the fact that the present author was told that a wooden bedstead at the Guildhall in Leicester had belonged to Richard III. Subsequent enquiries revealed that the bed in question is seventeenth century, was purchased for the Guildhall as part of a room display in the 1950s, and has absolutely no historic connection either with Leicester or with King Richard (I am grateful to Philip French, curator of Leicester City Museums, for this information). See also below, note 16.

12. Speede, *History*, p. 725.

13. See the case of Jeweyn Blakecote, *sortilega*, in J. Ashdown-Hill, *Mediaeval Colchester's Lost Landmarks*, Derby, 2009, p. 161. Regarding the Richard III Bow Bridge prophecy, the location, at a water crossing, may perhaps be significant. With the substitution of begging for washing, 'there is a hint of the Irish / Scottish "Washer at the Ford" folk motif. The Washer at the Ford is an Otherworld woman whose task it is to wash the clothes of those who are about to die': personal communication from Marie Barnfield.

14. *Crowland*, pp. 180–81.

15. Ellis/Vergil, pp. 221–22.

16. The chair at Coughton Court is said to be made from the bed in which Richard III slept the night before the Battle of Bosworth (thus 21/22 August). This must, therefore, have been his camp bed, and not the great royal bed, which had reportedly been left behind in Leicester. The tradition relating to this chair seems to be an old one, but lacks documentary evidence.

17. 'The malady was remarkably rapid in its course, being sometimes fatal even in two or three hours, and some patients died in less than that time. More commonly it was protracted to a period of twelve to twenty-four hours, beyond which it rarely lasted. Those who survived for twenty-four hours were considered safe.' It is said to have particularly attacked the rich and the idle: www.luminarium.org/encyclopedia/sweatingsickness.htm (consulted March 2009).

The exact cause of the disease remains unknown, but the symptoms did not include the rash or boils found in cases of typhus or plague. Some authorities consider *sudor anglicus* an early form of the Hantavirus pulmonary syndrome which struck parts of America during the summer of 1993: R. Putatunda, published 3/27/2008: www.buzzle.com/articles/sweating-sickness.html (consulted March 2009).

18. The sweating sickness was a fever and its most obvious symptom was sweating. There was no visible rash associated with it. If patients were kept quiet, in an equal temperature, they often survived the disease.

19. Ellis/Vergil, pp. 222–23, speaks of the royal army as a 'multitude' which struck terror into the hearts of those who saw it, and says that the king's forces outnumbered those of Henry 'Tudor' by two to one.

20. On the other hand, if the king was indeed suffering from an attack of sweating sickness, he is unlikely to have mentioned that, since it would have given grounds for disquiet as to his physical fitness for the coming conflict.

21. There has been much debate as to the identity of the Crowland chronicler, and the latest thinking is that he may not have been one single individual: A. Hanham, 'The Mysterious Affair at Crowland Abbey', *Ric.* 18, pp. 1–20. Some of the information in the chronicle does appear to have come from someone who had attended the Yorkist court – but of course the Abbot of Crowland would himself have sat in Parliament. We may also note that Henry VII's mother was an oblate of Crowland Abbey, not to mention its direct neighbour (through her tenure of Deeping).

8. 'He has now Departed from Amongst the Living'

1. *Iam enim è vivis abiit*: the words of the beautiful messenger who reported Richard III's death to the Infanta Joana of Portugal in a vision: P. Antonio Vasconcellio, *Anacephalaeoses, id est, summa capita actorum regum Lusitaniae*, Antwerp, 1621, p. 252.

2. *Crowland*, pp. 176–83; Ellis/Vergil, pp. 216–25. Pronay and Cox oppose the theory that Vergil saw and used the Crowland Chronicle as one of his sources: *Crowland*, p. 99.

3. Ellis/Vergil, p. 221; see also Jones, *Bosworth 1485*, p. 166.

4. *Circa* 1924: P.J. Foss, *The Field of Redemore*, Newtown Lindford, 1998, pp. 40, 63.

5. There is certainly no source earlier than the 1920s for this unlikely story, which appears to have been invented by the 'Fellowship of the White Boar' (later the Richard III Society) to provide an ecclesiastical focus for modern commemorations. It is regrettable that Sutton Cheney church was chosen, since nearby Dadlington church has an *authentic* historic connection with the battle. In the words of Henry VIII's chantry licence of 1511, Dadlington is specified as the church 'to þe wheche þe bodyes or bones of the men sleyne in þe seyde feelde beth broght and beryed': TNA, C 82/367, quoted in Foss, *The Field of Redemore*, p. 40.

6. *Crowland*, pp. 180–81.

7. BL, Add. MS 12060, ff. 19–20, as quoted in Foss, *The Field of Redemore*, p. 54. See also R.M. Warnicke, 'Sir Ralph Bigod: a loyal servant to King Richard III', *Ric.* 6 (1982–84), pp. 299–303. It should be noted that Morley was an old man in 1554, while Sir Ralph Bigod had died in 1515. It is also worth noting that similar tales exist relating to the losers of other battles, including Agincourt and Coutrai (see, for example, J.W. Verkaik, 'King Richard's Last Sacrament', *Ric.* 9, [1991–93], pp. 359–60).

8. Soc. Ant., accession no. 446. The measurements are those given on the Society of Antiquaries object file, and have not been checked.

9. Sharp's drawing of the crucifix, made in 1793, shows no damage at these extremities, but Sharp may simply have reinstated the missing sections of foliation in his drawing.

10. Oman describes the decoration on the reverse of the roundels as 'the Yorkist "sun in splendour"'. C. Oman, 'English medieval base metal church plate', *Archaeological Journal*, vol. 119, 1962, p. 200. However, the Bosworth Crucifix is not unique in having 'suns' on the back of its roundels. The very similar Lamport Crucifix (now in the treasury of Peterborough Cathedral) also has them, while other similar crucifixes have single or double roses in these positions.

11. J. Ashdown-Hill, 'The Bosworth Crucifix', *Transactions of the Leicestershire Archaeological & Historical Society*, vol. 78 (2004), pp. 83–96.

12. TNA, C 82/367 (Henry VIII's licence for a chantry for the battlefield dead at Dadlington church, 24 August 1511) refers to 'Bosworth feld otherwise called Dadlyngton feld': Foss, *The Field of Redemore*, p. 39. Only a small number of burials has actually so far been discovered at Dadlington.

13. C. Ross, *The Wars of the Roses, a concise history*, London, 1976, p. 131.

14. Ross, *The Wars of the Roses*, p. 131.

15. *Crowland*, pp. 180–81 implies that he rose at dawn. On 22 August 2009 the sun rose at 5.57 am BST. However, in the fifteenth century the medieval (Julian) calendar then in use was nine days behind the modern (Gregorian) calendar. Thus we actually need to consider the time of sunrise on 31 August, which in 2009 was at 6.12 am BST: www.timeanddate.com/worldclock/astronomy.html?n=136&month=8&year=2009&obj=sun&afl=-11&day=1 (consulted May 2009).

16. Fifteenth-century custom may have been less strict regarding the use of correct liturigal colours than has subsequently been the case: see Θ, subsection 5.9.

17. Of the possible introits for a mass celebrated in honour of martyrs, one included the following words from Psalm 20 (in the enumeration of the Vulgate), which may also have figured in Richard III's coronation service: *Quoniam praevenisti eum in benedictionibus dulcedinis: posuisti in capite eius coronam de lapide pretioso.* [For you have gone before him with blessings of sweetness: you have set on his head a crown of precious stones.]

18. Ashdown-Hill, 'Bosworth Crucifix', p. 85.

19. Ellis/Vergil, p. 223.

20. Lord Strange undoubtedly survived. However, there is no proof that the execution was ever actually ordered.

21. See Map 1: The Battle of Bosworth.

22. About 9 am.

23. It is doubtful whether Richard could have actually seen Henry's features, and in any case, he had probably never seen him before. He would have recognised him by the standard he was displaying.

24. *Il vint a tout sa bataille, lequelle estoit estimee plus de XVM homes, en criant: ces traictres francois aujour'uy sont cause de la perdition de nostre royaume.* Jones, *Bosworth 1485*, p. 222. This evidence does, however, seem to be at variance with the 'traditional' account of Richard's cavalry charge.

25. Jones, *Bosworth 1485*, pp. 194–95.

26. Jones, *Bosworth 1485*, pp. 196–97.

27. Which Stanley was in command depends on whether or not Lord Stanley himself was present (see above). Both Vergil and *Crowland* claim that he was but, as we have seen, Lord Stanley himself suggested otherwise.

28. Ellis/Vergil, p. 224.

29. See *Beloved Cousyn*, p. 115.

30. TNA, C 82/367, 24 August 1511.

31. Williams, 'The Portuguese Connection …', p. 142; Vasconcellio, *Anacephalaeoses*, pp. 251–52. Williams refers incorrectly to the page numbers of Vasconcellio's text.

9. 'A Sorry Spectacle'

1. Polydore Vergil, as quoted in C.J. Billson, *Mediaeval Leicester*, Leicester, 1920, p. 180.

2. The precise distance would depend, of course, on the point of departure.

3. Ellis/Vergil, p. 226.

4. The sun probably set at about 7.55 pm that evening: see www.canterbury-weather.co.uk/sun/ukmap.php?d=31&m=8&y=2009 (consulted May 2009).

5. By the late fifteenth century most churches had more than one bell: a small *Sanctus* bell, which was rung at mass to signal the consecration, and also a 'great bell' for Requiems and anniversaries. Some churches may have had a third bell for ringing the *Angelus*. Those which did not would have used the *Sanctus* bell for this purpose.

6. Kendall *R3*, p. 369. See also Speede's account (appendix 4).

7. Kendall was probably misled by the large nineteenth-century stone plaque erected near the river to commemorate Richard III by Benjamin Broadbent.

8. Kendall's account of the exposure of Richard's body is based on the rather casual wording of Vergil (see below).

9. In a subsequent footnote he goes on to recount the very dubious tale of the exhumation of Richard III's remains at the time of the Dissolution as though this were an established fact, which is certainly not the case.

10. This interpretation is based on *Crowland*, pp. 194–95. However, the relevant passage does not, in fact, say that Henry antedated his accession, and there is no evidence to support such a claim in the surviving acts of attainder against Richard III's supporters.

11. C.R. Cheney, *Handbook of Dates*, RHS, 1945, reprinted Cambridge, 1996, p. 23.

12. Ellis/Vergil, pp. 220–26; *Crowland*, pp. 178–83.

13. Quoted in Billson, *Mediaeval Leicester*, p. 180. See also Ellis/Vergil, p. 226.

14. *Crowland*, pp. 182–83. It is possible (but not certain) that there is a gap in the text, as tentatively indicated.

15. D. Baldwin, 'King Richard's Grave in Leicester', *Transactions of the Leicestershire Archaeological and Historical Society*, vol. 60 (1986), pp. 21–24 (p. 21).

16. For details of John Howard's burial, see *Beloved Cousyn*, pp. 126–30. Also, J. Ashdown-Hill, 'The opening of the tombs of the Dukes of Richmond and Norfolk, Framlingham, April 1841: Darby's account', *Ric.* 18 (2008), pp. 100–07.

17. *Eleanor*, p. 184.

18. *Crowland*, pp. 182–83.

19. Examination of Richard III's skeleton revealed post mortem injuries to the face and to the right side, and evidence of a sword having been thrust up the anus. Obscene treatment of defeated and dead enemies has occured throughout the history of warfare. Modern examples were reported as recently as 2012.

20. If this detail is true, it can hardly have been done other than by Henry 'Tudor''s express command.

21. Throsby, *Leicester*, p. 62, contends that the fact that *Blanc Sanglier* accompanied Richard's body was at least a concession of some sort on the part of Henry VII.

22. Although Throsby, *Leicester*, p. 62 (following an earlier writer) suggests that the rope was 'more to insult the helpless dead than to fasten him to the horse', it is interesting to note that the second possibility had at least been considered.

23. C.W.C. Oman, *The Art of War in the Middle Ages, AD 378–1515*, New York, 1953, pp. 78, 103.

24. C. Weightman, *Margaret of York*, Gloucester, 1989, p. 102.

25. *Letters and Papers, Foreign and Domestic, of the reign of Henry VIII*, vol. 1(i), no. 2246, p. 1006, citing Lambeth MS 306, f. 204.

26. J. Ridley, *Henry VIII*, London, 1984, p. 72.

27. 'The 21st [September], confirmation of the news of the defeat of James IV, by a messenger, who brought the Scotch King's plaid [*paludiamentum seu tunicam*] with the royal arms upon it.' *Letters and Papers … Henry VIII*, vol. 1(i), no. 2391, pp. 1060–61.

28. Jones, *Bosworth 1485*, p. 160.
29. Benson, ed., *The Riverside Chaucer*, p. 39 (G. Chaucer, *The Canterbury Tales*, 'The Knight's Tale', lines 1001–08).
30. As with the case of James IV, it has been debated whether the bodies displayed as those of Edward II and Richard II were the authentic remains of those kings, but this point is not particularly significant in the present context.
31. This part of the plan was by no means always successful, of course, and royal martyr cults did tend to spring up around the royal bodies, in spite of their discreet burials.

10. The Franciscan Priory

1. *VCH, Leicestershire, vol. 2*, 1954, pp. 33–35.
2. TNA, C1/206/69 recto, lines 4 and 5. For the precise words, see chapter 11 below.
3. Ellis/Vergil, p. 226.
4. For an explanation of the differences, see J. Ashdown-Hill, *Mediaeval Colchester's Lost Landmarks*, Derby, 2009, p. 65.
5. See above: Kendall.
6. As we shall see shortly, Richard was buried in the choir of the priory church: a part of the building normally accessible only to the friars themselves.
7. Ashdown-Hill, *Mediaeval Colchester*, p. 74.
8. My italics. R. Baker, *Chronicle of the Kings of England*, London, 1684, p. 235. For Speede's text see below, appendix 4.
9. Green, *Legends*, p. 22, asserts that the friars 'begged for the body', but as usual, she cites no source. The guardian (religious superior) of the Leicester Greyfriars in 1485 may have shared the dead king's name. The guardian in office in 1479 had certainly been called Richard: VCH, *Leicestershire*, vol. 2, pp. 32–35 and n. 19.
10. Richard III's parents had employed a Franciscan chaplain, and later his sister, Margaret of York, Duchess of Burgundy, chose to be buried in the Franciscan conventual church in Mechelen.
11. Stow, *Annals* (ed. 1615), p. 327, cited in W. Page (ed.), *VCH*, London, vol. 1, Section 12, London 1909.
12. Accounts suggesting that Richard III was buried in a stone coffin date only from the seventeenth century and are anachronistic (see below). When his body was excavated in 2012, it was clear that he had been buried only in a shroud.
13. See above: description of Queen Anne Neville's funeral rites.
14. *Calendar of State Papers – Venetian, vol 1, 1202–1509*, p. 156.

11. 'King Richard's Tombe'

1. BL, Add. MS 7099, f. 129.
2. By comparison, Henry VI, for example, had had to wait thirteen years for his new tomb.
3. Will of Cecily Neville, dowager Duchess of York: Nicholls and Bruce, eds, *Wills from Doctors' Commons*, p. 8.
4. TNA, C1/206/69 *recto*, lines 4 and 5.
5. He witnessed a deed on 10 August 1490: Nottinghamshire Archives, DD/P/CD/13. See also http://en.wikipedia.org/wiki/Lord_Mayor_of_Nottingham (consulted June 2009).
6. R. Edwards, 'King Richard's Tomb at Leicester', *Ric.* 3 (no. 50, Sept. 1975), pp. 8–9, citing PRO [TNA], C1/206/69. This is a record of a chancery case brought by Rauf Hill of Nottingham against Walter Hylton, alleging the fraudulent insertion of Rauf's name in indentures between Hylton and Sir Reynold Bray and Sir Thomas Lovell, concerning the making of a tomb for Richard III. About one-third of this manuscript is now virtually unreadable. The supposed figure of £50 for the cost of the tomb is an interpretation advanced by a previous researcher – who may indeed have been able to decipher more of the text than is now legible. However, my examination of the manuscript did not succeed in substantiating this figure, though two separate references to 'xv li' and 'xx li' respectively were found.
7. See Edwards, 'King Richard's Tomb at Leicester'.
8. J. Blair and N. Ramsey, eds, *English Medieval Industries*, London, 1991, p. 37.
9. Blair and Ramsey, *English Medieval Industries*, p. 35; J.C. Cox, *Memorials of Old Derbyshire*, London, 1907, p. 108.
10. M. Hicks, *Richard III and his Rivals*, London, 1991, p. 342; NA, PROB 11/11, will of Richard Lessy, 1498. I am grateful to Marie Barnfield for these references. The hard stone tomb with brass memorials for Thomas Howard, 2nd Duke of Norfolk, and his second wife cost 400 marks (or about £267) in 1524.
11. The tomb of William Shore, erstwhile husband of Edward IV's last mistress, is marked by an incised alabaster effigy, similar in appearance to a 'brass'. See *Beloved Cousyn*, figure 19.
12. The Latin texts of these two royal epitaphs are given in appendix 6, for comparison with the Latin text of the Richard III epitaph.
13. The manuscript texts give *vano* rather than *vario* (i.e. 'vain' or 'ostentatious' marble).
14. Sandford and BL, Add. MS 45131, f. 10v: 'Was by many called Richard the Third'.
15. 'Exactly' or 'merely'. The word means 'just' in both senses.
16. The extant manuscripts give a variant version of this line: '… and caused a non-king to be revered with the honour of a king'.

17. 2 x 5 = 10, - 4 = 6. An alternative possible (but less likely) reading of this line
    would be: 'When [in] twice four years less five' (i.e. 2 x 4 = 8, - 5 = 3).

18. 300 x 5 = 1500, minus the figure given in the previous line (either 6 or 3)
    would give 1494 (or – less probably – 1497). This dating technique is a complex
    numbers game. The punctuation given here assumes that the writer's intention
    was to convey the date of the inauguration of the tomb and epitaph. With
    different punctuation, however, one could argue that the intention was to give
    the date of Richard's death – in which case the writer evidently became so tied
    up in his own cleverness that he got it wrong!

19. On 22 August.

20. Sandford and BL, Add. MS 45131, f. 10v: '… the right it claimed'.

21. Henry VII himself referred to this first Yorkist pretender simply as *spurium
    quemdam puerum* ('some illegitimate boy'): J. Gairdner, ed., *Letters and Papers
    illustrative of the reigns of Richard III and Henry VII*, London, 1857, p. 95, citing BL,
    Add. MS 15385, f. 315.

22. The real identity of this person is not known for certain, but Henry VII later
    sought to establish that he was one Pierre Werbecque of Tournai, and he is
    therefore usually referred to as 'Perkin Warbeck'.

23. J. Ashdown-Hill, 'Coins attributed to the Yorkist Pretenders, 1487–1498', *Ric.* 19
    (2009), pp. 69–89 (pp. 81–86).

12. 'Here Lies the Body'

1. Seventeenth-century inscription from Alderman Herrick's pillar marking the
   gravesite of Richard III: C. Wren, *Parentalia, or Memoirs of the Family of the Wrens*,
   London, 1750, p. 144.

2. A tomb effigy which fits the description of Richard's, and which shows signs of
   weathering, is now preserved in Tamworth church. P. Tudor-Craig, ed., *Richard
   III Exhibition Catalogue*, National Portrait Gallery, London, 1972, no. 172.

3. Wren, *Parentalia*, p. 144; D. Baldwin, 'King Richard's Grave in Leicester',
   Transactions of the Leicestershire Archaeological and Historical Society, vol. 60 (1986),
   p. 22.

4. Richard III Society, Barton Library, personal communication from S.H.
   Skillington, Hon. Secretary, Leicester Archaeological Society, to Saxon Barton,
   29 October 1935.

5. In the present Social Services Department car park on the former Greyfriars
   site.

6. See Richard Corbet's *Iter Boreale* (*c.* 1620–25), cited in J. Ashdown-Hill, 'the
   Location of the 1485 Battle and the Fate of Richard III's Body', *Ricardian
   Bulletin*, Autumn 2004, pp. 34–35.

7. Such violent exhumations did sometimes occur in the seventeenth century, during the Civil War. It is perhaps significant, therefore, that the story of the digging up of Richard's body was disseminated at about that period.

8. The Commons were protesting against Cardinal Wolsey's attempt to enforce a 'benevolence', thus contravening a statute against these forced taxes, enacted by Richard III. Wolsey rebuked the MPs, saying: 'I marvel that you speak of Richard III, which was a usurper and murderer of his own nephews.' They, however, responded robustly: 'Although he did evil, yet in his time were many good Acts made': J. Potter, *Good King Richard?* London, 1983, p. 23.

9. It would be interesting to compare the DNA of this skull with that of Richard III (as revealed below), were it not for the fact that carbon-14 dating has already shown the skull to date from before the Norman Conquest (A. Wakelin, 'Is there a king under this bridge?', *Leicester Mercury*, 8 October 2002, p. 10).

10. VCH, *Leicestershire*, vol. 2, p. 33. The superior of a Franciscan Priory has the title not of 'prior' but of 'guardian'.

11. See, for example, the extensive but roofless remains of the former Greyfriars at Little Walsingham in Norfolk.

12. Speede, *History*, p. 725 (see appendix 4).

13. Wren, *Parentalia*, p. 144.

14. Speede, *History*, p. 725 (see appendix 4).

13. 'The Honour of a King'

1. Richard III's epitaph.

2. The bishop of St David's so described him, and in August 1485 the city of York noted in its records its deep regret at his death: *Road*, pp. 135, 223. We have also seen that the House of Commons recalled him as a good king in the presence of a rather astonished Cardinal Wolsey during the reign of Henry VIII.

3. Although Richard III had two known illegitimate children, they seem to have been older than his legitimate son. They are thus likely to have been begotten before Richard married.

4. '… our father, King Edward the Fourth, whom God assoile': letter from Henry VII to Sir Gilbert Talbot, quoted in J. Gairdner, *History of the Life and Reign of Richard the Third*, Cambridge, 1898, p. 276.

5. 'Very truth it is and well-known that at such time as Sir James Tyrell was in the Tower for treason committed against the most famous prince, King Henry the Seventh, both Dighton and he were examined and confessed the murder [of Edward V and Richard Duke of York]': R.S. Sylvester, ed., St Thomas More, *The History of King Richard III*, New Haven & London,

1976, pp. 88–89. Tyrell was executed in May 1502 for his support of the Yorkist prince Edmund de la Pole (son of Richard III's sister, Elizabeth of York, Duchess of Suffolk, and younger brother of John de la Pole, Earl of Lincoln).

6. See *R3MK*; *Eleanor, Beloved Cousyn*.

14. Richard III's Genes part I – the Fifteenth Century and Before

1. For Richard's books, see the series of articles by A.F. Sutton and L. Visser-Fuchs, *Ric.* 9 and 10 (1991–96). For his handwriting, see B. Hickey, 'Richard III – a character analysis', published by P. Stirling-Langley, *Ricardian Bulletin*, September 2000, pp. 27–34, and March 2001, pp. 16–22. This article also refers to earlier published material on the same subject. For Richard's horoscope, see J. Elliott, 'The Birth Chart of Richard III', *Astrological Quarterly*, vol. 70, no. 3 (Summer 2000), pp. 19–37.

2. Richard III certainly had two illegitimate children. His daughter, Catherine, was married but died childless. His son, John of Gloucester, was put to death by Henry VII. There is also the curious story of Richard Plantagenet of Eastwell, an old man who died in Sussex in the reign of Elizabeth I, and who reportedly claimed to be Richard's son. See P.W. Hammond, 'The Illegitimate Children of Richard III', *Ric.* 5 (1977–81), pp. 92–96.

3. As far as is known. John of Gloucester might conceivably have had illegitimate offspring of his own, but if so, no record of them survives.

4. A letter dated 20 February 1478 mentions plans for Clarence's burial at Tewkesbury.

5. Bodl, MS Top. Glouc. D.2, f. 40r-v.

6. R.K. Morris and R, Shoesmith, eds, *Tewkesbury Abbey, History, Art and Architecture*, Almeley, 2003, pp. 32–40.

7. The account which follows is based upon P. De Win, '*Danse Macabre* around the tomb and bones of Margaret of York', *Ric.* 15 (2005), pp. 53–69.

8. Her heart and intestines were buried in the Carthusian monasteries at Herne and Scheut respectively.

9. *Sub limine ostii huius chori*. Paris, Bibliothèque nationale de France, Département des manuscrits, fr. 5234, f. 146.

10. P. De Win, '*Danse Macabre* rond graf en gebeente van Margareta van York', *Handelingen van de Koninklijke Kring voor Oudheidkunde, Letteren an Kunst van Mechelen*, 2003, pp. 61–86; English version published as '*Danse Macabre* around the tomb and bones of Margaret of York', *Ric.* 15 (2005), pp. 53–69.

11. The precise location of the original tomb was somewhat unclear. See De Win, '*Danse Macabre*', *Handelingen*, p. 63 (*Ric.* 15, p. 55) & *passim*.

12. Three skeletons found, one of them female; the latter aged between 50 and 60, and 1.54 metres in height.

13. Two skeletons found, one of them female.

14. Partial skeleton (secondary burial?), with hair, belonging to a woman of about 50.

15. *Dienst Archeologie*.

16. Information supplied by Dieter Viaene, Mechelen Town Archives, 29 June 2007.

17. B. Sykes, *The Seven Daughters of Eve*, New York & London, 2001, p. 27.

18. E. Hagelberg, B. Sykes and R.E.M. Hedges, 'Ancient bone DNA amplified', *Nature*, vol. 342 (1989), p. 485.

19. A.J. Klotzko, *A Clone of Your Own?* Oxford, 2004, p. 52.

20. J. Marks, *What it means to be 98% Chimpanzee*, London and Berkeley, 2002, p. 34.

21. The designations, lifetimes and places of origin of the clan mothers as given here are derived from Sykes, *The Seven Daughters of Eve*, p. 195 and *passim*. It was Professor Sykes who named the clan mothers.

22. D. Brewer, *Chaucer and his World*, London, 1978, p. 89.

23. *Ibid.*

24. These adjectives of nationality are, of course, anachronistic in a fifteenth-century context, but it is convenient to employ them.

25. One recent writer suggests the contrary, stating that 'it is possible to speculate that, given [Gilles'] time in the court of the English King and Queen, his wife or wives were of English origin'. J. Lucraft, *Katherine Swynford, the History of a Medieval Mistress*, Stroud, 2006, p. 2. However, there is actually little evidence that Gilles spent a great deal of time at the English court.

26. J. Gardner, *The Life and Times of Chaucer*, London, 1977, p. 118.

27. J. Perry, 'Philippa Chaucer's Tomb' (2002), http://members.cox.net/judy-perry/Philippa.html (consulted June 2009), p. 2. The tomb, with an effigy of a lady in a wimple, is uninscribed. It is identified as Philippa's on the basis of the de Roët wheel badge which the lady wears on her breast. Philippa's son, Thomas Chaucer, held the manor of East Worldham from 1418–1434.

28. *ODNB*, vol. 30, pp. 888–89.

29. Later Marquess of Somerset and Dorset.

30. G.C. Coulton, *Chaucer and his England*, London, 1908, p. 31. Chaucer's sons were apparently proud of their de Roët heritage. It has been claimed that they abandoned their father's coat of arms, preferring to use the de Roët arms which came to them from their mother. G.K. Chesterton, *Chaucer*, London, 1932, p. 80.

31. Reported in J. Ashdown-Hill, 'Alive and Well in Canada – the Mitochondrial DNA of Richard III', *Ric.* 16 (2006), pp. 1–14.

15. Richard III's Genes part II – the mtDNA Line

1. Kendall, *Richard the Third*, pp. 261, 274.

2. *ODNB*, vol. 13, p. 22.

3. *ODNB*, vol. 13, p. 22.

4. J.D. Mackie, *The Earlier Tudors, 1485–1558*, Oxford 1952, p. 387.

5. *ODNB*, vol. 13, p. 22.

6. All of Margaret Babthorpe's (Cholmley) daughters married, some of them more than once, however, only one bloodline – the one followed here – has successfully been traced to the present day.

7. One who conformed in public as an Anglican, but who was a Catholic in private.

8. *ODNB*, vol. 50, p. 939, quoting Slingsby's diary.

9. Joy Ibsen, personal letter, 13 November 2004.

10. TNA, PCC Wills, Prob 11/884, ff. 161r-162v.

11. TNA, PCC Wills, Prob 11/884, f. 161v.

12. Curiously, given Barbara Yelverton's royalist ancestry, Sir Robert Reynolds was the Solicitor General under the Commonwealth. He purchased Elvetham from William Seymour, Duke of Somerset.

13. R. Furneaux, *William Wilberforce*, London 1974, pp. 165; 166.

14. Furneaux, *William Wilberforce*, p. 162.

15. J. Pollock, *Wilberforce*, London 1977, p. 159.

16. Furneaux, *William Wilberforce*, p. 166.

17. Pollock, *Wilberforce*, p. 305.

18. The only living descendants of Barbara Spooner [Wilberforce] are in through her sons: J. Ashdown-Hill, 'A Granddaughter of William Wilberforce', *Genealogists' Magazine*, September 2004 (28:3, 2004), pp. 110–11.

19. E. Adams, ed., *Mrs J. Comyns Carr's Reminiscences*, London 1926, p. 16.

20. Joy Ibsen, 1 August 2006.

21. Joy Ibsen, 13 December 2005.

22. A. Comyns Carr, *J. Comyns Carr – Stray Memories*, London 1920, p. 53.

23. Adams, ed., *Mrs J. Comyns Carr's Reminiscences*, pp. 13–14.

24. Adams, ed., *Mrs J. Comyns Carr's Reminiscences*, pp. 14–15.

25. Joy Ibsen, 13 November 2004.

26. Comyns Carr, *Stray Memories*, p. 21.

27. Comyns Carr, *Stray Memories*, p. 2.

28. Arthur was the eldest of the three Strettell children, born in 1845. Alice was born in 1850 and Alma in 1854.

29. He died, at the young age of 36, on 24 January 1882 at Colorada Springs, though his will was not proved in England until 13 December 1890.

30. Comyns Carr, *Stray Memories*, p. 112. Henry Irving made his debut on the London stage in 1866, where he was reputed the greatest English actor of his

time. Born in Somerset in 1838, Irving began his acting career in the provinces. In 1878 he formed a partnership with Ellen Terry at the Lyceum Theatre, where he became actor-manager. The first actor in British history to receive a knighthood, Sir Henry Irving died in 1905.

31. W.C. Homes, 'An English Lady at Glen Eyrie, the 1902-03 Diary of Dorothy Comyns Carr', *Kiva, the Journal of the Cheyenne Mountain Heritage Center*, Vol. 4, no. 2 (Spring 2000), pp 3–11 (p. 4).

32. Comyns Carr, *Stray Memories*, p. 8.

33. E. Terry, *The Story of my Life*, London 1908, p. 350.

34. The portrait is now in the Tate Gallery.

35. Comyns Carr, *Stray Memories*, p. 132.

36. Consort of King Carol and, after September 1914, Queen Dowager.

37. Comyns Carr, *Stray Memories*, p. 44.

38. Homes, 'An English Lady at Glen Eyrie', pp. 8–11.

39. Homes, 'An English Lady at Glen Eyrie', p. 4.

40. Homes, 'An English Lady at Glen Eyrie', pp. 3–4.

41. Homes, 'An English Lady at Glen Eyrie', p. 11.

42. Dame Ellen Terry's memorial service was held at St Paul's Church, Covent Garden, in July 1928.

43. Joy Ibsen, 1 August 2006.

44. Joy Ibsen, 2 July 2004.

45. His mother's second cousin; one of the two sons of Alice Strettell (Comyns Carr).

46. Joy Ibsen, 21 May 2004.

47. His will was proved on 5 January 1940.

48. A.F.G. Stokes, *A Moorland Princess: A Romance of Lyonesse* (1904); *From Land's End to the Lizard* (1909); *From Devon to St Ives* (1910); *From St Ives to Land's End* [DATE?]; *The Cornish Coast and Moors* (1912).

49. Joy Ibsen, 11 August 2004.

50. Joy Ibsen, 1 August 2006.

51. Joy Ibsen, 1 August 2006.

52. Joy Ibsen, 1 August 2006.

53. Joy Ibsen, 1 August 2006.

54. Joy Ibsen, 1 August 2006.

55. Joy Ibsen, 2 July 2004.

16. The Future of Richard III

1. W.C. Sellars and R.J. Yeatman, *1066 and All That*, London, 1930: 'a memorable history of England, comprising all the parts you can remember, including 103 Good Things, 5 Bad Kings and 2 Genuine Dates'.

2. There is always an element of presumption in tracing patrilineal descent, since the paternity of a child can never be taken for granted. For this reason it would be impossible to absolutely guarantee that the Plantagenet Y-chromosome survives in the Somerset family.

3. They were not, of course, 'princes': either one of them was a king, or both of them were bastards.

Appendix 1: Richard III's Itinerary for 1485

1. Taken from R. Edwards, *The Itinerary of King Richard III*, London, 1983.

Appendix 2: Calendar for 1485 (March to August)

1. Solar eclipse, death of Queen Anne Neville.
2. Feast of the Annunciation (Lady Day); the first day of 1485 according to the medieval English calendar. Burial of Queen Anne Neville.
3. Palm Sunday.
4. Maundy Thursday.
5. Good Friday.
6. Easter Sunday.
7. Ascension Day.
8. Anniversary of the death of Henry VI(?).
9. Feast of Pentecost (Whit Sunday).
10. Trinity Sunday.
11. Feast of Corpus Christi.
12. Anniversary of Richard III's accession and start of his third regnal year.
13. Battle of Bosworth. Death of Richard III.
14. Feast of St Louis IX of France: burial of Richard III at the Franciscan Priory Church, Leicester.

Appendix 4: John Speede's Account of the Burial of Richard III

1. From Speede, *History*, p. 725.
2. It is not the case that all coins of the Emperor Caligula were destroyed.
3. It is noteworthy that Speede does not say (as is usually reported) that Richard III's body was thrown into the river, but rather that it was reburied under one end of the bridge.

Appendix 5: DNA evidence relating to the putative remains of Margaret of York preserved in Mechelen, Belgium

1. When the bones were found, the precise location of the original tomb was somewhat unclear. See De Win, '*Danse Macabre*', *Handelingen*, p. 63 (*Ric.* 15, 2003, p. 55) & passim.

2. Three skeletons found, one of them female; the latter aged between fifty and sixty, and 1.54m in height.

3. Two skeletons found, one of them female.

4. Partial skeleton (secondary burial?) with hair, belonging to a woman of about fifty.

5. Information supplied by Dieter Viaene, Mechelen Town Archives, 29 June 2007.

6. V812/2 appears to constitute part of the 1955 (Twiesselmann) remains. What appears to be another *part* of these same remains is stored under the number V812/4. Information supplied by Professor Cassiman and Dieter Viaene.

7. For V812/1 and V812/2 only a partial DNA sequence was obtained.

8. Taken from the femur of V812/2.

9. All the other samples from V812/2 yielded at least one double reading (see below: Table 2).

10. As has been stated, when analysing mtDNA it is standard practice to concentrate on a 'control region' of four hundred nucleotide bases. In terms of its control region, Joy Ibsen's mtDNA is identical to that of the 'clan mother' for haplogroup J. It follows that Margaret of York cannot have displayed mutations in the control region of her mtDNA which Joy Ibsen does not possess.

11. Joy Ibsen has 'C' at 146, whereas V812/3 is identical to the Cambridge Reference Sequence (CRS) at this point. Also V812/3 differs from the CRS at three other points (16311, 152 and 228) where Joy Ibsen's sequence does not.

12. It has been estimated than one mutation will arise in the control region of the mitochondrial DNA every 20,000 years (B. Sykes, *The Seven Daughters of Eve*, London 2001, p. 155). However, I know of no estimated chronology for mutations outside of the control region (which happens to be where the four mutations which distinguish Joy Ibsen's mtDNA and that of V812/3 are located). Since the 'clan mother' of haplogroup J is estimated to have lived approximately 10,000 years ago, it follows that the last common maternal-line ancestress of Joy Ibsen and V812/3 must have lived less than 10,000 years ago.

13. For the female bone samples examined, carbon-14 dating produced death dates of approximately 1245 and 1367 [De Win, '*Danse Macabre*', *Handelingen*, pp. 80-1 (*Ricardian*, pp. 65-6)]. These dates appear to refer to the Steurs and Winders bones, though sadly the confusion over the remains found in the 1930s means that it is unclear which date refers to which bones.

14. Personal communication from Dieter Viaene, 29 June 2007.

Appendix 6: Richard III's Epitaph

1. p. 149.
2. pp. 217–18.
3. See below, note 31.
4. There is no reason to assume that Buck's published punctuation is authentic. As we shall see, the extant manuscript copies of the epitaph contain no punctuation.
5. Arguably, Sandford's text may reflect the original tomb inscription more closely than Buck's, but as we shall see, there is no great difference in the meaning.
6. Buck 1647: *Richardi*.
7. Buck 1647: *ad*.
8. Buck 1647: *Sti*.
9. These words are not given by Sandford. Presumably they did not form part of the original inscription, but were in the nature of a heading, supplied by Buck's manuscript source (since it seems unlikely that Buck himself would have chosen to apply to Henry VII the adjective *sanctus*).
10. Sandford: *multa*.
11. Buck 1647: *Richardus*.
12. Sandford: *Nam patrie tutor*.
13. Buck 1647 and Sandford: *patrius*.
14. Buck 1647: *duntaxat*.
15. Buck 1647: *Aetatesque*; Sandford: *Estatesque*.
16. Sandford: *non*.
17. Buck 1647 has a marginal note here: *Annos 2 & 51 dies*. Buck 1619 has *Annos 2 et 52 dies*. This misinterprets the text, which gives the length of Richard's reign as 'two summers and fifty-eight days' (it actually lasted two years and fifty-seven days).
18. Sandford: *merito*.
19. Buck 1647: *dicaras*.
20. Buck 1647 and Sandford: *quatuor*.
21. Buck 1647: *quinq.*; Sandford: *quinqζ*.
22. Sandford: *tricenta*.
23. Buck 1647 here inserts a marginal note: *Anno Domini 1484*. Buck 1619 sets this note next to the preceding line. Both texts seem to take the convoluted date as referring to the Battle of Bosworth.
24. Buck 1647: *antique*; Sandford: *anteqζ*.
25. Buck 1647 has a marginal note at this point reading *Die 21 Aug*. Buck 1619 has *Die 22 Augusti*. The latter is clearly the correct reading.
26. Buck 1647 and Sandford: *Redideram*.
27. Sandford: *rubre*.

28. Sandford: *debita iura*.

29. Sandford: *rose*.

30. Buck 1647: *precarem*.

31. Buck 1619: *levat*; Sandford: *pena fienda*.

32. Curiously, Nichols published a composite text containing elements of Buck 1619 (which was not published in his day) and Buck 1647. Nichols also noted the variant readings of Sandford. Despite occasional errors, Nichols notes more of Sandford's variant readings than does Kincaid in his edition of Buck 1619.

33. W. Hutton (with additions by J. Nichols), *The Battle of Bosworth Field*, second edition, London, 1813 (reprinted Dursley, 1974), pp. 220–22. The translation may indeed be by Buck, but curiously it does not figure in the published editions of Buck's *History of Richard the Third*.

34. This is an error, the Latin text does not say this.

35. The year date is incorrectly given in this translation.

36. J. Nichols, *History and Antiquities of the County of Leicester* (4 vols, London, 1795–1811), vol. 1, part 2, p. 298.

37. J. Weever, *Ancient Funeral Monuments*, London, 1631, p. 475; London, 1767, pp. 253–54.

38. Weever, *Funeral Monuments*, 1631 edition, p. 476; 1767 edition, p. 254. For the positioning of this epitaph around the top of the tomb chest, see R. Marks and P. Williamson, *Gothic; Art for England 1400–1547*, London, 2003, p. 83.

39. Weever gives *benigne*; the inscription on the tomb reads *benigna*.

List of Abbreviations

Beloved Cousyn	J. Ashdown-Hill, *Richard III's 'Beloved Cousyn'*
BL	British Library
Crowland	N. Pronay & J. Cox, eds, *The Crowland Chronicle Continuations*
Eleanor	J. Ashdown-Hill, *Eleanor, the Secret Queen*
Ellis/Vergil	H. Ellis, ed., *Three Books of Polydore Vergil's English History*
Harl. 433	+ folio number: BL, Harl. MS 433
	+ vol. number, + page number: R. Horrox and P. W. Hammond, *British Library Harleian Manuscript 433*
HHB	A. Crawford, ed., *Howard Household Books*
Itinerary	R. Edwards, *The Itinerary of King Richard III*
Kendall *R3*	P. M. Kendall, *Richard the Third*
Myers/Buck	A.R. Myers, ed., G. Buck, *The History of the Life and Reigne of Richard the Third*
Nicolas	N.H. Nicolas, ed., *Privy Purse Expenses of Elizabeth of York: Wardrobe Accounts of Edward the Fourth*
ODNB	*Oxford Dictionary of National Biography*
Road	P.W. Hammond and A.F Sutton, *Richard III, The Road to Bosworth Field*
R3MK	A. Carson, *Richard III the Maligned King*
Ric.	*The Ricardian*
Soc. Ant.	Society of Antiquaries of London
Speede, *History*	J. Speede, *The History of Great Britaine*
TNA	The National Archives
Θ	L.J.F. Ashdown-Hill, 'The client network, connections and patronage of Sir John Howard' (&c), unpublished PhD thesis, University of Essex, 2008
V&A	Victoria and Albert Museum
VCH	Victoria County History

Acknowledgements

I should like to thank Antonio Marques for his help in accessing Portuguese sources relating to Richard III's marriage projects of 1485, and also my fellow student at the University of Essex, Carolina Barbara, for checking my translations of the Portuguese texts which I have published. I am most grateful to the staff of the Leicestershire, Leicester and Rutland Record Office and to the staff of the Leicester Museum Service for their assistance, and I also owe many thanks to Sally Henshaw (Secretary of the Richard III Society East Midlands Branch) for her help in tracking down Thomas Clarke, mayor of Leicester, and in pursuing rumours of Richard III's bed. I should also like to thank Marie Barnfield, Annette Carson, Dr Mike Jones and Lynda Pidgeon for reading draft versions of my text (or parts of it) and providing very valuable comments and advice. I also owe an enormous debt of gratitude to Lindsey Smith, my current editor, and to all the team at The History Press, for all their help and encouragement in bringing to completion this new and updated second edition of *The Last Days of Richard III*. Finally I should like to thank the late Joy Ibsen and her family, Richard Mackinder (operations manager, Bosworth Battlefield Centre), Eddie Smallwood (Bosworth Battlefield guide), Philippa Langley, and all my colleagues in the Leicester University 'Search for Richard III' team. As usual, Annette Carson and Dave Perry have helped me to avoid the more obvious typographical errors. Any mistakes which remain, are, of course, my responsibility!

Bibliography

Books and Booklets

Adams E, ed., *Mrs J. Comyns Carr's Reminiscences*, London 1926

Anderson, J.E., *see* Bloch

Ashdown-Hill, J., *Eleanor, the Secret Queen – the Woman who put Richard III on the Throne* (Stroud, 2009).

———, *Mediaeval Colchester's Lost Landmarks* (Derby, 2009).

———, *Richard III's 'Beloved Cousyn' – John Howard and the House of York* (Stroud, 2009).

Ashdown-Hill J, *Royal Marriage Secrets*, Stroud 2013 (forthcoming).

Attreed, L.C., ed., *York House Books 1461–1490*, vol. 1 (Stroud, 1991).

Austin, J.D., *Merevale and Atherstone 1485: Recent Bosworth Discoveries* (Friends of Atherstone Heritage, 2004).

Baker, R., *Chronicle of the Kings of England* (London, 1684).

Beltz, G.F., *Memorials of the most Noble Order of the Garter from its foundation to the present time* (London, 1841).

Bennett, M., *The Battle of Bosworth* (Stroud, 1985, 2000).

———, *Lambert Simnel and the Battle of Stoke* (New York, 1987).

Benson, L.D., ed., *The Riverside Chaucer* (Oxford, 1987).

Billson, C.J., *Mediaeval Leicester* (Leicester, 1920).

Black, M., *The Medieval Cookbook* (London, 1992).

Blair, J. & Ramsey, N., eds, *English Medieval Industries* (London, 1991).

Bloch, M. (trans. Anderson, J.E.), *The Royal Touch, Sacred Monarchy and Scrofula in England and France* (London, 1973).

Brewer, D., *Chaucer and his World* (London, 1978).

Buck, G., *see* Myers

Calendar of State Papers – Venetian, vol 1, 1202–1509.

Carson, A., *Richard III, the Maligned King* (Stroud, 2008).

Cheney, C.R., *Handbook of Dates* (RHS, 1945, reprinted Cambridge, 1996).

Chesterton, G.K., *Chaucer* (London, 1932).

Coldwells, A., *St George's Chapel, Windsor Castle* (guide book, 1993).

Comyns Carr A, *J. Comyns Carr – Stray Memories*, London 1920

Corbet, R., *Iter Boreale, see* Gilchrist

Coulton, G.C., *Chaucer and his England* (London, 1908).

Cox, J.C., *Memorials of Old Derbyshire* (London, 1907).

Crawford, A., ed., *The Household Books of John Howard, Duke of Norfolk, 1462–1471, 1481–1483* (Stroud, 1992).

Cunningham, S., *Richard III: a royal enigma* (TNA, Kew, 2003).

Davis, N., ed., *Paston Letters and Papers of the Fifteenth Century*, 2 vols (Oxford: Clarendon, 1971 & 1976).

Edwards, R., *The Itinerary of King Richard III* (London, 1983).

Ellis, H., ed., *Three Books of Polydore Vergil's English History* (London, 1844).

Foss, P.J., *The Field of Redemore* (Newtown Linford, 1990, 1998).

Furneaux R, *William Wilberforce*, London 1974

Gairdner, J., ed., *Letters and Papers illustrative of the reigns of Richard III and Henry VII* (London, 1857).

Gairdner, J., *History of the Life and Reign of Richard the Third* (Cambridge, 1898).

Gardner, J., *The Life and Times of Chaucer* (London, 1977).

Gilchrist, O.G., *The Poems of Richard Corbet* (London, 1807).

Gill, H., *A Short History of Nottingham Castle* (Nottingham, 1904).

Gomes dos Santos, D.M., *O Mosteiro de Jesus de Aveiro*, 3 vols (Lisboa, 1963).

Green, S.E., *Selected Legends of Leicestershire* (Leicester, 1971 [1982]).

Griffiths, R.A., 'Henry VI', *ODNB*.

Halsted, C.A., *Richard III* (London, 1844).

Hammond, P.W. & Sutton, A.F., *Richard III, the Road to Bosworth Field* (London, 1985).

Hammond, P.W., *Food & Feast in Medieval England* (Stroud, 1993).

Hartley, D. & Elliot, M.M., *Life and Work of the People of England in the Fifteenth Century* (London, 1925).

Hartopp, H., *The Roll of the Mayors of the Borough and Lord Mayors of the City of Leicester 1209–1935* (Leicester, 1935).

Hicks, M.A., *Richard III and his Rivals* (London, 1991).

Horrox, R. & Hammond, P.W., *British Library Harleian Manuscript 433*, vol. 2 (Upminster, 1980); vol. 3 (London, 1982).

Horrox, R., *British Library Harleian Manuscript 433*, vol. 4 (London, 1983).

Hughes, J., *The Religious Life of Richard III* (Stroud, 1997).

Hutton, W. (with additions by Nichols, J.), *The Battle of Bosworth Field* (second edition London, 1813; reprinted Dursley, 1974).

Jones, M.K., *Bosworth 1485, Psychology of a Battle* (Stroud, 2002).

Jowett, J., ed., *The Tragedy of King Richard III* (Oxford, 2000).

Kendall, P.M., *Richard the Third* (London, 1955).

Klotzko, A.J., *A Clone of Your Own?* (Oxford, 2004).

Laing, L. & J., *Medieval Britain, the Age of Chivalry* (London, 1996).

Langland, W., *see* Skeat

Laynesmith, J., *The Last Medieval Queens* (Oxford, 2004).

Letters and Papers, Foreign and Domestic, of the reign of Henry VIII, vol. 1(i).

Lucraft, J., *Katherine Swynford: the History of a Medieval Mistress* (Stroud, 2006).

Mackie J D, *The Earlier Tudors, 1485-1558*, Oxford 1952

Marks, J., *What it means to be 98% Chimpanzee* (London and Berkeley, 2002).

Marks, R. & Williamson, P., *Gothic; Art for England 1400–1547* (London, 2003).

More, T., *The History of King Richard III, see* Sylvester

Morris, R.K. & Shoesmith, R., eds, *Tewkesbury Abbey, History, Art and Architecture* (Almeley, 2003).

Myers, A.R., ed. Buck, G., *The History of the Life and Reigne of Richard the Third* (London, 1646, 1973).

Nicholls, J. & Bruce, J., eds, *Wills from Doctors' Commons. A selection of Wills of eminent persons proved in the PCC 1495–1695*, Camden old series, vol. 83 (London, 1863).

Nichols, J., *History and Antiquities of the County of Leicester* (London, 1795–1811).

Nicolas, N.H., ed., *Privy Purse Expenses of Elizabeth of York: Wardrobe Accounts of Edward the Fourth* (London, 1830).

Oman, C.W.C., *The Art of War in the Middle Ages, AD 378–1515* (New York, 1953).

Page, W., ed., *VCH London*, vol. 1 (London 1909).

Pollard, A.J., *North-Eastern England during the Wars of the Roses: Lay Society, War and Politics 1450–1500* (Oxford, 1990).

Pollock J, *Wilberforce*, (London 1977).

Porter, R., *The Greatest Benefit to Mankind* (London, 1997).

Poston, E., ed., *The Penguin Book of Christmas Carols* (Harmondsworth, 1965).

Potter, J., *Good King Richard?* (London, 1983).

Power, E., ed., *The Goodman of Paris (Le Ménagier de Paris) a Treatise on Moral and Domestic Economy by a Citizen of Paris c. 1393* (London, 1928 [1992]).

Prockter, A. & Taylor, R., *The A to Z of Elizabethan London* (London, 1979).

Pronay, N. & Cox, J., *The Crowland Chronicle Continuations 1459–1486* (London, 1986).

Ratcliffe, E.E. & Wright, P.A., *The Royal Maundy, a brief outline of its history and ceremonial* (The Royal Almonry, Buckingham Palace, seventh edition, 1960).

Reeves, C., *Pleasures and Pastimes in Medieval England* (Stroud, 1995).

Ricks, C., ed., *The Penguin History of Literature vol. 3: English Drama to 1710* (Harmondsworth, 1971).

Ridgard, J., ed., *Medieval Framlingham*, Suffolk Record Society, vol. 27 (Woodbridge, 1985).

Ridley, J., *Henry VIII* (London, 1984).

Roe, F., *Old Oak Furniture* (London, 1908).

Ross, C., *Richard III* (London, 1981).

Scully, T., *The Art of Cookery in the Middle Ages* (Woodbridge, 1995).

Sellars, W.C. & Yeatman, R.J., *1066 and All That* (London, 1930).

Skeat, W.W., ed. W. Langland, *The Vision of William concerning Piers the Plowman*, (Oxford, 1869).

de Somogyi, N., ed., *The Shakespeare Folios: Richard III* (London, 2002).

Speede [Speed], J., *The History of Great Britaine* (London, 1611, 1614).

Stow, *Annals* (ed. 1615); see Page, W.

Sutton, A.F. & Hammond, P.W., eds, *The Coronation of Richard III: the extant documents* (Gloucester, 1983).

Sutton, A.F. & Visser-Fuchs, L., *The Hours of Richard III* (Stroud, 1990).

———, with Griffiths, R.A., *The Royal Funerals of the House of York at Windsor* (London, 2005).

Sykes, B., *The Seven Daughters of Eve* (New York & London, 2001).

———, *Adam's Curse* (London, 2003).

Sylvester, R.S., ed., St Thomas More, *The History of King Richard III* (New Haven & London, 1976).

Terry, E., *The Story of My Life* (London, 1908).

Throsby, J., *The Memoirs of the Town and County of Leicester* (Leicester 1777).

Twining, A.G., *Our Kings and Westminster Abbey* (London, 1911).

Vasconcellio, P.A., *Anacephalaeoses, id est, summa capita actorum regum Lusitaniae*, (Antwerp, 1621).

VCH, *Leicestershire*, vol. 2 (1954).

Vergil, P., *see* Ellis

Weever, J., *Ancient Funeral Monuments* (London, 1631, 1767).

Weightman, C., *Margaret of York* (Gloucester, 1989).

Wolffe, B., *Henry VI* (London, 1981).

Woolf, N., *The Sovereign Remedy, Touch Pieces and the King's Evil* (British Association of Numismatic Societies, 1990).

Woolgar, C.M., Sejeantson, D. & Waldron, T., *Food in Medieval England – Diet & Nutrition* (Oxford, 2006).

Woolley, L., *Medieval Life and Leisure in the Devonshire Hunting Tapestries* (London:V&A, 2002).

Wren, C., *Parentalia, or Memoirs of the Family of the Wrens* (London, 1750).

York, Edward, Duke of (d. 1415), trans. Foix, Gaston III, Comte de, *Livre de Chasse*.

Articles

Ashdown-Hill, J., 'Queen Elizabeth Woodville and the *Angelus*', *Ric.* 10 (1994–96), pp. 326–27.

———, 'The Lancastrian Claim to the Throne', *Ric.* 13 (2003), pp. 27–38.

————, 'The Bosworth Crucifix', *Transactions of the Leicestershire Archaeological & Historical Society*, vol. 78 (2004), pp. 83–96.

————, 'A Granddaughter of William Wilberforce', *Genealogists' Magazine*, September 2004 (28:3, 2004), pp. 110–11.

————, 'the Location of the 1485 Battle and the Fate of Richard III's Body', *Ricardian Bulletin*, Autumn 2004, pp. 34–35.

————, 'Yesterday my Lord of Gloucester came to Colchester', *Essex Archaeology and History*, vol. 36 (2005), pp. 212–17.

————, 'Alive and Well in Canada – the Mitochondrial DNA of Richard III', *Ric.* 16 (2006), pp. 1–14.

————, 'Margaret of York's Dance of Death – the DNA evidence', *Handelingen van de Koninklijke Kring voor Oudheidkunde, Letteren an Kunst van Mechelen*, 111 (2007), pp. 193–207.

————, 'The opening of the tombs of the Dukes of Richmond and Norfolk, Framlingham, April 1841: Darby's account', *Ric.* 18 (2008), pp. 100–07.

————, 'Coins attributed to the Yorkist Pretenders, 1487–1498', *Ric.* 19 (2009), pp. 69–89.

Baldwin, D., 'King Richard's Grave in Leicester', *Transactions of the Leicestershire Archaeological and Historical Society*, vol. 60 (1986), pp. 21–24.

Barnfield, M., 'Diriment Impediments, Dispensations and Divorce: Richard III and Matrimony', *Ric.* 17 (2007), pp. 84–98.

Breeze, A., 'A Welsh Poem of 1485 on Richard III', *Ric.* 18 (2008), pp. 46–53.

Carpenter, C., 'Edward, called Earl of Warwick', *ODNB*.

De Win, P., '*Danse Macabre* rond graf en gebeente van Margareta van York', *Handelingen van de Koninklijke Kring voor Oudheidkunde, Letteren an Kunst van Mechelen* (2003), pp. 61–86.

————, '*Danse Macabre* around the tomb and bones of Margaret of York', *Ric.* 15 (2005), pp. 53–69.

Edwards, R., 'King Richard's Tomb at Leicester', *Ric.* 3 (no. 50, Sept. 1975), pp. 8–9

Elliott, J., 'The Birth Chart of Richard III', *Astrological Quarterly*, vol. 70, no. 3 (Summer 2000).

Hagelberg, E., Sykes, B. & Hedges, R.E.M., 'Ancient bone DNA amplified', *Nature*, vol. 342 (1989).

Hammond, P.W., 'The Illegitimate Children of Richard III', *Ric.* 5, (1977–81), pp. 92–96.

Hanham, A., 'Henry VI and his Miracles', *Ric.* 12 (2000–02), pp. 2–16 [numbered in error, pp. 638–52].

————, 'The Mysterious Affair at Crowland Abbey', *Ric.* 18 (2008), pp. 1–20.

Hickey, B. & Stirling-Langley, P., 'Richard III – a character analysis', *Ricardian Bulletin*, September 2000, pp. 27–34, and March 2001, pp. 16–22.

Homes W C, 'An English Lady at Glen Eyrie, the 1902–03 Diary of Dorothy

Comyns Carr', *Kiva, the Journal of the Cheyenne Mountain Heritage Center*, Vol. 4, no. 2 (Spring 2000), pp. 3-11.

Horrox, R., 'John de la Pole, Earl of Lincoln', *ODNB*.

Knox, R., 'Bosworth Battlefield Archaeology Project Update', *Ricardian Bulletin*, Winter 2007, pp. 22–24.

Marques, A.S., 'Álvaro Lopes de Cheves [*sic*]: A Portuguese Source', *Ricardian Bulletin*, Autumn 2008, pp. 25–27.

St John Hope, W.H., 'The Discovery of the remains of King Henry VI in St George's Chapel, Windsor Castle', *Archaeologia*, vol. 62, part 2, pp. 533–42.

Sheppard Routh, P., '"Lady Scroop Daughter of K. Edward": an Enquiry', *Ric.* 9 (1991–93), pp. 410–16.

Sutton, A.F., 'Richard III's "Castle of Care"', *Ric.* 3 (no. 49, June 1975), pp. 10–12.

Sutton, A.F. & Visser-Fuchs, L., 'Richard III's Books', *Ric.* 7–10 (1985–96).

Verkaik, J.W., 'King Richard's Last Sacrament', *Ric.* 9 (1991–93), pp. 359–60.

Visser-Fuchs, L., 'A Commentary on the Continuation', *Ric.* 7 (1985–87), pp. 520–22.

Warnicke, R.M., 'Sir Ralph Bigod: a loyal servant to King Richard III', *Ric.* 6 (1982–84), pp. 299–303.

White, W.J., 'The Death and Burial of Henry VI, part 1', *Ric.* 6 (1982–84), pp. 70–80; part 2, *Ric* 6, pp. 106–17.

Williams, B., 'Rui de Sousa's embassy and the fate of Richard, Duke of York', *Ric.* 5, pp. 341–45.

Williams, B., 'The Portuguese Connection and the Significance of "the Holy Princess"', *Ric.* 6 (1983), pp. 138–45.

Unpublished Theses

Ashdown-Hill, J., 'The client network, connections and patronage of Sir John Howard (Lord Howard, first Duke of Norfolk) in north-east Essex and south Suffolk', unpublished PhD thesis, University of Essex, 2008.

Internet

http://members.cox.net/judy-perry/Philippa.html (consulted June 2009).

www.buzzle.com/articles/sweating-sickness.html (consulted March 2009).

www.1911encyclopedia.org/Pheasant (consulted January 2009).

www.bbc.co.uk/nottingham/content/articles/2008/09/18/robin_hood_and_ bestwood_feature.shtml (consulted December 2008).

www.bw-bestwoodlodge.co.uk/HistoryoftheLodge.asp (consulted December 2008).

http://en.wikipedia.org/wiki/Coventry_Mystery_Plays (consulted January 2009).

http://en.wikipedia.org/wiki/Lord_Mayor_of_Nottingham (consulted June 2009).

http://en.wikipedia.org/wiki/Sweating_sickness (consulted March 2009).

www.girders.net/Wo/Woodville,%20Sir%20Edward,%20(d.1488).doc (consulted January 2009) © I.S. Rogers.

www.godecookery.com/how2cook/howto05.htm (consulted December 2008).

http://ls.kuleuven.ac.be/cgi-bin/wa?A2=ind0103&L=vvs&P=1445.

www.luminarium.org/encyclopedia/sweatingsickness.htm (consulted March 2009).

www.maney.co.uk/files/misc/HenryChapter3.pdf (consulted January 2009).

www.nottshistory.org.uk/Brown1896/arnold.htm (consulted December 2008).

www.nottshistory.org.uk/gill1904/charlesi.htm (consulted January 2009).

www.probertencyclopaedia.com/cgi-bin/res.pl?keyword=Fifteenth&offset=0 (consulted December 2008).

www.r3.org/bookcase/croyland/index.html (consulted June 2009).

www.springsgov.com/Page.aspx?NavID=1368 (consulted June 2009).

http://sunearth.gsfc.nasa.gov/eclipse/SEsaros/SEsaros121.html.

www.susanhigginbotham.com/richard_woodville,_third_earl_rivers.htm (consulted January 2009).

www.woodmillshootings.com/holiday_packages.htm (consulted November 2008).

Index

Kings are listed under their first names. Other individuals are listed under surnames, rather than titles, and women are listed under maiden surname if this is known, but all entries are cross-referenced.